WORKPLACE PARTNERSHIP IN PRACTICE

Securing Sustainable Mutual Gains at Waterford Glass and Aughinish Alumina?

Tony Dobbins

The Liffey Press

Published by
The Liffey Press
Ashbrook House, 10 Main Street
Raheny, Dublin 5, Ireland
www.theliffeypress.com

A catalogue record of this book is
available from the British Library.

ISBN 978-1-905785-54-4

Printed in Ireland by Colour Books.

CONTENTS

ACKNOWLEDGEMENTS

This book would not have been possible without the information, encouragement, support and advice provided by a number of people.

First of all, I would like to thank all the employees, trade union representatives and managers at both Waterford Crystal and Aughinish Alumina who contributed to the study, and, in many cases, provided rich insights, which undoubtedly added greatly to my knowledge of workplace industrial relations. Reading books on the subject is vital, but there is no substitute for the cut and thrust of frontline research. Particular thanks go to the respective 'gatekeepers' in each company: Senan Cooke, training manager at Waterford Crystal, and Pat Sweeney, personnel manager at Aughinish Alumina. Special thanks also go to Dan Miller, TEEU official, who represents workers at Aughinish.

Special thanks also go to Professor Patrick Gunnigle, University of Limerick, for his invaluable assistance and supervision during the doctoral research on which this book is based. The love of my wife Paula was also particularly important during the course of the research, and I am extremely grateful for her support.

I would also like to express gratitude to the Labour Relations Commission and its Chief Executive, Kieran Mulvey, for sponsorship and financial assistance. Since its inception in January 1991, the Labour Relations Commission has played a vital role in resolving industrial relations disputes, not just in Waterford Glass and Aughinish Alumina, but in many other organisations. Many thanks also to The Liffey Press for agreeing to publish this book

This book is dedicated to family and friends past and present.

About the Author

Dr. Tony Dobbins is a Post-Doctoral Research Fellow at the Centre for Innovation & Structural Change (CISC), National University of Ireland Galway. Previously, he was a journalist with the independent weekly industrial relations magazine, *Industrial Relations News* (IRN). Tony has also been national correspondent on Irish industrial relations for the European Industrial Relations Observatory (EIRO) since 1997. He has a BA, MA, and Doctorate in industrial relations.

Chapter 1

INTRODUCTION

As the traditional pluralist model of industrial relations – predominantly based on adversarial collective bargaining negotiations between employers and trade unions on the distribution of pay and conditions of employment – has retreated in the face of intense competitive pressures and related factors, the concept of workplace partnership has attracted attention from employers, unions, academics and policy-makers. This has been particularly so in Ireland, where national agreements ('social partnership') have long characterised the industrial relations system. The following broad working definition of workplace partnership was agreed by the social partners in Ireland, and is contained in Chapter 9 of the *Partnership 2000* national agreement (1997: 52):

> Partnership is an active relationship based on recognition of a common interest to secure the competitiveness, viability and prosperity of the enterprise. It involves a continuing commitment from employees to improvements in efficiency and quality; and the acceptance by employers of employees as stakeholders with rights and interests to be considered in the context of major decisions affecting their employment.

In addition, a specific state body, the National Centre for Partnership and Performance (NCPP), was also established some years ago to promote workplace partnership. Other institutions, notably the Labour Relations Commission, have also played a vital role in supporting cooperative workplace IR initiatives.

The practices commonly associated with workplace partnership are partnership between management and worker representatives ('representative participation' (RP)); direct employee participation (DP) practices such as teamwork; and a range of complementary Human Resource Management (HRM) practices, notably employee financial stakeholding practices like gainsharing and profit-sharing, employment security policies, training, single status conditions of employment (as far as possible terms and conditions of employment are broadly similar for different occupational grades), and two-way communication channels between managers and employees.

'Truncated' Partnership

But despite national-level centralised partnership being seen by many as well developed in Ireland (see Hastings et al., 2007), genuine workplace partnership remains quite rare (see Gunnigle, 1998; Wallace et al., 2004; Roche, 2006) – reflected by what Roche calls 'truncated' partnership. Crucially, in the context of Ireland's voluntarist industrial relations traditions, employers possess the sole authority to initiate workplace partnership. In other words, regardless of whether workers and their representatives want (or do not want) partnership, the ultimate decision rests with employers. In relation to this, partnership is but one of many policy options open to employers in Ireland and employment relations are characterised by growing diversity (Roche, 2006). Other options include managerial unilateralism, traditional collective bargaining and weak forms of employee involvement.

In contrast to workplace partnership, so-called traditional adversarial industrial relations were, and still are, characterised by arms-length collective bargaining negotiations between employers and trade unions. Also under the adversarial model, management has traditionally tended to use various control mechanisms at its disposal, such as close supervision and a range of formal bureaucratic rules, to secure the requisite level of worker compliance with its objectives. However, with the advent of more intense competitive pressures, it is more often deemed to be the case now that mere worker compliance is not enough for employers to achieve their goals, and that higher levels of active cooperation and creative input are required from workers and their representatives.

Mutual Gains Premise

A key premise of workplace partnership is that it can deliver mutual gains for all workplace stakeholders (Kochan and Osterman, 1994). Great emphasis is placed on the concept of mutuality: management engages workers, both directly as individuals and indirectly through representatives, in a cooperative and integrated relationship to pursue mutual gains such as participation, employment security and productivity. Differing interests among independent stakeholders are acknowledged, but the focus is on reconciling common interests for mutual gain (Guest and Peccei, 2001).

Aim of Study

The rationale for this study is to bring clarity to the continued polarisation between competing perspectives about the dynamics of workplace partnership, the balance of mutual gains and costs accruing to employers, workers and unions, and the conditions sustaining or retarding partnership. Workplace partnership is a contested terrain, with three perspectives discernible in the mutual gains academic literature: 'advocates', 'critics', and 'pragmatic contingency' perspectives.

Ambiguity on Partnership

Furthermore, polarised views on workplace partnership in the academic literature are accompanied by ambiguity surrounding the broad nature and thrust of workplace partnership practices among employment relations practitioners and policy-makers. While management-trade union cooperation tends to be the most commonly associated manifestation of workplace partnership, it is not the only one. In the non-union sector, many employers would claim to have management-employee partnerships in place, based on direct employee involvement and communication, rather than through the indirect channel of independent worker representatives. In view of this, while employer representative bodies, such as the Irish Business and Employers Confederation (IBEC) (2002), argue that direct employee involvement practices (such as teamwork, two-way communications, and suggestion schemes) in non-union firms can constitute partnership, trade union representative bodies, such as the Irish Congress of Trade Unions (ICTU) (1995, 2003), argue that partnership in any true sense must entail independent collective representation for workers. This ambiguity surrounding the broad nature of workplace partnership is reflected in many policy statements in Ireland on the subject, which, while often fervently embracing the need to introduce new forms of employee involvement to boost competitiveness and workplace innovation, commonly suggest that partnership arrangements need to be tailored to fit different employment settings and circumstances (IBEC, 2002; Department of Enterprise, Trade and Employment, 2003; NCPP, 2004).

Need Clearer Political Vision

At the level of Government policy, while politicians often espouse the benefits of workplace partnership and innovation, there are few signs of a clear and coherent political vision of what constitutes quality work and 'good work relations'. Most importantly, more could be done to actively promote the relationship between 'good work relations', strong economic performance and the role of the state in promoting quality employment. The absence of a coherent political vision of good workplace governance is one barrier to the potential of pluralist mutual gains partnership. A related barrier is that Government and many employers (and unions for that matter) tend to view employment laws and regulations 'as something to be complied with', rather than as something that can be proactively used as a springboard to producing mutual gains and improving the productivity and performance of firms. The response of the Government and employer representatives to the EU information and consultation is an example of this 'lowest common denominator' approach to employment regulation. Also, while the primary authority for workplace partnership ultimately resides with the employer, unions too, by and large, have been slow to mobilize around the concept of 'good work relations' and new forms of worker voice–influenced by the fact that their historical mindset and role has centred on an adversarial 'defence' of pay and conditions. These issues will be revisited in the final chapter.

This book attempts to address this polarization and ambiguity among academics, practitioners and policy-makers by providing an in-depth examination of the practical realities and outcomes of partnership – and hopefully contribute something to knowledge and understanding of workplace cooperation.

Views of all Stakeholders

Accordingly, this study focuses on whether or not partnership practices generate mutual gains for employers, workers and worker representatives, and the contextual conditions sustaining or retarding partnership. The balance of mutuality arising from workplace partnership is a crucial area requiring further examination. In particular, case studies embracing all workplace stakeholders are necessary due to over-reliance on surveys of partnership garnered primarily from management respondents – a somewhat paradoxical phenomenon when one considers that partnership involves multiple stakeholders. This book originated from a doctoral thesis examining the nature and outcomes of workplace partnership in two case study organisations in Ireland (Waterford Crystal (WC) and Aughinish Alumina (AAL). The case studies were in-depth and longitudinal (the fieldwork was conducted over a two-year period), which was facilitated by extremely good access to multiple respondents and perspectives (drawn from all levels of management, external and internal trade union representatives, and samples of workers across various grades and occupations). The main research methods deployed were semi-structured interviews, ethnography, and use of internal and external archival and documentary material. The study outlines the main case findings in the two companies and, in particular, synthesises the balance of mutual gains (and losses) for all workplace stakeholders and addresses the durability of partnership.

Outline of Book

The book is structured as follows. The next chapter provides a general synthesis of the existing theoretical literature. It examines competing theories and perspectives on workplace partnership, and argues that 'pragmatic contingency' perspectives emphasizing the importance of contextual conditions promoting or retarding partnership are the best means of understanding the dynamics and consequences of partnership. Key conceptual tools associated with contingency theory provide the analytical framework to the rest of the book. The literature review chapter also reviews recent empirical studies of workplace partnership, with emphasis on the Irish context, but also taking account of international evidence. Chapters three and four outline the case study findings at Waterford Crystal and Aughinish Alumina respectively. The two chapters provide background information on both companies, in terms of ownership, financial position, business strategy, organisational structure, structure of production, technology, work organisation, and industrial relations. The findings relating to historical patterns of IR and then, more recently, the nature of workplace partnership and its consequences, are then outlined.

The book finishes with a discussion and some conclusions in chapter five, which discusses the empirical findings of the two case studies and relates them to the existing literature. A number of conclusions are provided. In particular, partnership delivered gains for all stakeholders at Aughinish Alumina, and the balance was quite equally divided. In contrast, while partnership delivered most gains for management at Waterford Crystal, and some for the union, worker gains were less. The Waterford partnership 'died' after ten years, and the company has been rocked by successive rounds of redundancies with large portions of production being relocated overseas. Meanwhile, the AAL partnership survives fifteen years on. Espousing a 'pragmatic contingency' perspective, it is concluded that the mutual gains potential of partnership, and its sustainability, is contingent on contextual conditions – notably how competently employers manage the uncertainties and competing demands of work relations, and the extent firms are exposed to/insulated from market pressures. Pluralist 'productivity coalitions' can 'work' for all workplace stakeholders, but they rely on supporting contextual conditions, which are not easily replicable in an industrial relations system bequeathed with a 'non interventionist' voluntarist legacy. Finally, chapter five outlines some policy implications and issues for future research. In particular, an observation is made that if pluralist-oriented mutual gains partnership is to increase more generally across the Irish economy, it would appear that more supportive and synergistic jointly 'beneficial institutional constraints' would be required to promote 'good work relations'. The Employee Information and Consultation Act 2006 offers one potential building block for institutionalising pluralist mutual gains partnerships in Ireland, but, if this potential is to be realised, much depends on the choices made by Government, employers and unions.

Appendix 1 briefly outlines the research methodology. It explains why an intensive qualitative case study method was deemed to be the most appropriate research strategy to examine the nature and consequences of workplace partnership. It outlines the various research techniques deployed and includes a table summarising all interviewees.

Chapter 2

THEORIES OF WORKPLACE COOPERATION

As noted in the introduction, the rationale for this book is to add to our understanding of the nature, outcomes and contextual conditions associated with voluntary workplace partnership (WP) – in particular, to add to knowledge on the balance of mutuality arising from WP, and the conditions supporting it. For many years the debate was largely polarised around positions which were either supportive or critical of partnership. More recently, all sides have become more aware of the influence of context and contingency on workplace partnership and, in some regards, there is now greater overlap between various industrial relations perspectives. Notwithstanding this common ground, there remain important analytical differences between various perspectives on the broad thrust of workplace partnership and the underlying nature of employment relations.

'Advocates'

Unitarist Advocates

Optimistic perspectives on employment relations have long portrayed partnership between management and employees as a means of generating mutual gains. Advocates of partnership can be separated into two strands: unitarist and pluralist – a distinction made long ago by Fox (1966) – and which can be applied to perspectives on workplace cooperation today. First, unitarist accounts of partnership often assume that management is concerned with moving away from controlling workers towards empowering them, that the interests of employers and employees are broadly similar, and that management-employee partnership can strengthen this common bond. Management is seen as the sole source of authority. Little mention is made of trade unions, because it is assumed there is no fundamental conflict of interest between employers and employees (Walton, 1985; Hamel and Prahalad, 1994; Huselid, 1995; MacDuffie, 1995; Boxall, 1996; Ichniowski et al., 1996; Pfeffer, 1994, 1998).

Walton (1985: 48-51) was an early advocate in the mutual gains literature identifying a positive direct link between what he called policies of mutuality and resulting benefits for the main workplace stakeholders. Walton described a high commitment model consisting of various policies of mutuality, notably new forms of job design, teamwork, flat organisational structures, employment security policies, extensive employee voice and information provision, and new forms of employee financial stakeholding such as gainsharing. According to Walton, employers are moving away from what he called the traditional control model towards a new high commitment model. There are clear mutual gains for workplace stakeholders in so doing, Walton argued. For employers, it enhances competitiveness, in terms of quality, cost and adaptation to change. For employees, it provides a more humane work environment and greater job satisfaction. Walton suggests that mutuality practices associated with the commitment model are applicable in most contexts.

Pluralist Advocates

Second, optimistic pluralist perspectives on partnership are fundamentally distinct from unitarist perspectives because they acknowledge competing workplace interests (rather than one sole authority, the employer), and often explicitly consider the role of worker representative bodies, especially unions. Consequently, pluralist perspectives accept the inevitability of conflict between the interests of employers and workers, but consider ways in which conflict can be contained and institutionalised to maintain workplace consensus and order (cf. Flanders, 1970; Clegg, 1979). Traditionally, pluralism was commonly associated with the institutions of collective bargaining, and influential British pluralists like Flanders (1970) and Clegg (1979), in particular, optimistically viewed collective bargaining as the best means of institutionalising conflict. Instead, as Fox (1985) argues, collective bargaining often became synonymous with conflict.

The core assumption of many modern pluralist optimists is that the traditional adversarial model of collective bargaining is now unsuitable for generating the cooperative and proactive problem-solving inputs required under more intense competitive conditions. In contrast to the unitarist perspectives above, however, unions are deemed to still have a vital role in governing work relations, and thus the pluralist nature of industrial relations is emphasised. To this end, under more intense competitive conditions, pluralist advocates of partnership view cooperation between management, employees and their representatives as a means of generating mutual gains for all workplace stakeholders, and promoting workplace consensus (Kochan and Osterman, 1994; Kochan and Rubenstein, 2000; Rubenstein, 2000 Guest and Peccei, 2001; Rubenstein and Kochan, 2001; Ackers, 2002; O'Dowd, 2006; Roche and Geary, 2006; Roche, 2008).

Kochan and Osterman (1994) are the most widely quoted pluralist advocates of the benefits of mutual gains partnership for all stakeholders. They identify mutual gains practices encompassing union-management forums, direct employee participation practices (e.g. teamwork) and bundles of complementary HRM practices, notably employment security clauses, training and financial stakeholding. Positive outcomes for employers include higher commitment, increased productivity, lower conflict, and improved product quality/innovation. Kochan and Osterman claim that workers also benefit, principally through enhanced employment security and opportunities for direct participation and representative voice at operational and strategic levels. Also, cooperative union-management structures provide unions with inputs into business decision making and, indeed, provide the only basis for union renewal. However, they do not claim that partnership can be applied universally, but requires supportive conditions, notably a differentiation-based competitive strategy and comprehensive management backing.

Rubinstein and Kochan (2001) identify mutual gains arising from WP at the American company Saturn (a General Motors subsidiary), which is lauded for the extent to which unions are involved in co-management initiatives from shopfloor level up to corporate strategy, and where workers participate in self-managed work teams and enjoy employment security. Management also benefits from better product quality and customer service. But despite the equal balance of mutual gains at Saturn, Rubinstein and Kochan identified contextual vulnerabilities, notably doubts over GM's commitment to the project, coupled with weak external institutional supports (America's corporate governance and labour relations system is seen to retard WP). Elsewhere, Rubinstein and Heckscher (2003) suggest limited diffusion of WP may be due to employer perceptions that the stability and job security associated with partnership may constrain, and clash with, the priority of achieving flexibility and cost containment in turbulent competitive conditions.

Drawing on the Saturn experience in another paper, Kochan and Rubinstein (2000) outline a theory of the stakeholder firm based around three key questions. First, under what conditions do stakeholder firms emerge? Kochan and Rubinstein argue that company stakeholders must hold assets (like knowledge) critical to competitive success, stakeholders must be willing to risk assets and must have sufficient power, and shareholder and stakeholder leaders must trust that partnership can work, thus preventing exit. Second, Kochan and Rubinstein ask what organisational/ governance features contribute to successful outcomes? Stakeholders need to add value to achieve high performance, employment and governance systems need to support employee stakeholding in company performance, and stakeholder interests must be aggregated and conflict carefully managed. Finally, for partnership to endure, Kochan and Rubinstein believe stakeholders must have a voice in leadership succession and leaders must be held accountable to all stakeholders. Also, resistance to the legitimacy of stakeholders other than shareholders needs to be overcome. But, they argue, "ultimately, a change in the political environment from one that reinforces the ideology of unregulated capital markets and enterprises to one that legitimates other stakeholders is likely to be necessary to sustain these alternative organizational forms" (2000: 384).

In Ireland, a number of empirical studies report mutual gains arising from workplace partnership. Roche and Geary (2006) identified mutual gains for all stakeholders arising from the now defunct partnership at Irish semi-state airline management company Aer Rianta. Known as the 'Compact for Constructive Participation' (CP), workers and union representatives had a joint decision-making role in areas of corporate strategy.

The Aer Rianta CP dated back to the mid-1990s, when a Joint Union Company Group (JUCG) was set up to govern multi-level partnership in three Irish airports: Dublin, Shannon and Cork. A central principle of the Compact was 'jointness': no party would impose its will unilaterally, and all change proposals would go through agreed partnership processes prior to any decision being made. The CP envisaged multi-level partnership arrangements granting employees and unions a role in decision-making on task participation, department and business unit strategy, and competitive strategy for the company. Unions received guarantees of institutional security and employees were assured of employment security. The company received assurances from unions on improving performance, and the CP dealt with important strategic challenges facing the company.

Using data from the Economic and Social Research Institute (ESRI)/National Centre for Partnership and Performance (NCPP) survey of 3,500 employees (O'Connell et al., 2004), Roche (2008) concludes that employers, employees and unions all gain relatively equally from partnership. Employees gain with respect to intrinsic aspects, such as autonomy, information provision, job satisfaction and fairness. Partnership practices are neither more nor less likely to lead to onerous work regimes, in terms of work intensity or stress. For Roche (2008), employers gain with respect to organisational commitment and the IR climate. With regard to unions, Roche suggests that, on balance, positive net gains appear to arise with respect to union influence and union membership. Arguably, Roche observes, these findings do not point to any major asymmetry in the balance of mutuality or advantage. He feels that over and above the indirect effects on employee attitudes and behaviour, partnership practices do not exert direct influence on outcomes. Rather, partnership practices appeared to affect outcomes on the simple basis that more practices are better than fewer.

Drawing on a survey of managers examining the extent and outcomes of representative partnership arrangements in Ireland, O'Dowd (2006) identified what he perceived to be about 150 workplace partnerships in unionised firms. O'Dowd suggests that the rate of formation of new partnerships had tailed off towards the end of the 1990s, as the early momentum provided by the first national framework agreement covering workplace partnerships (Partnership, 2000), and the availability of EU funding for partnership initiatives, receded. In terms of outcomes, managers in O'Dowd's survey identify a series of positive outcomes for organisations, including higher business performance and workforce productivity. Most managers surveyed also held the view that partnership was linked to higher levels of job satisfaction and better pay and conditions for workers. However, less than half attributed higher job security to partnership and only one fifth reported a positive link between partnership and staffing levels. Just over 50 per cent of managers recorded higher levels of union involvement on a day-to-day basis, and 76 per cent associated partnership with higher levels of union influence over management decision-making. Large numbers of managers reported positive outcomes in areas such as trust levels, quality of communications, and the incidences of disputes and grievances. Overall, O'Dowd concludes that the most positive outcomes from partnership are in the areas benefiting employers (better quality relationships and performance), with less pronounced benefits in areas favourable for unions (union influence in decision-making) and employees (job satisfaction, pay and conditions, employment security).

'Constrained Mutuality'

While emphasising that bundle's of partnership practices can produce mutual gains, but do not work as well in isolation, Guest and Peccei (2001) also argue that management benefit most. In their survey of 54 management and employee representatives in the UK, Guest and Peccei conclude that the most positive mutual gains outcomes for all emanate from combined bundles of representative participation in company decision-making, direct employee participation in work decisions, flexible job design, focus on quality, employment security, and financial participation. Gains for employers include superior productivity and better IR. Employees benefit from greater involvement, satisfaction and voice, and representatives benefit from engagement in business decision-making. Guest and Peccei argue that partnership bundles do not exert direct effects on outcomes, but exert indirect effects by shaping the psychological contract in relation to worker perceptions of trust relations, fairness, and management's delivery of its promises. The state of the psychological contract determines attitudinal and behavioural outcomes, such as job satisfaction, commitment, innovative behaviour, and labour turnover. Although Guest and Peccei (2001: 231) are optimistic about mutual gains potential, they talk of 'constrained mutuality with the balance of advantage leaning clearly towards management'. But they suggest that this 'constrained mutuality' is not an argument against the benefits of partnership.

'Critics'

Partnership Bad for Workers and Unions

The claims of advocates have been criticised by commentators considerably more pessimistic about partnership and its capacity to deliver mutual gains; many of whom would classify themselves as 'Marxists'. Critics tend to view partnership as a new vehicle for employers to recast control over workers and argue that while it may deliver significant benefits for employers, it delivers very few benefits for workers, and may even entail significant costs, such as work intensification and job insecurity (Sennett, 1998; Danford et al., 2005; Tailby et al., 2007). Furthermore, critics of management-union partnership claim employers are intent, at best, on incorporating unions into a managerial agenda and, at worst, marginalising and even eradicating unions (Kelly, 1996, 1998, 2004; Allen, 2000; Terry, 2003; Danford et al., 2005).

Danford et al. (2005) examined partnership initiatives in two British aerospace firms, and concluded that while management accrued significant gains, notably higher productivity and reduced costs, workers and unions experienced few benefits but significant costs. Employees experienced work intensification, job insecurity and reduced autonomy. They further argue that participation in direct and representative partnership structures resulted in unions and their members being incorporated into a managerially dominated agenda, while reaping very few gains. Tailby et al. (2007) reach similar conclusions in their case study of a UK insurance company, with employees and union representatives accruing little benefit from partnership, which primarily benefited management.

One of the most strident critics of management-union partnership from a Marxist perspective is John Kelly (1996, 1998, 2004), who argues that it clearly favours management, with few benefits for unions and their members. For Kelly, unions are best served by engaging in independent militant strategies, because there are irredeemable conflicts of interest and employers are increasingly hostile to unions. He feels that where unions engage in partnership, worker benefits are negligible, while the incorporation of unions in partnership reduces workers' capacity to mobilise and resist employers. His later (2004) study of 22 UK partnership agreements contrasts what he calls 'employer-dominant' and 'labour-parity' partnerships. Under the former, partnership agendas reflect employer interests and unions are compliant. Labour-parity partnerships reflect a more equal power balance, unions are better organised, partnership agendas reflect the interests of both parties more, and employers are more dependent on co-operation. Although labour parity partnerships are more likely to generate some mutual gains than employer-dominant forms, even here Kelly concludes that unions and their members gain little benefit (in relation to issues such as employment security, wages, union influence and density).

In the Irish literature, also from an avowedly Marxist perspective, Allen (2000) argues that adversarial militancy is the best means of advancing the interests of working people and trade unionism. Allen has been a prominent critic of social partnership in Ireland, both at national and workplace level. Indeed, the title of one of his books sums up his thoughts on the potential for consensus: 'The myth of social partnership in Ireland'. Allen (2000: 117-120) notes that the increasing embrace of the market by trade union representatives in Ireland, and the advent of what he calls American-style 'business unionism', have led to the desire to establish 'high trust' relations with employers:

> Increasingly this involves a strategy of deepening partnership structures, so that they are embedded at workplace level and begin to encroach on the traditional adversarial structures of collective bargaining.... The focus on partnership arrangements at workplace level means that the union leaders often seem to share a similar outlook to human resource managers.... Business unionism has a certain appeal in a booming economy when profits are rising and where the avenues of traditional trade unionism seem to be closed.

However, it contains many dangers, Allen warns, adding that employers are refusing to operate as partners in any real sense. Referring to one quoted example of workplace partnership, Allen notes that, rather than accept a small fall in profits in response to deteriorating competitive conditions, 'the company demanded that workers take a major cut in their wage packets and agree to increase their production targets'.

Deep-rooted Conflict

According to critics, conflict is far more deep-rooted in capitalist employment relationships than advocates accept and, accordingly, the conditions retarding partnership are far more acute than those sustaining it (Kelly, 1998; Thompson, 2003; D'Art and Turner, 2005). In Ireland, D'Art and Turner (2005) conducted a survey of 2,000 members of the Amalgamated Transport and General Workers Union in 43 firms, and uncovered very little evidence of mutual gains partnership. D'Art and Turner examine the impact of partnership practices in Irish organisations, including joint union-management committees, teamwork, profit sharing. Overall, diffusion was limited: 39 per cent of employees surveyed reported none of six partnership practices in their workplace, and only 29 per cent reported more than two. A fundamental premise of advocates of partnership is that it reduces/eliminates 'them and us' attitudes. D'Art and Turner's (2005) findings do not support this premise. While just over half of respondents reported no change, almost one-third felt that the 'them and us' divide had increased, as against one-fifth reporting a decrease. Turning to the impact on unions, no change was reported by just less than half of respondents. However, where respondent's felt the union role had changed, this was more likely to result in a perceived decrease (38 per cent), rather than an increase (15 per cent) in union influence. D'Art and Turner (2005:138-139) conclude that diffusion of a 'genuine sense of partnership at firm level has not occurred to any significant degree'. Responding to conditions such as intensified competition, employees in the firms they surveyed had apparently become more cooperative, as indicated by a decline in overt conflict. Yet, old adversarial attitudes persisted. D'Art and Turner (2005: 139) attribute this paradox to the contradiction in employment relations: 'while workers may co-operate with management in pursuit of mutual survival, the antagonism integral to the capital labour relationship remains'.

Thompson (2003) pessimistically refers to a 'disconnected capitalism' as the reason why employers find it so difficult to create and sustain workplace partnerships. He does not question the desirability of mutual gains, but argues that a disconnected, uncoordinated capitalist system generates mainly negative consequences for workers, such as precarious employment and work intensification. Rather than promoting conditions for mutual gains partnership, Thompson (2003) argues that capitalism's current instabilities are producing significant evidence of sharp declines in employee commitment and morale related to factors such as job insecurity and work stress.

'Pragmatic Contingency' Perspectives

Contingent on Context

Aside from advocates and critics, a third theoretical strand can be identified in the literature, which will here, for convenience, be labelled 'pragmatic contingency' perspectives (Fox, 1985; Edwards, 1986, 2003; Streeck, 1987; Batstone, 1988; Regini, 1995; Gallie et al., 1998; Korczynski et al., 2000, Geary and Dobbins, 2001). These writers are grouped together here because they all provide generic analytical observations on industrial relations; in particular, showing how employment relations are characterised by inherent structural contradictions, which generate different outcomes in different contextual conditions. In essence, contingency perspectives – some of which evolved as a so-called 'radical' semi-critique (but not abandonment) of traditional pluralist perspectives – emphasise the pragmatism often at the core of the search for cooperative work relations. Contingency perspectives observe that the adoption and outcomes of partnership, and its sustainability, are contingent on multiple contextual conditions, including economic pressures, technology, labour market and institutional factors, and different management and worker choices. Practices and outcomes are likely to vary, because they are contingent on the context in which partnership is located. The implication is that advocates and critics can both be right or wrong about partnership. It all depends on context.

Extends Pluralist Theory

'Pragmatic contingency' perspectives build on traditional pluralist analysis, while also offering a partial critique from what has in the past been termed a 'radical' industrial relations orientation (cf. Fox, 1985) in order to advance theoretical understanding of the paradox of workplace cooperation and conflict. In this way, pluralist IR theory has proven itself to be adaptable and to refine and take on board new ideas. In a nutshell, the key difference between conventional pluralism – associated with the likes of Flanders (1970) and Clegg (1979) and more recently Kochan and Osterman (1994) – and the contingency perspectives cited above is that the former underestimate and are not theoretically explicit about the underlying balance of power, authority and control relations in the employment relationship. Watson (1995: 289) provides the following definition of what he calls 'radical pluralism' to distinguish it from conventional pluralism:

> [radical pluralism] recognises the plurality of groups and interests in society (and welcomes social pluralism in principle) whilst observing the more basic patterns of power and inequality which tend to shape, and be shaped by it.

In terms of extending pluralist theory, contingency or 'radical' perspectives go further than traditional pluralist analysis by explaining why workplace conflict and cooperation have deeper structural roots in the employment relationship than surface issues concerning IR institutions and procedures. In short, a deeper level of analysis allows us to go beneath the surface of specific industrial relations phenomena and outcomes to explain the general underlying structural pressures and contradictions driving IR. The task for practitioners and scholars is not just to focus on the specific IR issues between employers and workers emerging at the surface level, but, crucially, to also understand the general structural forces underneath giving rise to them.

Core Conceptual Arguments

The core conceptual ideas associated with a 'pragmatic contingency' perspective, many of which have been described by Edwards (1986, 2003) elsewhere, can be summarised as follows:

- The concept of *contradiction* is vital for illustrating how managing the employment relationship involves balancing contradictory forces pushing in opposite directions. This 'contradiction' operates at two main levels: employers have to manage uncertainties associated with external economic pressures (notably pressures to accumulate profits, which are particularly acute when competition intensifies), and external contradictions feed into the internal contradictions of managing employment relations (a need to balance the competing requirements to generate employee cooperation with management goals while also maintaining control over employees).

- The need for employers to pursue the contradictory objectives of worker *cooperation* and *control* means that management adopt a mix of cooperative and controlling employment relations practices in pursuit of this objective.

- The balancing of these contradictions means the employment relationship is potentially unstable and that the generation of worker cooperation is uncertain.

- Employers and workers are locked together in a relation of *structured antagonism*: they enter into an employment relationship because they depend on each other, but they also have divergent interests. 'Structured antagonism is built into the employment relationship because managerial practices are concerned with ensuring that employees agree to undertake work under the authority of their employer, who, in the process, face an imperative to secure a surplus in the process of production/service delivery and, ultimately, accumulate profits. Employees enter into an employment contract to earn a living, and the employer has the authority to deploy employees in various ways in return for a given payment/reward.

- The employment contract is *indeterminate* because it cannot stipulate in more than general terms the nature of the ongoing day-to-day employee contribution.

- Structured antagonism indirectly shapes the day-to-day balance of cooperation and conflict, in terms of the extent to which employers and employees have shared or conflicting interests. At the most basic level, a certain degree of cooperation is ensured because both parties depend on the survival of the enterprise.

- The vital concept that workplaces are *negotiated orders* (Strauss et al., 1971) bringing together stakeholders with divergent as well as shared interests means that patterns of work relations, and accompanying workplace rules, expectations and norms (formal and informal, explicit and implicit) are (re)created by the outcomes of interactions and power relations between employers and workers.

- The balance of *power* influences the employment relationship (cf. Lukes, 2005). It is a truism to say 'it's all about power'.

- The prevailing rules, expectations and norms of the employment relationship at any given time make-up the *psychological contract* between employers and employees, which may be explicit and implicit, and sets the terms for day-to-day interaction.

'Contradiction' and 'Structured Antagonism'

Paul Edwards' (1986, 2003) theoretical work is valuable for illustrating how contextual conditions can promote or retard partnership, notably his emphasis on the concepts of 'contradiction' and 'structured antagonism', described above. Edwards (2003) illustrates how the management of the employment relationship involves balancing contradictory forces pushing in opposite directions. Employers have to manage uncertainties associated with external economic pressures, and also the internal contradictions of employment relations. The most fundamental external contradiction relates to the periodical volatility and uncertainty of capitalism as an economic system and resultant uncertainty in product and financial markets. Employer actions, at some level, are shaped by a drive to produce goods and services to accumulate profit or stay within budget. The system is susceptible to volatility and uncertainty (Hyman, 1987; Streeck, 1987; Edwards, 1990), because the drive for profit accumulation is in contradiction with a general tendency for the rate of profit to fall as competition intensifies. Significantly, product market contradictions have become more turbulent in recent decades as international competition has intensified, although some sectors and firms are more exposed than others.

To varying degrees, these external pressures filter internally into the workplace, and Edwards (2003: 16-17) describes how the task of management is 'an uncertain process', and that workplace consensus 'cannot be total because of the structural conditions in which employers and workers find themselves'. According to Edwards (2003: 16-17), managers and workers are locked into a relationship that is contradictory and antagonistic. 'It is contradictory not in the sense of logical incompatibility but because managements have to pursue the objectives of control and releasing creativity, both of which call for different approaches'. Similarly, Watson (1995: 292) suggests that patterns of employment regulation 'involve both the direction, surveillance and discipline of subordinates whose enthusiastic commitment to corporate objectives cannot be taken for granted, *and* the mobilisation of discretion, initiative and diligence which coercive supervision, far from guaranteeing, is likely to destroy'. Management faces the continuous problem of trying to reconcile this contradiction in the people management process, together with responding to uncertain external contradictions, and the search for a solution is likely to encompass a pragmatic combination of policies, none of which can be permanently successful.

Edwards (2003: 16-17) also explains that the employment relationship is 'antagonistic' because managerial strategies are 'about the deployment of workers' labour power in ways which permit the generation of a surplus'. Workers are the only people who produce a surplus in the production process, but, they do not usually determine how their labour power is deployed to meet this objective, Edwards argues. There is thus a relation of structured antagonism between employer and worker. He uses this term to emphasise that the 'antagonism is built into the basis of the employment relationship', even though on a day-to-day level cooperation is also important. Edwards distinguishes the concept of 'structured antagonism' from the more usual one of conflicts of interest. 'The latter has the problem of implying that the real or fundamental interests of capital and labour are opposed. The fact that workers have several interests confounds this idea'. A structured antagonism is a basic aspect of the employment relationship which shapes how day-to-day relations are handled but is not something feeding directly into the interests of the parties. 'Firms have to find ways to continue to extract a surplus, and if they do not then both they and their workers will suffer'. Balancing the needs of controlling workers and securing cooperation ultimately rests on ensuring that a surplus continues to be generated, Edwards observes.

Power and the 'Negotiation of Order'

The generation of workforce consensus in an employment relationship characterised by contradiction and structured antagonism defines the ongoing and uncertain task facing employers, namely the 'negotiation of order' (Strauss et al., 1971). According to Strauss et al. (1971: 103-4):

> Order is something at which members of any society, any organization, must work. For the shared agreements ... are not binding for all time ... review is called for ... the bases of concerted action (social order) must be constituted continually, or 'worked out'. Such considerations have led us to emphasize the importance of negotiation.

'Status' and 'Contract'

By using these conceptual tools provided by contingency perspectives we can see that employment relationships in Ireland and other industrialised economies are therefore subject to contradictory pressures. Recent contradictory trends in employment relations can best be conceptualised by using Streeck's (1987) distinction between 'contract' and 'status' in the employment relationship. In a highly influential paper, Streeck (1987:290) argued that moves away from traditional pluralist collective bargaining in many industrialised economies, and changes in workplace relations generally, are being shaped by the requirement to increase efficiency and flexibility in order to respond to an 'unprecedented degree of economic uncertainty'. This requirement has necessitated an increasingly close integration of industrial relations and wider business strategy, whereas in the past the two were largely disconnected under a more stable era of profit accumulation. Economic pressures have resulted in the gradual unravelling of traditional IR institutions such as collective bargaining, which have been insulated from efficiency considerations, and which are perceived by many employers as constituting rigidities that obstruct flexible work organisation and labour deployment.

Streeck (1987: 292-5) distinguishes between management by 'contract' and 'status' when explaining the decline of traditional pluralist collective bargaining. Streeck suggests that employers may use two broad means to dismantle perceived workplace rigidities, and to secure the requisite degree of worker compliance or cooperation to the adjustments deemed to be required in the face of new market pressures: a 'return to contract' or an 'extension of status'. A 'return to contract' is characterised by a short-term disposable 'hire and fire' approach, the widespread use of insecure atypical employment contracts, agency work, subcontracting and outsourcing, the dismantling or rejection of traditional workers 'status rights' (such as collective bargaining/trade union representation), with employers adopting unilateral control policies to extract concessions and force workers to comply with flexibility and change. Workers are expected to comply with formal rules and performance targets (with rewards being strictly linked to measurement against performance), are granted very little autonomy and are largely excluded from decision-making. It is made very clear that management is the sole source of authority.

Alternatively, under what Streeck (1987) calls 'extension of status', employers may move towards an integrative collaborative partnership approach in an attempt to secure a higher intensity of worker commitment to change and closer identification with company goals. To this end, employers may introduce new status rights, such as union-employer partnership forums, works councils, joint consultative councils, direct employee participation schemes such as teamwork, and new HR policies such as employment security guarantees, financial participation schemes, skills training, and single status terms and conditions. This more inclusive approach usually incorporates some devolving of autonomy, voice and decision-making power to employees and their representatives and is based on mutual relations of high trust. There may be a concern by employers to move beyond a simple cash nexus relationship, to build trust, reciprocal obligations and shared interests. Approaches based on extending status correspond with workplace partnership.

Crucially, Streeck (1987: 297) is careful to emphasise that contract and status are not mutually exclusive and are often used in combination, given that management has to manage external and internal uncertainties, and he noted the 'possible contradictions inherent in a simultaneous pursuit of restored contract and extended status'. Lower skill workers on insecure atypical contracts, such as temporary agency workers, are more likely to be managed on the basis of a return to contract. In contrast, permanent skilled core workers are more likely to be managed on the basis of an extension of status rights. But Streeck argues that elements of status and contract often co-exist in the same workplace, and even permanent core workers may work in semi-autonomous teams (status) but at the same time be subject to explicit tighter performance measurement (contract). The contrasting characteristics of management by contract and status are outlined below, drawing from Streeck's (1987:294) own table.

Table 2.1: Management by Contract and Status

	Return to Contract	**Extension of Status**
Employment status	Temporary	Permanent
Numerical flexibility	Hire and fire	Flexible working time
Functional flexibility	Hire and fire	Self-regulated, job rotation
Work organisation	Taylorist	Teamwork
Qualifications sought	Narrow	Broad
Wage determination	Industrial engineering	Payment by ability
Management style	Unilateral prerogative	Consultation, participation

Contingency Case Studies

The significance of context and the key concept of 'contradiction' are supported by empirical research on partnership. In a case study of partnership at a pharmaceutical plant in Ireland, Geary and Dobbins (2001) identify partial mutual gains from teamwork, but this coincided with a re-casting of managerial control, reflecting contradictions in managing employment relations. Management repositioned competitive strategy around the manufacture of differentiated small-batch products. This new quality-oriented strategy was complemented by continuous process technology, teamwork, employment security, training, and engaging unions in partnership. Management were the main beneficiaries, with improved productivity, less conflict and better product quality. Fewer gains were accrued by unions and workers, but the gains were nevertheless welcomed. Unions experienced greater input into company decision-making, but partnership was something of a double-edged sword because traditional collective bargaining power waned. Workers cited various benefits, such as modest increases in autonomy and more job satisfaction. But workers also experienced costs. They were still subject to controls, such as residual direct supervision and tighter performance targets. Many workers experienced work intensification. Significantly, many workers accepted working harder in a more orderly and better-managed work process where management had removed old irritants provoking conflict. Yet despite partial mutual gains, conflicting interests remained. Most workers saw a need for unions, pockets of distrust existed, and there were few signs of wider commitment to the employer.

In his nuanced study of industrial relations partnership arrangements in four Irish unionised semi-state companies (the ESB, An Post, Aer Lingus and Eircom), Hastings (2003: 215-16) suggests that marketisation appears to trigger a series of distinctive responses within companies, involving different but strongly interconnected modes of political engagement, different modes of strategy development and implementation, and different sequences with respect to IR and HR postures. According to Hastings, the types of responses found, and the distinctive patterns that emerge, depend primarily on variable external and internal conditions, including the pace and nature of marketisation, social and geographical embeddedness, and internal conditions such as the tradition and structure of industrial relations. He argues that politics works in different ways, commercial strategy works in different ways, and that the handling of IR and HR works in accordance with what he calls 'different sequences of forcing and fostering' (cf. Walton et al., 1994). This 'forcing' and 'fostering' distinction echoes Streeck's 'contract' and 'status' distinction.

In view of this, Hastings remarks that management in his four case studies used two general approaches to restructuring in response to greater competitive pressures for marketisation and liberalisation: forcing and fostering. Significantly, he noted that forcing and fostering were often used in parallel, which corresponds with the observations made in this book. He identifies fostering as constituting either collective partnership relationships and/or direct employee participation – encompassing, for instance, new Employee Share Ownership Schemes (ESOP) or other new partnership arrangements. Hastings notes that having a fostering culture at the apex of an organisation does not necessarily mean it will percolate downwards to all levels, with adversarialism continuing to exist. In the ESB, he observed that management used both fostering and forcing in parallel. At Eircom, meanwhile, a fostering approach underpinned by partnership was facilitated by the commercial conditions, and strong union power was a big factor in going down the partnership route. Sequential forcing and fostering was used at An Post and Aer Lingus, which reflected the financial difficulties in both organisations. In An Post, this took the form of a viability plan involving job losses and the introduction of atypical forms of work (both forms of forcing). This resulted in an adversarial climate for a period, until there was a move towards partnership and ESOPs (fostering). Hastings emphasises the continuing importance of informality and informal contacts in managing the industrial relations process. At ESB, for instance, Hastings notes that although formal channels of bargaining set the basis for change, informality was crucial at national and local level.

Drawing on 32 case studies of information and consultation (IC) initiatives in Irish firms, Dundon et al. (2006) refer to contingent and contradictory dynamics and outcomes. Most of the 32 cases they studied constituted managerial sponsorship, in the sense that management set the agenda, with direct IC methods taking precedence over representative participation. Only two of the 32 cases could be described as robust partnerships with strong employee representative forums. Dundon et al. add that although studies have consistently shown a link between bundles of IR/HR practices (notably information and consultation forums) and better performance, and that workers want more information and consultation than provided by employers, few employers in Ireland involve and consult their employees to any real extent, the result being a representation gap. They point to the contradiction that managers tended to guard their own decision-making prerogative, while at the same time articulating the need to tap into employee ideas for successful change. Also, Dundon et al. refer to the rather different meanings often ascribed to information and consultation by managers and employees/unions respectively. Indeed, many employees and representatives interviewed in their case studies appeared more sceptical of the depth and extent of consultation and partnership than managers. There are a number of tensions/barriers retarding effective employee consultation, they argue, including opposition from corporate HQ; line managers being preoccupied and having their own agendas; and insufficient skills for management and worker representatives to engage in joint consultation. Dundon et al. (2006) conclude that partnership-oriented IC methods were most effective when they were integrated, when direct and indirect methods were combined, when senior management strongly endorsed practices, and when informal dialogue supported formal arrangements. Without informal dialogue, trust and goodwill, it is difficult to progress with formal partnerships. They suggest organisations are not undifferentiated, and it is wrong to assume what works in one place will work elsewhere.

Sustainability of Partnership

A vital theme that has been addressed by contingency perspectives is partnership's sustainability. Oxenbridge and Brown (2004) conducted case studies of UK firms, distinguishing between robust and shallow partnerships. They conclude that managers and union representatives are more likely to report mutual gains where cooperative union-management partnerships are robust, but observe that these partnerships are difficult to sustain. They argue that cooperative relationships are more sustainable where employers wish to maintain independent employee voice, especially where union density is high and informal partnerships exist. Shallow partnerships give unions and their members little influence, and employers benefited disproportionately from these weak forms. Significantly, though one of their cases had successfully negotiated a second partnership agreement, most had not yet been tested by time.

As well as identifying positive mutual gains for all stakeholders arising from workplace partnership at the Irish Airports' Authority, Aer Rianta, Roche and Geary (2006) describe how the experiment broke down after eight years, with the authors attributing this to weak internal institutional bulwarks; tensions between supporters and critics of the 'Compact'; a succession crisis after key management and union advocates retired; failure to vertically align interlocking partnership architecture from top to bottom by implementing direct participation and complementary

HR policies alongside representative forums (WP at Aer Rianta was largely restricted to representative level). These factors interacted with external obstacles, notably 'prolonged indecision and inaction by government regarding the future of Aer Rianta' (2006: 252).

Conditions Promoting or Retarding Workplace Partnership

More generally, the contingency literature also examines a range of contextual conditions deemed to promote or retard partnership. Batstone's (1988) framework identifying five conditions underpinning patterns of work relations is an effective tool for the purposes of this book: namely identifying the conditions influencing workplace partnership. The five key contextual conditions identified by Batstone as influencing particular patterns of work relations are: the production system and the technology used; the role of markets: both for labour and products; 'institutionalisation', in terms of the structures and institutions regulating the employment relationship, with the state as a key actor; and the strategies and structures of employers and trade unions/workers.

Product Markets and Technology

Many commentators agree that product market competition is *the* driving force influencing employer moves from adversarial/control approaches towards partnership approaches. There is disagreement in the literature, however, as to the nature and extent of this trend. Some of the more optimistic writers have suggested that an intensification of product market competition – often accompanied by advanced new technologies – is promoting a transformation in employment relations away from control towards empowerment and commitment approaches (Piore and Sabel, 1984; Walton, 1985; Womack et al., 1990; Pfeffer, 1994, 1998). In contrast, more nuanced contingency perspectives (Locke et al., 1995; Regini, 1995; Cappelli et al., 1997; Crouch and Streeck, 1997; Godard, 2001, 2004) accept that product market competition, particularly exposure to international competition, is a key condition promoting moves towards partnership, and also recognise the influence of advanced technology, but refute grandiose claims by some of the more utopian optimists that we are witnessing anything that could be interpreted as a uniform transformation of employment relations in the direction of high commitment HRM/partnership. According to the contingency literature, it is more accurate to suggest that certain conditions may promote tendencies towards mutual gains partnership in some competitive circumstances. But it is just as possible, if not more so, that employers will respond to competitive pressures by tightening unilateral control and engaging in cost cutting, contracting-out, outsourcing, redundancies, rationalisation.

In reality, firms have responded to new market pressures in contingent ways. Competitive postures and employment relations practices are characterised by what Regini (1995: 104-5) calls 'pragmatic eclecticism'. Cappelli et al. (1997: 106) suggest that it is not intensity of competition which is crucial, but the manner in which competition relates to the competitive posture of the firm: moves towards partnership are most likely where 'quality competition' is emphasised and firms are exposed to international competition. Locke et al. (1995) suggest that the main point of divergence is between high value-added capital intensive competitive postures focusing on product customisation, innovation and quality competition, and more traditional low value-added labour intensive competitive postures focusing on product standardisation and cost minimisation; although in practice many firms use both, either simultaneously or sequentially.

According to Streeck (1995: 325-6):

> As long as management finds it in its rational interest to operate a mode of production that requires peaceful, cooperative labor relations – perhaps even giving workers an institutionalised, collective voice in the firm – workers and unions may be able to extract concessions by threatening to withdraw from cooperation. However, as long as management can respond by restructuring towards alternative modes of production that function profitably with less demanding or no labour co-operation, it will take place largely on management's terms.

A similar point was emphasised by Streeck at an International Industrial Relations Association Conference in Dublin in 1997, when he posed the question, 'how much pluralism is needed for high performance?', delivering the sobering answer that many employers simply do not need high levels of employee representation, consultation and partnership to achieve high performance outcomes.

For Godard (2001), employers that primarily focus on high value-added competitive postures are more likely to perceive an economic requirement to invest in human resources and move towards partnership. In contrast, employers that compete primarily on product standardisation and cost minimisation are likely to view partnership and HRM practices as unnecessary and expensive, and continue to rely on unilateral prerogative to secure compliance. The financial and time resources required to introduce partnership – particularly in a comprehensive bundle – can be considerable, with large profitable firms having obvious advantages over smaller firms in this regard. In a later paper, Godard (2004) accepts there is little reason to doubt that partnership practices are highly effective in some workplaces, and that the adoption of at least some progressive work practices can deliver mutual gains in many workplaces. But he believes the premise of a high-performance paradigm may be a false one, and that it may be more fruitful for employers to adopt what have always been considered 'good' work practices (e.g. formal training, group-based work organisation, information-sharing, and accommodative union relations policies). He argues that advocates may not only overestimate the positive effects of partnership, but also underestimate the costs. 'As a result it may be that, for most employers, the full adoption of the high performance paradigm often yields little or no overall advantage over traditional personnel practices...' Godard (2004: 366) supports a 'political economy approach', which holds that conflicts embedded in the employment relationship may limit the effectiveness of the high-performance paradigm for employers, render it highly fragile, and explain its variable adoption, which depends on workplace context variables. 'In short, it may simply be that it is in the interests of only a minority of employers to adopt the high-performance paradigm fully...' (Godard 2004: 371). Elsewhere, Godard says, given the costs of partnership and HRM, many employers may see their interests best served by a labour intensification approach.

Institutional Conditions – 'Checks and Balances'

A number of contingency perspectives stress the importance of institutional factors and historical starting points for promoting or retarding moves towards workplace partnership: that change is, to some degree at least, path dependent on institutional starting points and legacies (Locke et al. 1995; Regini, 1995; Streeck, 1997; Roche and Geary, 2000; Hutton, 2002). Streeck (1997) remarks that certain institutional and historical conditions may constrain price competition and management unilateralism, and persuade employers to compete on the basis of quality competition and develop productivity coalitions. Northern European countries such as Germany (Streeck, 1997), Sweden (Pontusson, 1992), and the Netherlands (Visser, 1998), are frequently quoted as possessing institutional frameworks supporting quality competition and collaborative production. Each of these countries has a different institutional framework, but they all support workplace collaboration and partnership to some degree.

For example, in Sweden, the durability of workplace consensus reflects institutional and cultural factors that include strong unions, as well as statutory institutional supports such as the 1976 Co-determination Act and the 1982 'Development Agreement' on co-determination (UVA) (Pontusson, 1992). In relation to Germany, Streeck (1995) cites five major institutional factors that promote quality competition/consensus approaches and constrain cost competition/ management prerogative: strong proactive trade unions, comprehensive employment protection legislation, a co-ordinated wage bargaining system promoting and extending high wages, a comprehensive national vocational training system, and a set of binding rules enshrined in the Work Constitution Act, 1972, which obliges employers to establish works councils to consult workers.

While in countries like Sweden, Denmark, Finland and Germany – frequently held up as beacons of high consensus – institutions promoting consensus are coming under considerable pressure from global market forces (Crouch and Streeck, 1997), these pluralist high consensus collaborative economies remain the most economically competitive and socially cohesive in the world, combining economic efficiency with fairness by embedding institutional 'checks and balances' governing and channelling the power and demands of the various interest groups, as Hutton (2002) argues.

In contrast, in traditionally voluntarist institutional contexts found in more liberal market economies such as the UK (Edwards, 2003), the US

(Cappelli et al., 1997), and Ireland (Roche and Geary, 2000), institutional conditions have historically tended to encourage adversarial power relations, cost competition and management prerogative, more than quality competition and workplace collaboration. As a result of this legacy, workplace partnership is only likely to be adopted by employers in these countries where it is seen as more economically advantageous than unilateral workplace governance – i.e. the benefits for employers outweigh the costs. Adoption of partnership will likely reflect rather 'unique' conditions such as niche high-value added competitive strategies, advanced capital intensive technologies, competent management 'champions' and strong proactive unions. Belanger and Edwards (2007: 713) conclude that conditions generating sustainable partnerships in liberal labour markets like the UK, US and Ireland are feasible but rare, and that stronger 'beneficial constraints' are necessary if partnership is to increase – in the form of coherent institutional supports requiring proactive state interventions.

In relation to Ireland specifically, there are few legal and institutional pressures obliging employers to share power with workers and their representatives over the key operational and strategic issues facing company stakeholders. Workplace partnership is still a voluntary endeavour. Existing institutions charged with promoting workplace partnership, notably the National Centre for Partnership and Performance (NCPP), can try and cajole organisations to enter into voluntary partnerships by selling it as a method of good industrial relations, but there are limits to this influence.

The upshot is that despite centralised bargaining being in place in Ireland for twenty years, it has not yet filtered down to workplace level to any great extent – a finding contained in the most comprehensive survey of workplace relations in Ireland to date, conducted by the ESRI and the NCPP (O'Connell et al., 2004; Williams et al., 2004). Drawing on the ESRI/NCPP survey data, Roche (2006: 25-30) concludes that partnership in Irish workplaces 'remains more a guiding vision than a reality'. The degree to which workplace partnership 'even remains a compelling vision for some of the parties to social partnership, or for sections of their constituencies, is also open to question'. Accordingly, Roche suggests, 'it is hard to maintain the 'high road' optimism of those who suppose that workplace partnership is, or might become, the template for the future of Irish employment relations'. Beginning with employees in unionised workplaces, Roche says the incidence of partnership practices varies significantly. About 17 per cent of employees report formal policies for avoiding compulsory redundancies/lay-offs. Just under 20 per cent are involved in profit sharing/gainsharing. Just over one in two employees were in receipt of paid training. Just under one third of employees in unionised workplaces experienced direct involvement, and less than four in 10 worked in enterprises with representative partnership arrangements involving unions. When the incidence of multiple partnership practices is examined, Roche says it is striking that less than 10 per cent of employees in unionised workplaces experienced four or five of these practices. Meanwhile, only about 5 per cent of employees in non-unionised workplaces reported three out of four possible partnership practices above.

One line of explanation for the limited spread of partnership, Roche (2006: 25-30) observes, is that 'the emergence, viability or durability and outcomes of partnership may be dependent on multiple contingencies that vary across workplaces and enterprises and that may also vary within them over time'. However, he adds:

> While this line of explanation seems compelling, it appears necessary to integrate the insights involved within a broader perspective that emphasizes the growing latitude available to employers to tailor employment relations arrangements to their commercial circumstances and postures.

The upshot is that diversity in employment relation's patterns constitutes the key trend:

> Partnership is implemented by some employers, where permitted by contingencies and prompted by more general postures. But frequently other types of regimes develop, some incorporating aspects of partnership and others still few or any such attributes.

Many employers may attempt 'serial and piecemeal experimentation with fashionable new practices that are grafted on to existing practices with little resulting coherence or concern for its realization'.

Management Competence

The importance of management competence for the negotiation of workplace order is recognised in a long line of studies dating back to the time of the British Donovan Report in the late 1960s, which transmit the simple but crucial message that good management is ultimately what matters for workplace consensus (Donovan Commission, 1968; Nichols, 1986; Batstone, 1986, 1988; Lazonick, 1990; Hodson, 1999, 2005; Edwards and Wright, 2001; Nolan and O'Donnell, 2003).

Rather than simply identifying unions and workers as the sole scapegoat for shop-floor disorder and strife in British workplaces during the 1960s, the Donovan Commission (1968) analysis was more complex and subtle. While not excusing it, the Donovan report interpreted the emergence of informal union and worker job controls (often referred to as restrictive practices) at the time as a rational response to management behaviour, particularly in situations where basic pay was often low and many managements had reneged on their responsibility to properly manage work organisations. This analysis runs against the common tide of opinion that unions and work groups developed job controls to prevent management from introducing more efficient forms of work organisation, innovative production techniques, and new technology. This may have been the case in some instances, but many employers, according to the Donovan analysis, made little attempt to co-ordinate and plan their businesses in a coherent fashion, the inference being that mismanagement and neglect was a key source of disorder, although organised workers and politicised union activists undoubtedly played a major part in fuelling workplace strife.

Since the time of Donovan, other commentators also claim that mismanagement is a key reason for retarding cooperation. Batstone (1986) argues that in contrast to the dominant opinion that poor industrial relations causes distrust and conflict, the opposite scenario may be more accurate: it is what he calls management sclerosis and badly planned and organised production and work systems that provokes poor IR.

Developing this 'good' management theme, a key issue emerging again in recent contingency literature is that outcomes of partnership may simply reflect a more competent and coherent management style and that a higher number of progressive practices will deliver better outcomes than few or none. Progressive partnership practices exert indirect, rather than direct, effects on outcomes. What matters directly is overall managerial competence, not just in employment relations, but production, sales, etc. Edwards and Wright (2001: 570-575) make the vital point that recent studies of partnership-based work systems 'may only be showing that managing people in a coherent and disciplined way is more effective than not doing so'. Partnership practices may complement such improvement without being a direct cause. Edwards and Wright (2001) reject claims by advocates of direct links between partnership practices and high performance. It does not follow, despite the pretensions of some quantitative studies to place a cash effect of adopting a given set of HR practices, that a firm following suit will reap the rewards. Effects may arise due to location in a specific context, and thus not be reproducible. Partnership and HRM may also be no more than the modern delivery mechanism of the simple principle that how well people are managed affects outcomes. Edwards and Wright note that many of the core ideas underpinning partnership existed in the 1960s or earlier, as with productivity bargaining and quality of work life programmes. Once stronger economic pressures forced a re-think, HRM and partnership may have been a convenient change vehicle.

Similarly, Hodson (1999) concludes that the critical factor influencing partnership is not the impact of specific practices, but whether management respects or violates the workplace norms defining the employment relationship in a given context. Workers expect management to deliver on its promises and to adhere to various norms underpinning workplace order: particularly fairness, participation, security, and a workable system of production. Workers are malleable to a certain extent, and may be prepared to adjust to workplace change and new management practices, but are less likely to accept constant 'chopping and changing' by management; particularly where there is no clear direction or reason for change. Serious management violation of established workplace norms may provoke distrust and conflict. For Hodson (1999: 5), the influence of IR practices occurs indirectly through the association of different practices with 'different levels of management abuse and incompetence'. Direct management control involving close supervision is most susceptible to management abuse and negative worker responses. In contrast, sophisticated partnership practices that integrate workers into decision-making are more likely to be associated with good management and mutual gains.

The actions and choices of workers and their representatives will also obviously be crucial for influencing whether or not cooperative relations prosper. In particular, where they are present, the ways in which unions respond to managerial policies will influence whether an adversarial or a cooperative approach emerges. Much depends on whether unions are able and willing to move away from defensive adversarial postures towards proactive collaborative postures, and critically, whether management support this. Historically, trade unions in Ireland and the UK have often reacted defensively to change, wanting to preserve the status quo – and this may be with good reason where management ultimately aims to erode pay and conditions. But even where 'good' management has positive intentions, unions sometimes find it difficult to move beyond a defensive 'conservative' mindset, which can inhibit cooperation.

Conclusion

In summary, it is argued in this chapter that 'pragmatic contingency' perspectives provide the best means of analysing workplace partnership. Employers have to manage external pressures and internal contradictions (of employment relations), so the nature and outcomes of partnership will be diverse, not fixed and uniform. Much depends on the context in which partnership is located. Gaps remain in knowledge of partnership, which this study seeks to address, notably on the balance of mutuality, and the conditions sustaining (and retarding) partnership. Table 2.2 on the next page summarises competing theories and perspectives on workplace partnership. Figure 2.1 on the page after that outlines a 'contingency model' of workplace partnership summarising the linkage between management practices, outcomes and context.

Table 2.2: Competing Perspectives on Workplace Partnership

Core Assumptions	Unitarist Advocates	Pluralist Advocates	Pragmatic Contingency	Marxist Critics
Nature of workplace partnership	Employers increasingly introducing high commitment model of HRM. No role for trade unions. Fundamental break with past.	Mutual gains representative partnership replacing collective bargaining. Strong role for unions emphasized.	Partnership coincides with continued management control. Cooperation and control exist in 'contradiction', but tendencies in either direction. Control may be re-cast but still exists.	Pervasive management control. Partnership not possible. Nothing changed.
Worker experiences	Highly positive: numerous benefits, such as employee empowerment, higher skill, etc. Employees have common interests with employers (unitarism).	Broadly positive for workers and representatives. Mutual gains. Interests may differ, but also common interests (pluralism).	Variable. Mixed costs and benefits for workers and representatives. Interests may differ, but also common interests (pluralism).	Highly negative: degradation, work intensification. Unions marginalized. Employers and workers interests are fundamentally opposed (Marxism).
Industrial relations outcomes	Highly positive: high trust, high commitment, mutual gains for all. No conflict (seen as pathological aberration)	Broadly positive: reduced conflict, mutual gains for all stakeholders.	Variable. (Partial) mutual gains consensus co-exists with conflict. Can be tendencies in either direction.	Conflict between capital and labour endemic. No consensus.
Contextual conditions	Mgt-employee partnership potentially universally applicable in most circumstances.	Representative partnership most common in strongly unionised sectors.	Pluralist partnership can 'work' but requires 'special' conditions to take root and prosper in prevailing uncertain economic/institutional climate. Strong emphasis on context for shaping patterns of workplace IR.	Partnership not possible under capitalist economic system. Capitalism requires fundamental reform, and new type of society.

Figure 2.1: A 'Contingency Model' of Workplace Partnership

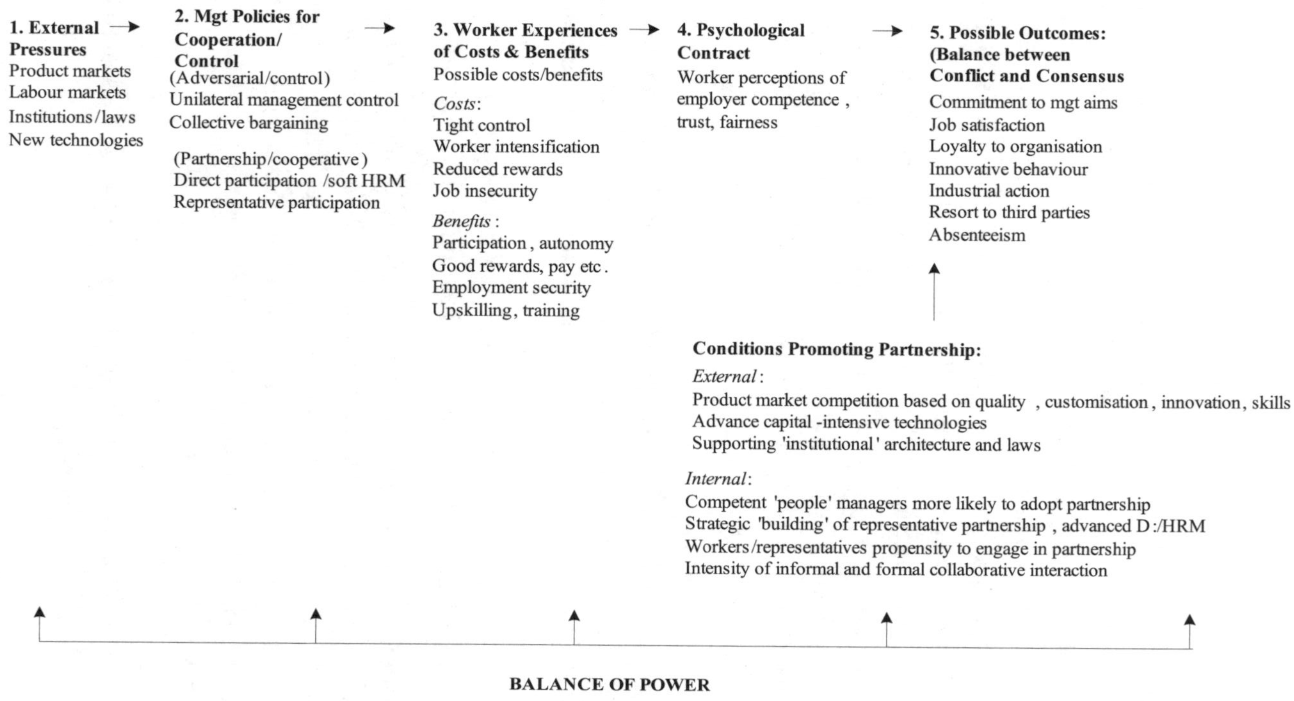

1. External Pressures
Product markets
Labour markets
Institutions/laws
New technologies

→

2. Mgt Policies for Cooperation/ Control
(Adversarial/control)
Unilateral management control
Collective bargaining

(Partnership/cooperative)
Direct participation /soft HRM
Representative participation

→

3. Worker Experiences of Costs & Benefits
Possible costs/benefits

Costs:
Tight control
Worker intensification
Reduced rewards
Job insecurity

Benefits :
Participation, autonomy
Good rewards, pay etc .
Employment security
Upskilling, training

→

4. Psychological Contract
Worker perceptions of employer competence , trust, fairness

→

5. Possible Outcomes: (Balance between Conflict and Consensus
Commitment to mgt aims
Job satisfaction
Loyalty to organisation
Innovative behaviour
Industrial action
Resort to third parties
Absenteeism

Conditions Promoting Partnership:

External:
Product market competition based on quality , customisation , innovation, skills
Advance capital -intensive technologies
Supporting 'institutional' architecture and laws

Internal:
Competent 'people' managers more likely to adopt partnership
Strategic 'building' of representative partnership , advanced D:/HRM
Workers/representatives propensity to engage in partnership
Intensity of informal and formal collaborative interaction

BALANCE OF POWER

Research Issues

Having reviewed perspectives and critiques on the potential of workplace partnership to deliver mutual gains, three important research issues arise:

- *How have employers tried to move towards partnership, and has it displaced management control practices?* A key issue is the pragmatic dynamics of how employers seek to cooperate with employees and their representatives in practice. It is important to examine how employers respond to stronger competitive pressures by attempting to move away from adversarial IR traditions towards adopting new practices commonly associated with workplace partnership. A key issue in the literature is whether or not workplace partnership is displacing adversarialism and management control. To examine what has happened in practice, it is vital to benchmark past patterns of employment regulation at our two case studies with current practice.

- *Does workplace partnership deliver mutual gains for workers, unions and employers, and what is the balance of mutuality?* A key premise of workplace partnership is that it can deliver mutual gains for the main stakeholders in the employment relationship (Kochan and Osterman, 1994). The balance of mutuality is a particularly important issue to explore, in terms of whether there is a fair and equitable balance between the various stakeholders. As noted, outcomes of partnership remain a 'contested terrain' in the literature.

- *How do external and internal contextual conditions influence the balance of mutual gains and the sustainability of partnership?* If mutual gains partnership 'works', why do relatively few employers adopt it? This book aims to enhance understanding about the complex external and internal conditions supporting and sustaining (or retarding) workplace partnership.

The next two chapters outline the case study findings at Waterford Crystal and Aughinish Alumina respectively.

Chapter 3

MANAGING CONFLICT AND COOPERATION
AT WATERFORD CRYSTAL

This chapter examines historical patterns of industrial relations at
Waterford Crystal (WC), and then considers why management attempted
to move away from adversarial IR towards workplace partnership with
workers and union representatives, the nature of workplace partnership,
the balance of mutual gains (and costs) accruing to employers, workers
and unions, and the conditions underpinning partnership.

Firstly, in order to address the first research issue raised in the
previous chapter, the chapter will pay attention to how WC management
decided to attempt to break away from adversarial relations and move
towards partnership from 1993. To this end, the motives behind, and the
nature of, new partnership practices will be described. A related issue is
whether new partnership practices constituted a fundamental break from
traditional IR at the factory, or whether they are combined with
management control practices. With regard to the second research issue,
the balance of mutual gains (and costs) for management, workers, and
the union, are considered. We shall examine whether partnership has
benefited management, in terms of contributing to higher productivity,
greater innovation, lower conflict, better IR, and so forth. We will also
consider the impact of partnership on the role of the union at WC. For
workers, we consider the gains and costs associated with partnership, in
terms of experience of the balance between management control and
worker participation, work effort and reward, employment security/
insecurity. Finally, in terms of the third research issue, the external and
internal conditions underpinning partnership is considered. We then
summarize the findings in the conclusion, and finish the chapter by

describing how partnership collapsed around 2003 (after the research fieldwork this book is based on was concluded), and the reasons for this collapse. We note that WC faces an uncertain future in the face of severe international competition.

The chapter begins with background information on Waterford Crystal in terms of ownership; financial position; business strategy; organisational structure; production system, technology, and work organization; and industrial relations.

Background Information

Waterford Crystal is a long-established indigenous Irish company. The main WC manufacturing operations are in Kilbarry on the outskirts of Waterford City. At the time the fieldwork was concluded, it employed about 1,750 people, but this has since decreased substantially following number of redundancy programmes, notably the closure of the Dungarvan plant in 2005, and with significant job losses announced early in 2008. WC is one of the leading producers of luxury crystal in the world and has gradually diversified its product range to supply the luxury gift market. WC exports to over 106 countries worldwide, with the United States by far its largest market. As such, the fortunes of the company are critically dependent on the buoyancy of the US economy and movements in the dollar.

The original Waterford Glass factory was founded in 1783 by George and William Penrose and established an international reputation for the manufacture of high quality crystal products. It closed in 1852, however, due to lack of capital and excessive taxation. The origins of the present company date back to 1947, when the factory was re-opened by an entrepreneurial Czech glassmaker, Charles Bacik, who received backing from a group of Irish entrepreneurs. The fortunes of the company began to take-off from the mid-1950s due to investment by the McGrath family and the influence of accountant Noel Griffin. The company recorded its first profit in 1955, and from then on recorded sustained growth during the so-called 'golden years' between 1957 and the mid-1980s. The company was hit by a severe crisis between 1987 and 1993, and then there was a significant improvement in its competitive position up to about 2002/2003. Since 2003, however, the company has experienced serious competitive difficulties.

Ownership

Up until 1986, WC was a single entity, but since then it has been part of the Waterford Wedgwood Group, which is comprised of four divisions. The first division is WC. The other three divisions are Wedgwood in the UK, which produces ceramics and was acquired in 1986. Rosenthal in Germany produces porcelain and was acquired in 1997. All-Clad in the United States produces luxury cookware and was acquired in June 1999. The expansion of the Group means that Waterford Wedgwood has secured a foothold in an increasing number of luxury goods markets. Sir Anthony O'Reilly and Peter John Goulandris are Group Chairman and Deputy Chairman respectively.

Financial Position

Between 1957 and 1987, WC made continuous profits buoyed by strong demand for its products, particularly in the US. The years between 1987 and 1993 were extremely precarious for the company, however, and between 1987 and 1992 it suffered substantial losses that left it close to the brink of financial ruin. From 1992, profits began to rise gradually, and 2000 was the most profitable in the company's history. Product demand from the United States market, in particular, was strong. In fact, WC commanded 50 per cent of the US crystal market. From about 2003, however, the financial situation facing the company began to deteriorate again.

Business Strategy

Up until 1990, WC was a single source producer of a single product. The traditional brand produced at the Waterford plants was a heavy glass, which was very ornate, in terms of cut. By the early to mid-1990s, however, the company had become a multi-source producer as a result of outsourcing. Thereafter, the company evolved to become a multi-source producer of multiple products. That is, it had become a supplier of a variety of luxury goods, rather than just a producer of a limited range of crystal products. Changes in branding strategy reflect the fact that the company has had to respond to new consumer tastes, partly because there is now a public preference for 'plain' crystal, rather than crystal with deep and ornate cuts. Competing at the high-value end of product markets is the key feature of WCs business strategy.

Over the course of the last twenty years or so, the company has had to react to intensified international competition, particularly from companies such as Lennox, Gorham and Mikasa from the United States, Baccarat and Lalique from France, Hoya and Noritake from Japan, and Orrefors from Sweden. Furthermore, competition has intensified from companies in low labour cost countries in Eastern Europe such as Slovenia, Hungary and the Czech Republic. Significantly, labour costs in some Eastern European glass companies are less than 15 per cent of total production costs. In comparison, labour costs at WC amount to approximately 50 per cent of total costs. Labour costs were much higher, however, in the 1980s and early 1990s, when they accounted for 70 per cent of total costs. Although WCs business strategy is not strictly geared towards low labour costs or price competition, containing and reducing total unit production costs by maximising efficiency is, nevertheless, a crucial aspect of competitiveness. Management has attempted to reduce production costs through introducing new technology, improving the design and process of manufacturing, and utilising new industrial engineering techniques. Significantly, the outsourcing of uncompetitive products, or 'dogs' as they are known at WC, has also been used to reduce costs. Outsourcing was first introduced in the early 1990s. Products have since been outsourced to countries such as Slovenia, Czech Republic, Portugal, India, China and the Phillipines. The decision by management on whether to outsource is based on:

> The competitive cost of manufacturing at our plants compared with other possible sources and the gross margin achievable on the sale of those products in the market place. This gross margin must be in line with the levels of gross margin generally achieved on luxury branded products internationally (Cost Improvement Agreement, 1993: 3).

As of 2003, 50 per cent of new products were made at WC in Ireland, while 50 per cent were outsourced. Many higher-end small batch products are still manufactured at Waterford, but many of the lower price range larger batch products are outsourced.

Business strategy is primarily based on new product development and innovation, enhancing customer service and product quality, and investing in new technology and human resources. Management has been concerned with strategically integrating these various facets of business strategy. Prior to 1993, relatively little attention was paid to such strategic issues.

Despite the serious threat from international competition, WC retains a competitive advantage as 'the recognised brand' at the luxury high end of the market; although, even here, competition is increasing. An engineer put it thus:

> As more and more countries come into the European Union, and the Eastern European countries start to catch-up with technology, they will be in a position to make products similar to our own, cheaper than our own. But I suppose the real ace in the pack that we have is that the Waterford Crystal brand is recognised as the world's leading brand in crystal.

As well as producing glassware, the company produces a wide range of luxury gift products. The various product categories include fabrics, sports trophies, tableware, lampshades, vases, and cut glass ornaments. For many years, the process was primarily production driven, rather than being driven by what was happening in the marketplace. That is, the production schedule was largely determined by what people inside the factory decided should be produced, rather than by what the customer wanted. To this end, a senior manager stated:

> The products that were easier to blow from the blowing rooms, they were the ones that travelled through the factory. They would then flow through into the distribution centre, and eventually to the outlets. But that wasn't what the customer necessarily wanted.

Most products are now manufactured in small batch sizes due to wide variations in customer demand, rather than being produced in larger batch sizes as they would have been up to about fifteen years ago. As a result, adaptability and the speed of product turnaround are crucial, as emphasised by a manager:

> Our customers are looking for new products on a regular basis. They are looking for product immediately. This leads to short runs and small batch sizes, which means a lot of experimentation, flexibility, innovation, creativity. It is all about speed and agility. It has to be that way. We are customer focused and customer driven. We have to supply the customer with what they want, at the time they want it, the quality they want it, and at the price they are prepared to pay for it.

Product quality is also a crucial aspect of business strategy, because customers are paying for an expensive luxury product. Quality has become all the more important as standards are continuously raised across the industry. Stringent quality standards and inspections have to be passed before a product can leave the factory. The current level of defective product is 1.5 per cent, which is a significant improvement on the pre-1992 period, when there were numerous problems with product quality, and there were no proper quality standards.

Organisation and Occupational Structure

The organisational structure of WC has traditionally been very bureaucratic and hierarchical. Although the structure is still quite bureaucratic, some layers of middle management have been removed, with more responsibility over decision-making and problem-solving being devolved down to front line managers (FLMs).

As of 2003, the organisational structure was comprised of the Chief Executive Officer (CEO) and Directors from the different functional areas, such as Manufacturing, Human Resources, Finance, Marketing and Sales. Below this level, are the managers in these functional areas who directly report to the respective Director. For instance, there are four plant managers who report directly to the Director of Manufacturing. The HR department is headed by the Human Resources Director who has four 'direct reports': Personnel and Administration Manager, Human Resources and Organisational Development Manager, Training and Communications Manager, and the Industrial Engineering Manager. Thereafter, there are approximately 120 front line managers who report to one of the four plant managers, as well as 180 professional and administrative support staff. Finally, there were approximately 1,300 shop-floor workers in 2003: in blowing, cutting, engraving, technician, maintenance craft, or machine/general operative positions. There has been a significant reduction in the number of craft workers over the years; whereas, in the past, the crafts outnumbered other grades. There were over 1,000 craft workers at the company in 1990, whereas in 2003 there were approximately 300. There are now a lot more semi-skilled and general workers than there are craft workers. The workforce has been reduced further as a result of the closure of the Dungarvan plant in 2005, as well as 490 voluntary redundancies at the main Waterford City plant announced in spring 2008.

The task of blowers is to form and shape the glass, and there are two distinct types of glass cutter: rhinetour cutters who perform flat cutting, and wedge cutters who perform deep cutting. In recent years, there has been an element of integration and multi-skilling between rhinetour and wedge cutters. The job of engravers is to decorate the glass. Technicians would be involved in programming the information technology to perform a particular production function, machine operatives are responsible for operating machines, while general operatives are responsible for general tasks such as packing and polishing. The job of electricians and fitters is to maintain and repair equipment round the factory.

The Structure of Production, Technology and Work Organisation

There are two different plants within the main WC manufacturing complex. In plant one, the biggest plant, advanced technology now plays a substantial part in the process of glass making, and production is semi-automatic. In contrast, glass production in the smaller plant two is still largely based on traditional handcraft skills. Plant two also serves as a 'tourist trail', where tourists are able to see for themselves the multitude of skills involved in traditional glass making. Traditional craft skills still play a crucial role in the promotion of the brand name, but, in practice, their use is in decline.

The process of producing glass has three distinct stages, which this author was able to observe at close quarters during time spent on the 'shopfloor'. The first stage of the production process is the production of the 'blank' (uncut crystal). The production of the 'blank' involves the melting and blowing of glass. Production of a high quality blank is crucial because it affects all other processes further along the production chain. The second stage is the cutting and engraving of glass. The third stage involves polishing and packing.

The production process has changed radically over the years from being solely hand craft-based, to technical-craft (technocraft), and more recently, technocraft-knowledge based. These changes have involved combining certain aspects of the handcraft with the advances provided by new automotive technology and information technology. There was no technological input for many years under the handcraft method, apart from a very small element of information technology. Over the course of the last decade or so, however, competitive pressures and technological advances have forced the company to introduce new technology to keep track with competitors. Therefore, the company has moved from a very low technological base to a high technological base. The most significant technological advance was a £10 million investment in a new state of the art tank furnace melting facility in 1995, which replaced all the old multi-pot furnaces that previously existed. The investment in the new furnace was considered vital to secure the future of the Waterford plant as the prime location for the manufacture of Waterford Crystal. Without this investment the plant would have faced a very uncertain future. New state of the art auto-cutting technology was also introduced.

Moves towards technocraft-knowledge based production have involved introducing advanced 'knowledge-based' information technologies with sophisticated software packages requiring special operating skills. The software system can be used to generate detailed information on aspects of production, such as how much product is made or lost, whether it is of the right quality, and so on. To facilitate this change, a number of craft workers have been retrained in computer and mechanical skills and re-deployed into machine operator and technician positions. The technology has contributed to a significant reduction in the number of craft workers and eliminated a great deal of the manual work that was subsidiary to the craft. According to senior management, the technology has facilitated significant improvements in product quality and product yield:

> The technology has been a terrific boost to our business. A machine will take the drudgery out of blowing. Instead of going into a traditional clay pot and humping out four kilos of crystal on the end of a blowing iron which is heavily contaminated with stone, you are now presented with pure crystal, and you just pick that up and blow it traditionally. If you were blowing out of a traditional clay pot, you could blow a hundred pieces and you might be very lucky to get a 20 per cent yield. That was hopeless. You need to be in the 70 per cent to 85 per cent category to compete.

The introduction of the tank furnace, and the fact that product runs come in small batch sizes requiring rapid turnaround to meet continuous changes in customer demand, prompted changes in work organisation aimed at enhancing worker flexibility. In 1995, management introduced cross-functional continuous shift-working teams of approximately 25 workers to operate the furnace, so that its productive capacity is fully maximised. Before shift work was introduced, work patterns were confined to days, Monday to Friday. Thus, continuous shiftwork was a major change in work organisation.

Trade Union Representation

Waterford Crystal is highly unionised. As of 2003, the Amalgamated Transport and General Workers Union (ATGWU) (now part of Unite), which is a UK-based general union, represented about 1200 shopfloor workers across all grades (about 95 per cent of the industrial workforce). Management and support staff are not represented by unions. The number of shop stewards has significantly reduced in recent years. In early 1990, before the major strike, there were 33 shop stewards in Kilbarry and 16 in Dungarvan, and two full-time convenors in each location, representing nearly 2,200 members. As such, there was a ratio of one union representative for every forty-two members. In 2003 there were three union convenors and a 22-member shop stewards committee representing approximately 1300 members. The main negotiating body is the Joint Negotiating Committee, comprised of 11 stewards. The JNC is divided into various section committees representing different grades:

blowers, cutters, semi-skilled and general workers. Some influential shop stewards held what would be perceived as 'far left' views as members of the Trotskyite Socialist Workers Party (SWP).

Historical Patterns of IR: 'Indulgency' and 'Adversarialism'

To fully understand the development of partnership at WC, it is vital to consider historical patterns of industrial relations. In view of this, three distinct phases or patterns of employment regulation at Waterford Crystal are examined below.

The first phase, which can be called the 'indulgency pattern', lasted from 1947 to 1985. Industrial relations were largely peaceful and management was concerned with securing consent from the workforce in a context of continuously high product demand, particularly in the US market. The 'indulgency pattern' constitutes a benchmark to measure future patterns of employment regulation. During the second period between 1986 and 1993 – which can be called the 'adversarial pattern' – management responded to a competitive crisis driven by new market pressures, by stripping away the indulgency pattern and tightening unilateral control over the employment relationship, often by coercive means, thereby forcing the workforce and the union to comply with its demands. Finally, once it had reasserted its authority, management attempted to generate a higher level of consent from the workforce and the union, as a central cog in a new product market strategy. Crucially, however, elements of conflict still remained, with new forms of control brought in alongside partnership practices. This third phase can be called the 'pragmatic partnership pattern'. It was pragmatic in the sense that a competitive crisis prompted management and union to engage and cooperate. The alternative was potential plant closure.

The indulgency and adversarial patterns are described in this section, and the pragmatic partnership pattern is outlined in the next section.

The 'Indulgency Pattern': 1947–1985

This section considers why an indulgency pattern developed, examines the nature of the indulgency pattern and its outcomes, and the conditions underpinning it.

Why Did Management 'Indulge' the Workforce and the Union?

Waterford Crystal, as we know it today, opened in 1947 and achieved its first profit in 1955. Between 1955 and 1985 the company prospered in the context of very benign economic and product market conditions. So much so, that it became a much lauded Irish indigenous industrial success story. Such was the continuous demand for its products that the company found it difficult to meet customer orders. Therefore, the problem was not in selling crystal, but in producing enough to satisfy demand. Concomitantly, the company was production led, in that the key objective was to manufacture as much glass as possible. Three features of the company during this period were particularly significant.

Firstly, there was unlimited demand for WC products, particularly in the huge and booming post world-war two US market. With US dollar sales accounting for 75 per cent of total sales, seemingly insatiable demand in the US helped to fuel the company's success. WC very much dominated the market for high quality crystal, and there was very little competition. But this did not happen by chance, because the company diligently honed its marketing strategy in America, selling its products in big stores such as Macy's. Secondly, the company developed a significant reputation for producing a handcrafted product. The skills developed by WC's craft workers were a key source of competitive advantage. As such, the company was highly dependent upon its craft workers, who, as a result, possessed considerable power, and autonomy from management control. Thirdly, the power of the local union organisation grew significantly during the indulgency period. The company operated as a closed shop and there was nearly 100 per cent union density. Aside from a small number of maintenance craft workers, all grades of shop-floor workers were members of the Amalgamated Transport and General Workers Union. Cutters, blowers, semi-skilled, female, general, and clerical sections were all represented by the ATGWU. The influence of a small group of political activists within the ATGWU was significant in building the power of the union: the Socialist Workers Party had up to 40 members in Waterford Crystal in the 1970s, mainly amongst shop stewards. Allied to this, the local union had sufficient resources to enable it to represent their members' interests, and union representatives had almost unrestricted time release.

In sum, in the context of a very benign product market environment, and with the power of the union growing all the time, management was concerned with negotiating worker and union consent to produce as much product as possible, in order to satisfy burgeoning demand. In order to achieve this, management 'indulged' the union and the workforce, and largely accommodated their demands.

Nature and Outcomes of Indulgency Pattern

i) Stable work organisation: Firstly, and most fundamentally, there was a sense of predictability and stability in terms of the external economic environment, which, in turn, had implications for the manner in which work was organised and regulated internally. The very benign external context facilitated a mutual gains arms-length accommodation acceptable to both sides – the result being that management largely ceded control of the shopfloor to craft workers, who had considerable autonomy. There was continuous demand for the product, employment was secure, workers knew what was expected of them, and there were few surprises. There were set patterns of work organisation and there was very little change from year to year. Workers responded positively to this stability and predictability.

ii) Financial indulgence – buying consensus: There was a high degree of financial indulgence, and management was not too concerned with securing a return on every cost. A primary feature of the indulgency pattern was the very high level of pay that workers received through collective bargaining negotiations and the piece rate pay system. In the context of seemingly unlimited product demand, management was concerned with 'buying' worker consent by exchanging the 'carrot' of pay in exchange for their discretionary effort at the point of production. To this end, a strong emphasis was placed on paying very high wages and bonuses, especially to 'elite' highly skilled craft workers. As a result, labour costs soared during the 1970s and 1980s. For instance, in a three-year collective agreement signed right at the end of the indulgency period in 1985, the unions negotiated a cumulative pay increase of 23 per cent, as well as other significant benefits, such as a reduction in the pension age for craft workers from 65 to 55. The company not only set the pace in pay terms in the local area, but the workforce was one of the highest paid in the country.

The economic exchange was primarily based on the piecework payment system. A manager observed:

> There was a piece rate system. There was a pool of product that had to be produced on an annual forecast, and the blowers and cutters blew and cut what they fancied, within reason. It was all about how do you ensure that people maintain their wages, and if we get the product out of the door at the right time, fine.

Management bought consent by paying workers on a particular craft bench team according to how many pieces of glass they manufactured on a gross production basis, rather than on a finished product net 'goods to store' basis. The rewards were then shared between the workers on each bench according to their status. Bench Masters received the highest rates, and apprentices the lowest. This production-led system frequently promoted runs of bad quality glass, due to the fact that payment was primarily based on quantity of glass produced rather than quality. Many workers welcomed the fact that they could earn substantial sums under this production-related piecework system. A blower commented, 'money was a crucial factor. As long as the money was ok, we were satisfied'.

iii) Union power and job controls: In relation to the above, a third feature of the indulgency pattern was the strong bargaining power and organising capabilities of the union and the various job controls it exercised over the wage-effort bargain. The strength of the union organisation meant that significant collective power could be mobilised. The unions used this power to continually negotiate substantial gains in the wages and living standards of members. A union representative suggested the union fought for these gains, rather than them being willingly handed down by management:

> Sometimes looking back, romanticism can sort of hide exactly what was happening, and you hear people referring to the good old days. Well there were a lot of the old days that weren't very good, and very bad in fact. So union organisation, and using our collective strength, was the way we moved forward on wages and

conditions. Again, some people, when they look back, quote people like Noel Griffin who was the Managing Director, and sort of paint a picture that he was handing down goodies and that there was no organisation demanding these improvements.

Another union representative observed that the bargaining power of the union was reinforced by the fact that the factory was the only source of production:

> The fact that we were the only source of production was a huge factor, and they had also succeeded in placing the product in the big American stores like Macy's. So you were able to pitch the product at a certain price as well. Maybe if you were selling in a high volume Woolworth's sort of store, you wouldn't be able to command such a high price for the product. So our battle was to say we want a fair share out of what is being achieved by the company.

Significantly, the union also controlled all communication channels with the workforce. Management made little attempt to communicate directly with the workforce, and all information had to go through the union first.

The union had extensive shopfloor controls over the wage-effort bargain. For instance, it had significant control over the setting of piecework rates, which were subject to negotiation through a piecework committee. To this end, a union representative remarked:

> If the company were launching a new piece of glass on the American market, they first of all had to come through our piece rate committee and we would put a price on how much we could produce the glass for. Management would then go through a process of putting a price on it from their side. So negotiations would take place over the price. That certainly gave us a big input into affecting our wages as against a system where the management went round asking individual workers how much they would do a glass for.

Moreover, the union also controlled issues such as overtime. Indeed, there was a widespread feeling that the union had grown so powerful that it largely controlled the shopfloor during the indulgency period. But, it also appeared to suit management at the time to cede control of the shopfloor. A union representative commented on this:

> Some people take the view that the union was running the place out there. The way I view it is we were just better negotiators than management at the time and we were able to secure good agreements from them at that stage. Later on we were accused of jeopardising the company by looking for too much, particularly in the late 1970s and early 1980s. The way we looked at that, it was our job to represent our members and to get the best pay and conditions, and it was up to the management to manage the place.

iv) Craft culture of 'responsible autonomy': Fourthly, the workforce – particularly the craft sections – possessed considerable skills and experienced 'responsible autonomy' (Friedman, 1977), in the sense that they had considerable freedom from direct management control, and controlled issues such as the allocation of work, the effort and pace at which they worked, and when to take breaks. By and large, work effort levels were not overly intense – it was up to workers how fast they worked. Thus, in terms of the 'frontier of control' over work organisation (Goodrich 1920, Batstone, 1988), the balance between management control and worker autonomy had swung towards the latter. To illustrate this, a blower commented, 'we were skilled craftsmen who could move around at will'.

The development of 'responsible autonomy' was partly attributable to the craft culture that had evolved at the company, the high levels of skill involved in producing hand-made crystal, and the fact that the pay structure was based on production-related piece rates. A union representative remarked:

> There was a fair amount of autonomy there. The craft sections kind of ran themselves. There wouldn't have been very strict supervision because they didn't need to have it. If you didn't work you didn't get paid, so the system kind of ran itself.

Furthermore, the autonomy of craft workers was shaped by the scale of union job controls, the sheer size of the factory, and because supervision tended to be quite informal and relaxed where it existed. There was no real front line management structure in place at the time and, significantly, the few front line managers (FLMs) that did exist were recruited from the ranks of craft workers. As a result, they were steeped in craft traditions and 'understood the system' and custom and practice on the shopfloor. Partly as a result of these various factors, management largely abdicated its responsibility for managing the shopfloor, and had little direct contact with workers.

This did not mean, however, that workers were subject to no control or discipline. There was a strong degree of self-discipline and peer control within the craft hierarchy. The Master Craftsmen or Bench Masters were at the top of the hierarchy and were responsible for 'managing' their particular bench team, while young apprentices were at the bottom, and were made very much made aware of their place at the bottom of the heap.

v) Bureaucratic control: The structure of the company was traditionally very bureaucratic and hierarchical. Despite the high level of shop-floor autonomy, there was an element of top-down bureaucratic control through a range of formal rules governing the behaviour expected of workers. However, there were differences across the factory, in terms of how frequently or strictly these rules were enforced, and formal rules were nowhere near as prevalent as they became after the indulgency pattern was dismantled.

vi) Paternalist management style: Senior management at the time placed a strong emphasis on promoting a paternalistic style, and life at the factory was very closely connected to, and shaped by, the tight-knit local working class community. Between the 1950s and the 1980s, the management style at the factory was closely associated with the major shareholder, the McGrath family, and the Chief Executive, Noel Griffin. During this period, the company had the feel of a family-owned business. Griffin placed a strong emphasis on visiting the factory floor. He knew workers on first name terms and often walked round the shopfloor informally conversing with people. Paternalism extended beyond the factory gates in the form of welfare schemes for workers, such as sports and social clubs, and assistance with house purchases. In particular, the numerous social clubs in the local community helped to cement workers' identity as Waterford Crystal workers. The fact that such a large workforce was situated within a relatively small city meant that the factory was very much part and parcel of the local community; and workers were primarily recruited from families across the local working class estates. All this helped to generate loyalty to the company and cement consensus.

A number of workers felt that there was quite an 'inclusive family atmosphere'. A general operator commented, 'in the past, it was more like a family environment'. A cutter suggested that there was 'a sense of belonging', while a worker in the repairs section, who was formerly a cutter, remarked:

> There used to be a feel good factor, and not too much pressure. You had the likes of Griffin and McGrath, who were top management. They would come down to the floor regularly and walk round. They knew workers on a first name basis.

vii) Absenteeism: Another feature of the indulgency pattern was the very high levels of absenteeism tolerated at the factory. For a long time, management made little effort to measure or control absenteeism, choosing to turn a blind eye as long as production was maintained. However, the problem was perceived to have become so bad that in December 1980 management issued the 3,000-plus workforce with an ultimatum to reduce absenteeism. The company claimed the amount of absenteeism was equivalent to the whole workforce working a four and a half day week, and was costing two million Irish pounds per year. This was one of the first indications that the company was concerned about its cost base.

The outcome of the indulgency pattern was that the majority of workers at WC believed that the benefits outweighed the costs – in particular, they had a high level of autonomy from management control, employment security, very good pay, with work effort not being very intense – and, as a result, relatively high levels of consensus and order were maintained for many years. Contrary to critical perspectives in the literature, which often tell us that workplace disorder is endemic, there was approximately thirty-five years of almost unbroken industrial peace at Waterford Crystal. During this period, there were no strikes and very little conflict. Where conflict did occur, it was dealt with internally, often informally, and sometimes brusquely, on the shopfloor, rather than being referred to senior management or third party institutions like the Labour Court. Many workers reminisced that trust levels were quite high at the time, and that they were loyal and committed to the company. Much of this may have been attributable to the fact that workers had considerable autonomy and were hardly ever in contact with management.

But, ultimately, the mutual gains indulgency pattern was based on a complex, fragile, and ultimately unsustainable power accommodation. It certainly was not a case of collaborative management-union partnership. Rather, while the economic good times rolled on, the two sides to the employment relationship largely kept their distance, and agreed an implicit 'truce', which removed much of the potential for industrial relations friction. Tension still existed, much of it among workers themselves. The main sources of tension in the early days were the poor working conditions in the factory and, in particular, the climate of fear and bullying promoted by certain benchmasters.

Conditions Underpinning the Indulgency Pattern

A combination of external and internal contextual conditions coincided at the time to underpin the consensus achieved under the thirty-year indulgency pattern, which meant that conflict more or less lay dormant for the entire period. First, and most fundamentally, very favourable and stable external product market conditions fed through into high levels of profitability, and meant that management believed it could 'afford' to indulge the union and the workforce. Demand for the product was seemingly never-ending, and it was a case of trying to get as much product out the door as possible. Management competence in employment relations was not really a serious consideration at the time, though in other management functions senior management had displayed considerable ability, notably in terms of marketing and selling glass in big American stores like Macy's. Second, the benign external market context shaped the relaxed way in which the employment relationship was regulated internally. In particular, management bought consensus through the carrot of high pay. The main forms of labour regulation were collective bargaining and direct worker participation. Management largely vacated its control of the shopfloor, with workers enjoying considerable autonomy. Third, the growing power of the union shaped management's approach to workplace regulation. The union secured extensive job controls over the wage-effort bargain and secured concessions from management through collective bargaining.

The 'Adversarial Pattern': 1986–1993

This section examines management strategies and outcomes during the 'adversarial' phase, which lasted between 1986 and 1993, and the conditions underpinning adversarial IR. It considers how management moved from an indulgency pattern to an adversarial approach based on a tightening of unilateral management control and concession bargaining, aimed at forcing worker and union compliance to change; resulting in a clampdown on union job controls and employee autonomy. This reassertion of unilateral management prerogative corresponds with what Streeck (1987) calls a 'return to contract' – and we shall see how, driven by new market contradictions and uncertainties, management imposed its authority on the employment relationship.

Why Did Management Impose Coercive Control?

Waterford Crystal entered a very difficult competitive period in the mid-1980s, and major changes were about to occur in the management of the employment relationship, notably a severe tightening of control, successive rounds of concession bargaining, and a corresponding weakening of union power and worker autonomy. Significantly, the McGrath family sold its majority shareholding in 1984 to the London based Globe Investment Trust. Meanwhile, management's adherence to the indulgency pattern continued into 1985. The pay agreement of 1985 – which incorporated pay increases of 23 per cent over three years – has been cited by management as one of the key mistakes of the time. The workforce had also reached a peak of approximately 3200. By 1985, labour costs had spiralled to such an extent that they constituted over seventy per cent of total unit production costs.

Almost immediately after the ink was dry on the 1985 pay agreement, it became apparent to senior management that the costs being incurred due to the indulgency pattern were unsustainable. The very success generated by the production driven model had sowed the seed for the severe crisis that was about to confront the company, and which undermined the indulgency pattern. Seemingly unlimited product demand had promoted a false sense of security. The eventual crisis that ensued was fuelled by a combination of spiralling internal costs, management neglect of the business's strategic development and technological base, and intensified international competition. Far too little attention had been focused on the strategic challenges facing the company. Costs were spiralling and product demand was falling simultaneously, international competition was intensifying, and technological advances were occurring elsewhere resulting in cheaper machine made crystal entering the marketplace. At that time, the management team was either ill-equipped to deal with this combination of challenges, or ignored them.

For the first time, a number of senior managers – known as outsiders because they came from outside Waterford Crystal – were externally head-hunted; in a bid to turn the company around. The first 'outsider', Paddy Hayes, was appointed as the new Chief Executive in 1985. Hayes had a tough reputation, having previously overseen the closure of the Ford Assembly plant in Cork. The workforce and the union had caught wind of his reputation, and were suspicious of his intentions.

Under Hayes, the company acquired Wedgwood in the UK in 1986, but the economic situation became serious from late 1986 onwards, when it was hit by a major crisis that would leave it on the brink of financial ruin. The US was hit by a recession in 1987, and the value of the dollar depreciated sharply. As a result, crystal sales fell in the US, by far the company's largest market. To make matters worse, lower cost international competition was gathering momentum. In response to the burgeoning crisis, the company increased prices in its key crystal markets. That the recently acquired Wedgwood division was profitable at the time provided something of a buffer against losses in the Crystal Division, but only for a short period.

The Nature and Outcomes of Adversarial IR

In such a harsh economic climate, the drive for efficiency and market responsiveness became an urgent priority for Hayes and his management team. Crucially, in this context, it was no longer possible to insulate industrial relations considerations from efficiency and productivity-driven considerations (cf. Streeck, 1987), as had been the case under the indulgency pattern. Hayes' response to crisis was to dismantle the indulgency pattern by forcing change in a coercive manner. In short, it was decided that managerial prerogative had to be won.

Therefore, between 1987 and 1993, Hayes and his successors introduced severe cost cutting plans in an attempt to increase efficiency and market responsiveness, and, ultimately, to restore profitability. Management asserted its authority over the wage-effort bargain and dismantled many union and workforce job controls. It set about reducing the financial rewards to workers. In addition, formal rules covering issues such as attendance and time keeping were strictly imposed and direct control and monitoring of workers was considerably tightened on the shopfloor. Significantly, from 1990, management continually communicated the threat of product outsourcing to the workforce to force compliance with change. In fact, outsourcing came to be management's 'trump card' for forcing change. Finally, there was also a considerable increase in the utilisation of temporary contract labour.

This tightening of management control, and uprooting of existing informal workplace rules and norms, was perceived by workers as a fundamental breach of their 'psychological contract' with management and sparked a seven-year period of industrial relations turbulence and intense conflict, and the long period of industrial peace came to an end. Distrust of management's intentions became acute and management found it difficult enough to force minimal compliance, never mind active co-operation. Events during this period are examined in detail below.

Hayes and his team implemented the first major cost-cutting plan in 1987. This took the form of a major rationalisation plan involving 955 voluntary redundancies, leaving a workforce of approximately 2,200. The union played no direct role in negotiating redundancy terms, choosing to oppose redundancies per se. As the redundancy terms were voluntary and the terms were perceived to be quite good – some individuals received up to £80,000 – resistance from the workforce and the union was relatively limited. Indeed, the company originally only requested 750 redundancies, but in the event 955 left. Management made what proved to be a serious blunder, however, because the redundancies resulted in the loss of highly skilled blowers, who were vital for the company's competitiveness. This led to serious production problems, and huge financial losses were incurred during the next few years (IRN 31 and 32, 1993).

The economic climate deteriorated further during 1988. The company policy of raising prices became unsustainable, because although it was maintaining its share of the high quality end of the market, that same market segment was declining, and competition intensified from companies producing cheaper machine made crystal. Furthermore, the dollar remained very weak and the Wedgwood division's profits began to decrease. Finally, Paddy Hayes was embroiled in an accountancy controversy that resulted in his resignation in April 1989.

In 1989, Paddy Galvin replaced Paddy Hayes as Chief Executive. A number of other key management figures were brought in during this period, notably Brian Patterson and Redmond O' Donoghue. A cost cutting 'agreement' with the union concluded in June 1989 incorporated a wage freeze and changes in work practices, and also provided for a profit sharing scheme and plans to introduce a company-union council and quality committee – early signs of attempts to develop partnership. The changes in work practices incorporated new shiftwork arrangements, increased flexibility and redeployment between sections, increased industrial engineering and work study methods to set piece rates, and eliminating unnecessary overtime.

Management had hoped that the 1989 agreement, and particularly the introduction of the profit-share scheme and the proposed cooperative company council, would help to improve the IR climate. This was not to be, however. The key problem was that the co-operative climate and trust necessary for the profit share scheme and the company council to succeed was simply not in place. More fundamentally, the company continued to lose money in an increasingly harsh economic environment. Although substantial cost cuts were achieved from the 1989 agreement, these savings were soon wiped out by decreases in the value of the dollar, and the crisis continued unabated.

Management's decision to tighten control and initiate cost cutting measures meant that its ability to secure consent was limited, as distrust spread. Management was widely perceived to be lacking direction and obsessed with cost cutting. In this context, a highly adversarial IR climate developed, and there was considerable resistance to change. The union became increasingly militant, and a showdown appeared imminent. The union was still very powerful and was determined to resist further cost-cutting measures in order to maintain members' living standards.

In January 1990, a further cost-cutting plan was put to the union, and was rejected. Shortly after, in March 1990, an international consortium headed by Dr Tony O'Reilly took a 29.9 per cent share in the company. The IR tensions that had built up finally came to a head in March 1990, when management withdrew a special 'bonanza payment' made to craft workers to coincide with bank holidays. This decision sparked a bitter 14-week strike, which commenced within two days of the withdrawal of the 'bonanza payment'. There was a perception amongst union representatives that management deliberately provoked the strike. There can be little doubt that management withdrew the special payment at a time of year when product demand was at its lowest, that it was prepared for a long strike, and was concerned with forcing a shift in the balance of power. Management denied, however, that it deliberately initiated the strike (IRN 32, 1993). During the strike, there was intense disagreement between the two sides over the issue of labour costs. While management wanted to negotiate further reductions in labour costs, the unions were vehemently opposed, particularly any wage cuts element, and had hired their own special adviser (Dr. Bryer from Warwick University) to produce a report on the company's proposals. The resultant Bryer Report concluded that the primary cause of the crisis facing the company was not high labour costs, but serious mismanagement, and that the only solution was to improve the efficiency of the manufacturing process.

After a protracted and bitter struggle, the strike finally ended following a settlement brokered by the Labour Court, under which several issues were – for the first, but not the last time – decided through binding arbitration. The company secured most of the cost cutting and flexibility measures it wanted, and the workforce gradually returned to work. The central feature of the 'Comprehensive Agreement', implemented in June 1990, was the withdrawal or buying out of traditional production-related bonuses and the introduction of new performance and profit-related bonus systems involving the use of industrial engineering techniques. Other measures included more flexibility between sections to match market demands, a reduction in contract staff by 250, a reduction in the cost of union activity, and an increase in the working week from 37.5 hours to 39 hours for five years without extra pay. As a trade-off, however, the union secured some concessions, in that basic wages remained untouched – indeed there was a pay increase for some lower paid grades (Comprehensive Agreement For Profit Improvement, 1990; IRN 28, 1990). At the time, Waterford craft workers were still very well paid relative to workers in the majority of other Irish factories. Figures for base weekly pay rates in 1990, and numbers employed, were as follows:

Table 3.1: Waterford Crystal Pay Rates in 1990

Section	Numbers	Amount (week)
Rheintour cutters	136	£496
Wedge cutters	493	£473
Blowers	466	£466
Semi-skilled	119	£312
Clerical	110	£291
General	393	£236
Female	396	£215

Source: Industrial Relations News 15, 1990.

For comparative purposes, according to the Central Statistics Office (CSO), average weekly earnings in manufacturing industries in 1990 stood at £222.40 (and £229.21 for all industries). Accordingly, even relatively unskilled general workers at Waterford Crystal earned above these average rates. However, there was a separate lower pay rate of £215 for the 396 female employees, as of 1990.

A senior manager described the events surrounding the strike as a 'watershed':

> It was the first time in the history of the company that the union had taken on the management and actually came back with less than when they went out. When they went out, management said we won't let them back until we get a new agreement. So through that fourteen-week period, they were giving up all the time.

Rather than negotiating to get back what we had taken away from them, we were actually negotiating to take more away from them. The balance of power had changed dramatically. Ultimately the union had to back down. The workforce and the union are two different things. The union had their own agenda. A lot of it was about maintaining their power base. The Socialist Workers Party has always had a strong influence in union activities in the Waterford area, and still does.

A union representative gave his opinion on the strike, and the events immediately preceding it:

They (management) decided to put forward proposals in 1990 to cut costs. We rejected these proposals. One of the proposals affected how the cutters were paid in a bank holiday period. The company decided to get rid of it. We argued that you couldn't unilaterally change any agreement. We felt that if we didn't take on that aspect of it, then they may as well just implement the rest of the plan and see whether we were going to react. We decided to take immediate strike action and we were resisting whatever proposal they had. When you are in a situation like that it becomes a defensive strike, so you are going to be coming back with some concessions made to the company. But we felt that even in those circumstances you were going to get a better deal by resisting what the company was trying to do as against trying to plead with them to lessen the impact.

Despite securing approximately £7 million in cost reductions, the fortunes of the company did not improve after the strike. Again, the savings were wiped out by the further weakening of the dollar. A new US recession had taken hold, international competition intensified further, and WC continued to lose its share of the crystal market. Significantly, it had become starkly apparent to management during and immediately after the strike that production capacity outweighed product demand by about 30 per cent. In particular, management realised that there were too many cutters. Therefore, management placed many employees, particularly cutters, on extensive short-time working from January 1991. Short-time working was to last intermittently for two years (IRN 31 and 32, 1993). A union representative remarked:

> There was short-time working in the cutting shops. In some cases it was as bad as working one of every three of four weeks. The workers took the position of sharing the work because I believe the company was trying to use the situation of short-time work to force people to take redundancies to reduce the numbers.

The events following the strike turned out to be a crucial catalyst for change. The balance of power swung firmly towards management. The decisive factor was that management was able to re-assert control by exposing the workforce and the union to market forces. In particular, the threat of outsourcing, and even closure, was used to extract significant concessions, with workers becoming more aware of their disposability. Political change in Eastern Europe at the time, following the collapse of the communist 'Iron Curtain', opened the 'floodgates' to competition from crystal manufacturers with very low labour costs. For the first time, there was a possibility that production could be relocated overseas, and, indeed, management began to outsource some new products from 1991. Management repeatedly communicated the threat of wider outsourcing. The union and the workforce eventually, but not immediately, took the threat seriously and realised there was a real danger that the company could either close, or that the bulk of manufacturing operations could be relocated to lower cost producers. Thus, the fear of production relocation, and the heightened sense of employment insecurity that this generated, had a dramatic impact on the workforce, and by implication, on the employment relationship. In connection with this, the ownership structure of the company had also changed from being an Irish-owned family dominated concern to one dominated by multinational ownership. The new owners were perceived by many to have less attachment to the indigenous traditions of the company.

But despite re-asserting its authority, the serious trust deficit meant that management found it extremely difficult to generate worker cooperation, and the implementation of the 1990 agreement was extremely problematic. A union representative remarked:

> The management took the view that they were going to shove it (the 1990 agreement) down our member's throats. This is the agreement; you are to do what we tell you. Rather than trying to understand our members' difficulties, they just tried to shove it

down their throats. However, the company wasn't improving, even after the gains the company got through the 1990 agreement. The company was getting worse; it was haemorrhaging more even from a debt point of view.

Moreover, and this was crucial, the workforce harboured considerable doubts over whether management had the ability to turn the place around. It would take management a long time to rebuild any sense of credibility and respect from the workforce. To this end, a blower commented:

Industrial relations went badly wrong for a period of time after the strike. People weren't happy. There was a lot of cost cutting. There was very much a them versus us attitude.

An engineer, who was a cutter at the time of the strike, made the following observation:

The level of trust after the strike was really non-existent. The company put up lots of figures to the JNC before the strike, during the strike, and after the strike, showing exactly the financial position of the company, and showing us losing huge amounts of money. But nobody believed it. The vast majority – I would say 90 per cent of the workers – didn't believe what the management were saying, that it was all a gimmick, and it was all about taking money out of our pockets. That suspicion lasted for a few years.

A union representative commented:

The workforce didn't have any trust in management. They didn't think that they had any ability to really turn the company around. If the only way that the company was going to be turned around was by cutting all the pay and conditions of the employees – the workers weren't buying into that. They wanted to see what the management plan was for the future in terms of how they were going to increase sales volume and how they were going to invest money in the company. If they weren't going to invest in the company, well the workers didn't think there was any future there.

In a similar vein, a manager remarked:

The return to work agreement involved an awful lot more flexibility. However, you still had the underlying attitude of a

> lack of trust ... and still to a fair degree, an authoritarian management. You had all the overhanging bitterness from the strike. You had the business still in serious difficulty. You had short time. So it was very insecure, and trust wasn't high.

The level of bitterness and resistance was highlighted in October 1991, when the workforce rejected management proposals relating to a variety of IR procedural issues by a ratio of three to one. A rash of unofficial disputes also illustrated the extent of conflict during 1991 and 1992. Management change proposals were constantly being delayed by worker resistance and the adversarial IR climate. Moreover, there was constant third party intervention. One company submission to the Labour Court described the IR climate pre-1993 as one of 'conflict and chaos'.

Management attempted to launch yet another cost reduction plan in summer 1992, which, according to a union representative was 'even more draconian than any of the ones before'. After being hit by the rationalisation plan of 1987 and the cost-cutting plans of 1989 and 1990, the workforce were expected to take more of the same medicine, as the company was still in deep crisis. There was a worldwide recession, the US dollar was still weak, the company still had surplus capacity, costs were still perceived to be too high in comparison with competitors, there was little investment in new technology, and the company was still not profitable. Management had no control over the first two factors, but was determined to address other factors. For the first time, the latest plan not only incorporated a continuation of the wage freeze in place since 1987, but went further in demanding substantial pay cuts. The message was starkly put to the workforce: without substantial pay cuts there would be no future for manufacturing operations at Waterford. The plan also contained proposals for 500 voluntary redundancies at all levels, the further removal of restrictive practices/job controls, the re-deployment of craft workers, the tightening of industrial engineering standards, the contracting out of non-core activities, and an industrial peace clause. More positively, from an employee perspective, there were also proposals to bring an end to short-time working, as well as a six-month moratorium on outsourcing.

Key changes in the senior management guard took place in the latter period of 1992, which were to have crucial ramifications for the later move towards a more cooperative IR trajectory. A new Personnel Director (Niall Saul) and a new Manufacturing Director (Michael Wilcock) were appointed. Brian Patterson and Redmond O'Donoghue occupied the top two senior management positions. In essence, these four highly able senior managers faced the formidable task of repairing the business and the employment relationship, following years of 'strategic neglect'. Understandably, given the level of distrust of management at the time, the workforce had very limited expectations of the new top management team. It appeared however that management had began to take onboard some important lessons from the failings of the past. From a management perspective it was imperative to open up direct communication channels with the workforce that were not distorted by the union, in an attempt to win back 'hearts and minds'. To this end, up to 60 meetings with small groups of about 40 workers, as well as larger meetings, were continually held right up until the vote whether to accept or reject the cost reduction plan was held in January 1993. During these meetings, workers were provided with detailed information on the external environment and the internal cost structure and were shown samples of glass made in Eastern Europe, in an attempt to convince them of the need for the plant to become more efficient. A manager remarked:

> We decided that communications with the workforce were no longer going to be through the union. The union had managed to get to the situation where they effectively stopped management discussing anything directly with the workforce.

Furthermore, an engineer, who was formerly a cutter, observed:

> Management used to give the information over to the union, and then it would be filtered down to the workers through meetings. The company expressed concern that the information had been distorted by that method, so they started coming across with the idea of these company-wide meetings so that they could give the message directly to the workers. That was the first real step in overstepping the union. On a number of occasions, direct mailings came from the company straight to your home outlining the companies' position.

In addition to the opening up of direct communication channels, the Labour Relations Commission and the Labour Court also played a crucial role during this extremely tense period (in subsequent years, the LRC and the Labour Court have continued to play a vital role in resolving various IR disputes at the glass factory). Although not an ideal situation, the use of third party institutions acted as something of a buffer against conflict because it facilitated a perception that the union was not being forced into conceding to the company's position – allowing it to save face. The parties had to go through a long and tortuous process involving the LRC, before a number of issues were referred to the Labour Court for binding arbitration. The Labour Court determination retained the companies' provisions for extensive pay cuts and 500 voluntary redundancies, and a tightening of industrial engineering standards; but, significantly, a few concessions were made to placate the workforce. For instance, the company's proposed 6 month moratorium on further outsourcing was extended to 12 months, and a maximum cap of 25 per cent for two years was placed on pay cuts – the union had feared that some workers would be hit by pay cuts of up to 40 per cent. The workforce pragmatically voted to accept the recommendation by a huge majority of 98 per cent. They were faced with a no choice scenario of accepting the deal or else risk seeing the company close or commence extensive outsourcing. This no choice scenario was exacerbated by high unemployment, which heightened employment insecurity. A union representative noted that the workforce was in no mood to engage in another strike to resist management's demands:

> In 1993, they put forward huge wage cut proposals across the board. We weren't on strike, and understandably I think. The workforce had gone through a short-time programme prior to 1993. Due to the effects of the strike on peoples' economic conditions, and their feelings on facing another strike, they decided to negotiate another agreement round those wage cuts. I have no doubt that because we weren't on strike, the company got a much better deal in 1993 (in comparison to 1990).

A senior manager remarked:

I came to Waterford Crystal in 1992. We had in this company a very, very restricted management view. We had a very highly unionised workforce, and it wouldn't be going too far to say it was anarchy. Management had lost control. The company was about to close. We did the deal with the union on 18th January 1993, which 98 per cent (of the workforce) voted in favour of. It reduced peoples' benefits by up to 25 per cent, eliminated all the demarcation, and became a landmark deal. But it was all done in a crisis. The decision was clear. Say yes and we will continue, say no and we will close. So it was crunch time – command and control. My job was to pick up the pieces with the people and to try and build the future.

The period following the acceptance of the 1993 agreement was very difficult for the workforce. They were hit by pay cuts averaging 15 per cent, and in some cases 20-25 per cent. But even after these pay cuts, craft wages were still higher than in many other workplaces. Approximate pay rates as of 1994 are detailed below:

Table 3.2: Waterford Crystal Pay Rates in 1994

Craft	£425 per week
Semi-skilled	£280 per week
General Grade A	£260 per week
General Grade B	£250 per week
General Grade C	£240 per week
General Grade D	£230 per week

Source: *Industrial Relations News* 29, 1994.

In comparison, according to Central Statistics Office (CSO) data, average weekly earnings in manufacturing industries in 1994 stood at £261.90 (and £269.90 for all industries).

There were also 500 voluntary redundancies, leaving a workforce of about 1,500. As in 1987, the union did not play a direct role in negotiating severance terms, preferring to oppose job losses per se.

In sum, prompted by new market pressures and uncertainties, management conducted a radical shift away from the indulgency pattern towards imposing unilateral control and its prerogative to manage, engaging in successive rounds of concession bargaining and cost-cutting. From a situation where the union tended to call the shots and extract concessions from management, and workers had a high level of autonomy, the reverse was happening, and management was continually forcing concessions from the workers and the union. In terms of how workers' experienced managerial policies, the overriding perception was a long way from mutual gains, the overwhelming feeling being that the costs far outweighed the benefits. In particular, workers autonomy was severely eroded as management tightened its control, work effort intensified, pay and rewards were slashed, and employment became much more insecure. The negatives for the union were also significant, leading to a considerable diminution of its power base. Even management reaped few tangible gains beyond reasserting authority. Although the balance of power shifted strongly in its favour, management was only able to force passive compliance at best from workers and the union, and conflict and disorder were rampant. Management made some rather half-hearted attempts to generate a higher level of consensus – including trying to bring in a profit share scheme and company council and quality committee – but these attempts failed given the competitive problems facing the company, and the extent of distrust and conflict at the time. The upshot of all this was that productivity and profitability were very poor, and left the company close to the brink.

The Conditions Underpinning the Adversarial Pattern

Closely corresponding to critical accounts in the literature, this shift towards coercive unilateral management control generated significant conflict because it breached the norms that workers had come to expect during the indulgency period. The main conditions underpinning adversarialism were as follows.

First, and most fundamentally, the deterioration in the company's external competitive position and falling profits – culminating in a crisis situation – prompted management to slash labour costs. Workers perceived this as an attack on their long-standing indulgency pattern, having become accustomed to high wages.

Second, management at all levels was generally deemed by the workforce to be directionless and incompetent for much of the adversarial period, until a new senior management team took hold of the reins in the early 1990's. This constituted a violation of worker expectations of predictability and set patterns of work, and the significance of management competence for maintaining workplace order is highlighted in a long-line of industrial relations literature (cf. Batstone, 1986; Nolan and O' Donnell, 1995, 2003; Hodson, 1999, 2005). During the indulgency period, workers had little day-to-day contact with management, which removed many of the irritants sparking conflict. But this changed dramatically during the adversarial phase, when management was perceived to be making changes on a regular basis and acting chaotically. Front line supervisors were commonly deemed to be 'dictatorial' and 'poor people managers'. Senior managers were widely deemed to have insufficient ability to turn the company round. A general operator commented, 'You didn't really know what they were doing. I don't think they knew themselves'. A cutter stated, 'there were problems with the management structure', while a blower remarked:

> There was a lot of anxiety and frustration due to the fact that management didn't seem to know where they were going. We had been used to set patterns in work, now things were forever changing. There was a lot of uncertainty and indecision amongst management as to the direction they were going to take. We were frustrated with all the chopping and changing and not being able to just come in and do a days work and go home.

Third, the redundancy programmes of 1987 and 1993 violated traditional worker expectations of employment security. At that time, many workers had been at the factory for twenty years or more, and had been conditioned to expect to spend their working lives at the factory. Employment insecurity is not conducive for generating consensus, and it was a new experience for many WC workers, after the security blanket of the indulgency pattern.

Fourth, the tightening of direct supervision at the point of production and the strict imposition of formal rules also violated worker expectations of 'responsible autonomy', the primacy of informal interaction, the freedom to use their own discretion, and to exert control over the wage-effort bargain. In particular, highly skilled craft workers deeply resented detailed management control of their work, constant interference, and did not believe that management really understood the production process, or had the competence to organise work properly.

Finally, the paternalist culture and management style associated with Noel Griffin and the McGrath's was severely eroded when new managers (labelled as 'outsiders') arrived. A 'them and us' climate permeated throughout the factory. Many of the vestiges of paternalism were stripped away as part of the cost-cutting agenda.

Moving to a 'Pragmatic Partnership' Pattern: 1993–2003

This section will examine why the senior management 'quartet' of Brian Patterson, Redmond O'Donoghue, Niall Saul and Michael Wilcock pragmatically moved away from an adversarial control strategy towards partnership from late 1993. It will then look in detail at the partnership practices management adopted to build cooperative relations with the union and workers. But it will also – guided by the contingency literature – examine how new forms of control have been utilised alongside attempts to develop partnership. Outcomes are then considered, in terms of the balance of mutual gains accruing to management, the union and workers. It is concluded that management benefited most from partnership at WC, and that gains were not shared equally, with workers benefiting less. Finally, the main conditions influencing the pragmatic partnership pattern will be outlined.

Why the Move Towards Partnership?

The move away from adversarial IR towards a partnership-oriented strategy was facilitated by a turnaround in the company's fortunes from late 1993. Crucially, in contrast to the 1989 and 1990 cost cutting agreements, the aftermath of the 1993 agreement coincided with a better economic environment. In particular, the United States was moving out of recession and the dollar began to recover. This bolstered WC's competitive position, and it achieved its first pre-tax profit for six years.

Significantly, at the same time, the new management team was displaying competence and credibility, and even earned some respect, and the workforce could at last see some light at the end of the dark tunnel. It helped that management was perceived to be showing some commitment to retaining manufacturing facilities at Waterford as a reward for the sacrifices made by the workforce. Indeed, management held out promises of investment in the factory over the next few years. This promise of some long-term security, however, was based on the proviso that competitiveness, efficiency and profitability had to improve. A powerful symbolic gesture by management during this time was the retention of the sports complex, which was originally due to be sold off as part of the 1993 cost cutting plan. Thus, the performance of the new management team was deemed by the workforce to represent an improvement on previous management, who were widely perceived to be lacking strategic direction (IRN 31 and 32, 1993). A union representative commented on the management style of the new Personnel Director, Niall Saul:

> He had a great way of moving things. He would look at a document and say leave it with me and I will be back in an hour. He would come back in an hour and he would make a decision be it right or wrong. What our union did before, they would go to management with what they were looking for, knowing that management would sleep on it and leave it. The new guy fuckin hit the ball back over the net straight away. We thought jesus that's quick, is he up to something. So, instead of management thinking what are they up to, it was us thinking what is he up to. He was totally different to what we dealt with. I thought he was very good.

Also, the backdrop of crisis and coercion – particularly the shock of job losses, substantial wage cuts, and the continuous threat of outsourcing – slowly promoted a pragmatic awareness among the union and workforce that change was unavoidable. In this context, there was a discernible shift in the balance of power, and once resistance from the union and the workforce had been overcome, management set about developing a more cooperative approach to workplace relations.

In short, three conditions in particular facilitated the start of a turnaround in the companies' fortunes from late 1993: the improvement in market conditions and exchange rates; the credibility gradually achieved by the new senior management team; and, once their resistance had been quashed, the pragmatic accommodations and sacrifices made by the workforce in difficult circumstances. A middle manager confirmed this:

> We employed a new Personnel Director and a new Manufacturing Director. That was probably the catalyst for the most significant change. But, you have got to remember, at the same time, the market returns for the business were improving, so the atmosphere and conditions were far better. You needed both. You needed the business fundamentals to improve, but you also needed the new (management) approach. The other key thing was, the workforce agreed to substantial pay cuts across the board, in order for the business to survive.

These conditions provided the foundations for the pragmatic move away towards cooperative relations. But they do not explain just why management moved towards a partnership type approach rather than remaining on a coercive control trajectory. So why did management choose to walk the cooperative path?

First, and most fundamentally, intensified competition in WC's international product markets persuaded the new management team to develop a new product market strategy and new technology, which required a more collaborative approach to employment relations. An adversarial approach based on forcing worker/union compliance with management aims was simply not viable, particularly given the necessity to tap into the voluntary discretionary inputs required from workers under the new product market strategy. This was emphasised by a manager:

> You wouldn't be competitive. You wouldn't have the co-operation, the inputs from employees. Under adversarialism, every move and every concession was fought over. It just wouldn't work. It is all about speed, flexibility and agility. We are customer focused and customer driven. Employees are expected to solve problems and to be proactive. It is a totally different approach from being passive and waiting to be told what to do.

The company had to find a new way to compete in turbulent international product markets. As it was positioned at the high end of the market and depended on the skill and creativity of its craft workers, WC could not hope to compete against companies with much lower labour costs. Rather, it chose to move towards the high wage, high productivity, and high technology route to gaining competitive advantage. To this end, management strategically set about developing a new market-led, multi-product business strategy characterised by brand diversification and new product development. In particular, it diversified into the luxury gift market. New product innovation and much better product quality were crucial for competitiveness. This, in turn, generated a need to enhance production efficiency, as well as speed of response, by tapping into employee skills and securing ongoing co-operation with change. Management consciously developed a new 'bundle' of employment relations practices to fit the new business strategy, which will be described below. By coherently linking its new business strategy to a new approach to employment relations, management earned some credibility from the workforce.

A second reason for the move towards partnership was the introduction of new advanced technologies, particularly a continuous melt tank furnace in 1994/95, which was required to support the new business strategy. The £10 million investment in the new technology was the centrepiece of the three-year 'Investment in Competitiveness' agreement, concluded in September 1994. A manager remarked:

> In 1994 we made an agreement with the unions called 'Investment in Competitiveness'. The central part of this was that the union agreed to flexible work practices that were required to work the technology. The company then put a huge amount of investment in to training and development to give people the new skills to work the technology.

A union representative described management's approach to the introduction of the new technology:

> In the past they tried to introduce major changes overnight and it just didn't work. The new manufacturing director's approach to it was much different than that, it was an incremental approach – that you get the best technology that is out there and you bring it in a way that you get the workers to go along with the change. If there were manpower implications as a result of that technology,

you dealt with this in the most humane way that you could deal
with it. I think they took a pragmatic approach, saying look there
is no point in us bringing in technology here and shoving it down
workers' throats and then having to switch it off because there is
a dispute over it.

Significantly, the whole agreement was negotiated directly between
management and the union on a cooperative basis, rather than being
referred to third party intervention. Both management and the union
were on common ground in perceiving that the new tank furnace was
vital for the company's future, particularly given that many of WC's
competitors already possessed advanced glass-making technologies. To
this end, a union representative remarked:

When we bought into the argument as to why you should have a
tank furnace – which is a 24 hour melt of glass, 7 days a week,
365 days a year – the choice we were faced with was a factory
with no investment, stagnating, or getting that 10 million pounds
investment in the tank furnace which gives you something to
build on in the future.

A manager commented:

Because we had high wages, to be competitive we needed to go
with high technology and high wages. We couldn't go for low
wages and high technology, and we couldn't go with low
technology and low wages.

The new technology facilitated major changes in the production process
by bringing together aspects of the traditional craft skills and the new
technology. It also promoted some changes in work organisation. In
particular, new work teams were introduced in the blowing section, and
there were significant moves towards continuous shift working across
the plant. A notable downside of the move towards automation from an
employee perspective was that the new furnace resulted in a surplus of
blowers, which led to a number of voluntary redundancies. Thus, the
investment constituted something of a double-edged sword for the
workforce. Significantly, however, the union implicitly acknowledged
that some redundancies were inevitable, and was actively involved in
negotiating severance terms for the first time, rather than simply

opposing them as in the past. The union insisted that compulsory redundancies were not on the agenda and negotiated alternative measures, such as voluntary re-deployment of craft workers into technician and semi-skilled operator positions. A union representative remarked:

> We took the approach in 1994 of negotiating (voluntary) redundancy and early retirement and redeployment. We took the view that if there was a surplus in one area, that the company had a responsibility to our members. So the options were that you could opt for redeployment – we negotiated a compensation package for craft workers moving into non-craft jobs. We had an early retirement package put in place so that people could retire from age 50. From our point of view we put in place a good agreement to deal with a surplus situation. We got them to agree that nobody would be forced into a compulsory situation. So we had an agreement drawn up so that all the voluntary options would be gone through.

The redundancy terms amounted to four and a half weeks pay per year of service plus statutory entitlements. The terms were much better than those offered to workers during the adversarial phase, which were not negotiated by the union, and amounted to about two weeks pay per year of service (IRN 29, 1994). In addition, payments for voluntary redeployment amongst craft workers to semi-skilled or general positions ranged from IEP£8,125 to £13,500.

Third, the fact that the workforce was highly unionised was a key reason promoting the move towards partnership. Management adopted a pragmatic perspective, in the sense that although the power balance had shifted markedly in its favour, it still needed to legitimize its actions and knew that attempts to marginalise the union would not have been viable and could have had a detrimental impact on securing broader workforce cooperation with change, notably the tank furnace. In short, management required legitimate its actions. There are strong parallels here with the existing literature on partnership initiatives in strongly unionised plants (cf. Marks et al, 1998; Geary and Dobbins, 2001; Oxenbridge and Brown, 2004). A union representative voiced his opinion on the new approach to industrial relations:

Management has changed their approach to dealing with the union, particularly since 1994. I think they have taken the view that you need to bring the union and the workforce along with you on issues. They knew that they were never going to be able to impose any changes. Rather than waking up one morning and having a change of heart and saying let's do things in a different way, I think it was a deliberate, strategic kind of decision to go into a different industrial relations structure. They said look, if the place is going to be turned around we need to move forward, we need to introduce new technology. The company knows that unless you utilise the union to manage the problem with you, the problem won't be managed. They needed the union's help to progress the issues that were there. I think, strategically they looked at what would be the quickest way of getting changes through at the lowest possible cost. One option was forcing the issues and seeing what the fallout would be, and whether the union would be strong enough to sustain that. I have no doubt that they looked at every single option in terms of what would be the quickest way to do it, and I think it came down to the fact that there was just no way any attempt to marginalise the union was going to work.

The Nature of Partnership Practices

We now consider how WC senior management went about trying to generate partnership in practice. From about mid-1993 onwards management set about tackling some of the major irritants that had been a source of conflict since the 1980s. Perhaps the most fundamental irritant was the perception that had taken root during the adversarial period that, by and large, management were incompetent and directionless. As part of a more strategic approach, encompassing the rolling out of new products, major investment in new technology, improving the design and organisation of production, and improving the quality of front line managers, the senior management team began to develop a 'bundle' of complementary partnership type practices to fit its new business strategy: management-union cooperation, investment in training and education, a re-vamped profit share scheme, two-way communication channels, a new facilitative style of line management, and equal opportunities policies. However, important parts of the IR/HR 'bundle' were missing at WC, particularly employment security and opportunities for direct worker job participation. These omissions, and the fact that traditional hierarchical structures largely remained intact, placed limits on the reach of mutual gains partnership, especially given that many workers had prior experience of employment security and 'responsible autonomy' during the indulgency phase.

While examining the nature of new partnership practices, the discussion below also illustrates how they were combined with various management control practices. The section after examines the balance of mutual gains accruing to management, the union and workers. In many respects, the findings validate contingency theoretical perspectives outlined in the last chapter.

Management-Union Cooperation

The most significant step by management, in terms of fostering more co-operative work relations, occurred from the second half of 1993, when there was a move away from a purely adversarial bargaining relationship with the union towards a more cooperative/joint decision-making approach. Given its ideological disposition, and a desire to maintain its independence from management, the union leadership never used the term partnership, and neither did management. A more accurate definition is 'pragmatic cooperation' in difficult circumstances. But what happens in practice matters much more than definitions, and the upshot was that new formal joint management/union decision-making structures operated in parallel with traditional collective bargaining. Traditional collective bargaining now tends to play a less prominent role than in the past, particularly given that, since 1987, basic pay levels have been set centrally through successive national wage deals, though local bargaining still takes place.

The central plank of the new cooperative approach was put in place in September 1993, when an innovative joint management-union task group was formed, which was the brainchild of Manufacturing Director, Michael Wilcock. The remit of the task group was to focus mainly on product strategy, an area of vital importance for the company and its employees. However, at various times, the task group also considered other aspects of business strategy, although joint decision-making powers afforded to the union were more limited with regard to the highest-levels of company strategic decision-making, with joint consultation rather than joint governance being the norm.

A manager remarked that it took 'six months to break the barriers down. I guess they (the union) were testing our credibility as a management team'. By striving to move away from adversarial IR towards co-operative relations with the union, management was concerned with fostering joint problem-solving over issues of common concern. The company needed the task group because 'they needed the input from the workers', a union representative noted. To secure this input, however, management had to share elements of strategic problem-solving with union representatives. Management was keen to engage with union representatives in a consensus-based forum to make it easier to promote acceptance of ongoing change amongst the workforce. While the union never used the term partnership to describe what was happening, they were now ready to independently and proactively engage with any initiative that could increase their capacity to represent their member's interests.

In practice, the task group provided the union with a joint input into a variety of operational and strategic issues facing the company, which would have traditionally been the domain of senior management alone. Therefore, the workforce – through union representatives – had significant voice in high-level decision-making, notably over product strategy. As a result, the role of the union changed quite radically from the adversarial period, and it spent significantly less time battling management. The main role of the task group was to collaborate and jointly devise creative ideas to keep products at WC. The task group proved very successful in improving existing products, securing new products, and even winning back products that had previously been outsourced. In addition, the task group also examined a wide range of other practical issues relating to the production process, new technology, financial issues, and work organisation. For instance, the task group was very instrumental in smoothing the introduction of the tank furnace in 1994, because the union was kept fully informed of events. A manager remarked:

> In the task group we show people the monthly accounts, at
> manufacturing operations level they see the margins, they also

see the sales numbers. We talk openly about the costs of various parts of the business.

Sometimes sub-working groups would be established under the auspices of the task group and asked to go off and investigate significant issues such as under-performing products. A union representative commented:

> We would go off and change things, like dogs (products that fall below the minimum gross margin). He (Manufacturing Director) would say go and have a look at it and see if you can do anything with it, and we would go off and change things and role it through the standards again. An awful lot of things have been saved. We might put a different process in to bring it over the margin, so it is no longer up for outsourcing.

Management and the union met much more often to discuss issues facing the business than was traditionally the case. The task group held meetings once a week, chaired by the Manufacturing Director. The task group was comprised of six union nominees and six management nominees, although this figure often increased to embrace additional shop stewards and managers when significant issues such as new technology were discussed. It was a forum designed to foster mutual gains consensus, and did not deal with traditional collective bargaining issues, such as pay, which were kept separate.

Another novel joint management-union structure was the monitoring committee. The monitoring committee was more informal than the task group and met once a week. It was comprised of three managers and three union convenors. The role of the monitoring committee was to serve as an early warning system for potential IR problems and flash points. A union representative commented that the monitoring committee might embrace a whole range of issues:

> It could be personal issues from certain workers. It could be an issue that the company feels strongly on. It would be an early warning system to avoid confrontation. Not that people are in there looking for confrontation. If two parties believe strongly on something and it comes to a head, they try to see a way of moving forward. While the monitoring committee would be the first line of avoiding confrontation, the task group would be for introducing new ideas.

There were a number of other joint management-union structures dealing with various IR, such as health and safety, pensions, and profit sharing. Shop stewards were closely involved in the operation of these committees, and would be regularly consulted by management.

Up until 1999, there was an industrial peace clause and binding arbitration mechanism at the company, the brainchild of the then Personnel Director, Niall Saul (who left WC in July 1997), who is a staunch advocate of binding arbitration because of the finality and certainty it affords. The company perceived the clause to be vital in achieving stability and finality in industrial relations. The union was opposed to the industrial peace clause, but reluctantly accepted it at the time. The clause was introduced as part of the 1993 cost savings agreement, and was extended in 1996 for a three-year period. It meant that any contentious issues that were left unresolved after local level industrial relations procedures had been exhausted could be referred to the Labour Court for a binding determination. Once the Court issued a binding determination, industrial action was forbidden. The peace clause expired, however, in 1999, after union members rejected any extension. A union representative remarked:

> The company had a thing called binding arbitration. They could do anything they liked. We weren't entitled to strike. There was a no strike clause. We were entitled to go to the Labour Court, but the Labour Court was always going to find in favour of the company. That ran out in 1999. We refused an extension.

The cooperative approach continued into 2002/2003. In summer 2002, workers accepted a new partnership style deal entitled, the 'Plan for Renewal and Growth', which dealt with surplus manpower, new working patterns, compensation for loss of shift premium, as well as a range of other issues (IRN 25/2002). In the introduction to the deal, management and the union observed that it provided a 'platform upon which both the company and its employees, through partnership, can share confidence in Waterford Crystal's future'. Both parties recognised their mutual interest in ensuring the future of the company and the inevitably of change. 'Change impacts on individuals, and accordingly it is important that the parties provide appropriately for the impact of such change on employees.'

As noted earlier, in the course of participating in these cooperative structures, the union possessed some right of veto over decision-making, which implies that their influence went beyond joint consultation to encompass a degree of joint governance. In this sense, it constituted one of the most advanced examples of mutual gains bargaining or management-union cooperation in Ireland, despite the union's reticence about the term partnership. In the literature, voluntary management-union partnership structures encompassing joint decision-making (like the WC task group) are viewed as particularly significant (cf. Kochan and Osterman, 1994; Roche and Turner, 1998). According to Roche and Turner (1998:93), formal joint decision-making partnerships are seen as significant because, 'more so than in relations between management and unions built around consultative arrangements, the parties bear joint responsibility for decisions. As decisions are arrived at, wherever possible, on a consensual basis, or through joint groups with parity of union and management representation, each of the parties – and not management alone – enjoys considerable power'.

Direct Worker Participation

As well as seeking cooperative relations with union representatives, management sought to generate employee consent directly by promoting a more positive and facilitative style of front line supervision. But apart from this, and the spread of shiftworking, the structures of work were not radically re-designed. For instance, where it exists, teamwork at WC is generally a very modest form of direct employee participation compared to the advanced semi-autonomous teams described in the literature (cf. Marchington, 2000; Geary, 2003). Employees have not been significantly empowered to participate in work tasks, with front line managers controlling all the major decisions pertaining to the organisation of work at the point of production. This was a marked change from the indulgency phase, when workers experienced substantial autonomy over the 'frontier of control' of work organisation. Employee autonomy was most developed in the tank furnace area. The manager in charge of the tank furnace remarked:

> We are going away from the command and control style of management towards empowerment. You have got to give people

enough space to do the job, and support them at the same time. So you are balancing those two. We would be striving towards a more hands off approach. Our machine operatives now take a lot more ownership and control of the process that they work than they did five years ago. That is because of the level of knowledge, skill, training, and hopefully, the level of empowerment.

A HR manager summarized the current nature of work organisation:

I would say we don't have teamwork in the way that I would understand it. We don't have the formal structures of teamwork. Teamwork to me is where you have a team of individuals who are responsible for organising work, and have a large amount of autonomy to do their work. We don't have that type of model at the moment. The other feature of teamwork is they wouldn't have a manager who is responsible for everything the team does. We don't have that situation. I think it probably could be introduced. I know it was discussed.

There has been intermittent talk of introducing the concept of team leaders at WC, but the idea never took off, partly because the union were concerned it would undermine their role. A union representative explained the thinking behind this opposition:

We wouldn't say to members don't get involved in these things. But it is preferable from our point of view to have union representatives negotiating on behalf of members rather than having our members directly involved. I think the company want to move that way, whereas from our point of view we don't see that as being as advantageous for our members as having the representatives involved in negotiations. We resisted team leaders. I don't think they have developed it to a stage where they are ready to move on that yet, but at some stage they will. I think they will start looking at what is the best way to start approaching this now in terms of trying to undermine the union role again, by having more direct contact with employees. But I don't think they'll achieve that in Waterford Crystal because of its history – some of the workers have been here 30 years. If it was a greenfield site it may be different.

In short, changes in work organisation were restricted to a new facilitative style of line management and work was re-organised on a shift basis after the introduction of the tank furnace. Management introduced five cross-functional teams of approximately 25 workers to operate the tank furnace on a continuous shiftwork basis. These larger teams replaced the small blowing teams that had previously existed when the multi-pot furnaces were there. The tank furnace teams incorporate a wide range of skill levels. They are generally comprised of six blowers, three craft maintenance workers, one technician, six machine operatives, six general operatives and one FLM acting as team leader. A middle manager described the changes associated with the new furnace:

> Firstly, the level of technology and technology-related skills in running the furnace were far higher. So you had a lot of craft people who had to re-deploy into technology areas, be retrained in computer skills, combined with mechanical skills, combined with glass-making skills. On top of that, they had the concept of shiftwork, which had been unknown in any significant volume prior to that. The third area that would have been different was teamwork.

There are now fewer job demarcations across the factory, and more evidence of job rotation, multi-skilling and labour flexibility. Before 1990, the vast majority of workers had worked in the same area since they started at the factory, but some have since changed jobs two or three times. Workers are now expected to engage in training to enhance their adaptability, and by implication, employability. There has been considerable training to enhance technology-related skills in the blowing and cutting sections. The following quotes illustrate the removal of traditional job demarcations:

> There are no demarcations and I mean that. Accept for those that are required by skill. In other words you have to be certified trained to operate this process. That is a demarcation. But that is different. It is not demarcation by protectionism (Manufacturing Director).

> People are far more flexible than they were before. Years ago your job was in that station, on that machine, on that wheel. In the past a manager would have been told it is not my job over there. Now, there is no problem saying to a person 'I need you over there today'. Some people don't like it, but generally, people just do it (FLM).

The ratio of FLMs to employees has increased significantly since the indulgency phase. At the time of the fieldwork, there were about 120 FLMs for a shopfloor workforce of about 1300. This constituted a ratio of approximately one FLM for every eleven employees. However, FLM's have been encouraged to be less authoritarian and to adopt a more open and facilitative management style. The role of the FLM includes co-ordinating the work of the team, setting targets, planning and scheduling work, solving problems, communicating information, and coaching the team. A manager remarked that the new role expected of FLMs is:

> Distinct from being a foreman, where they just watch and attend to things when they go wrong and tell people what to do. We are assuming now that people know what to do and do it. But at the end of the day the manager is responsible as well, so it is mix of facilitation and taking full responsibility. He will try to build up shared responsibility for results.

A union representative indicated that there have been some moves towards a more facilitative style:

> He (the FLM) will come down and say 'I want this glass through today, would you do that glass today'. There is no such thing as 'Do that'. They will say 'will you do it?' Common sense is one of the basic needs for anyone dealing with people. For a long time there were management who had absolutely no common sense. I have found that manager's who seem to be moving up the ladder in here now – the one thing they have is a lot of common sense.

But pockets of traditional coercive supervision remain. A manager observed:

> Some managers in difficult situations can be very dictatorial. In a normal situation they can be very open and motivational. There are pockets of authoritarianism. If there is an emergency you have to give orders. Like when trying to reach customer deadlines, reach targets, if there are breakdowns. You cannot sit down to talk about it, you just have to do it. A lot of it boils down to the personality of the manager as well. A lot of managers were brought up in the old school. Some are finding it difficult to leave the old school, and are not comfortable with the new style. Others love the new school. So it depends on circumstances and personality.

A union representative remarked:

> Even some of the new managers that they have brought in from the
> manufacturing end of it, their job is to get the product from one end
> of their department to the other end of their department. If it means
> blowing their cool and shouting and roaring at someone to do that,
> then they will do it, and they will just deal with the problem
> afterwards. In some cases it is an ongoing issue. Now, the
> management say we don't tolerate that, we won't accept, and we
> discipline our management the same as we discipline any union
> members. But, they just don't, unless it is a very serious issue, and
> the employee sees it is not being dealt with.

New HRM Practices

From 1993 to 2003 management introduced a range of new Human
Resource Management (HRM) practices to complement cooperative
work relations. It opened up *direct communication, information and
consultation* channels to the workforce. There was a concern that the
union should no longer be the sole means of communication. To this
end, direct communication structures were introduced in an attempt to
increase openness, create a more informed and business literate
workforce, and to win workers' 'hearts and minds'. Communication now
occurs through mechanisms such as twice yearly meetings between
senior management and groups of workers, monthly team briefing
sessions between FLM's and workers in their respective areas,
suggestion schemes, as well as the company newsletter, 'Crystal Clear'.
According to management, the information that is communicated at
meetings can incorporate many topics. Workers are free to ask questions
at these meetings, can voice concerns and 'blow off steam' to senior
management. This helps to diffuse any problems brewing. A senior
manager remarked:

> Every year, twice a year, the Chief Executive and a number of
> senior managers meet every member of the workforce. We are
> very open at those meetings. There are some constraints
> obviously. Within those limitations, we tell them what is going on
> in the business, what is good and what is bad. By continuing to
> do that twice a year, you build up a level of trust. When we
> started they didn't believe anything that came from management,

> but over a period of years when you give them consistent messages your credibility starts to rise because the things you say are seen to be true. We never try to use those meetings to manipulate things. If you are not honest, you are found out very quickly, and the whole process loses credibility.

The union view is slightly less sanguine:

> When the company says that you can have an input into what the company is about, they have suggestion schemes, which encourage people to put in suggestions, and there are rewards attached to the benefits coming from those suggestions. There is also a huge change in the way the company communicates with the workforce. They have shopfloor meetings on at least a quarterly basis where the whole workforce is met by top management. They then have inbriefing sessions, where the local manager brings their own group together. They are saying that if you put together their invitation to put in suggestions plus communication it means employee involvement. What we say is that you can get involved in a lot of issues which management are responsible for anyway, but nothing more than this.

The company also invested heavily in *training and education* to support its new business strategy and cooperative work relations. In 1994, investment in education and training amounted to £1.4 million or 4 per cent of payroll, while in 1999 it had risen to £2.3 million or 6 per cent of payroll. Workers are actively encouraged to participate in various education and training courses that promote upskilling. WC has a modern learning centre. Workers are also funded if they enrol on various courses in colleges outside the factory. In particular, workers are being encouraged to develop new IT/technological skills that will allow them to adjust to the rapid pace of technological change.

The union acknowledged that the company has made a significant investment in training, and they welcomed this. Nevertheless, while management believes that the amount of investment in training should be dictated by what is economically feasible, the union believes that all employees should have an equal right to training not just an 'elite group'. The management philosophy underpinning training is that by continuously updating their skill portfolio employees will enhance their employability, and will be less resistant to change. An engineer emphasised the importance of re-skilling for employability:

> The company is moving more and more towards new technology, and the traditional skills are starting to be replaced, or certainly complemented anyway, by technological skills. And people have to upgrade all the time, you have to keep renewing yourself. You could be doing an entirely different job in two years time than you are doing now. We all have to have the skills to be able to move, or your employability deteriorates. The company has changed from being a 'one job forever' situation. You have to be employable around here now.

There is no formal *employment security* guarantee as such, that is incorporated within a collective agreement or company policy; though there is a brief statement on employment security contained in the Waterford Wedgwood 'Group Code of Corporate Conduct':

> The group aims to help employees share in the group's success to which they have contributed by seeking to provide employment security based on performance whilst recognising individual achievement.

In reality, in a context of acute economic uncertainty, employment is insecure at WC – this was starkly illustrated after the demise of 'partnership' in 2003 when the Dungarvan factory closed in 2005, and, most recently, the announcement in spring 2008 of a further 490 redundancies.

On the pay front, a revamped *profit-share* scheme was introduced in 1993. Payments are made on an annual basis. While the annual profit share payment was negligible in 1993, it was £2500 (£50 pw) per employee in 1999. It helped that 1999/2000 was the most profitable year in WC's history. Management saw the profit-share scheme as an important mechanism for building consensus, and linking the interests of workers to company performance. It has also helped to promote the perception among employees that they had some stake in the company. Both management and the union thought the profit-share scheme produced mutual gains. A senior manager remarked:

Every employee in 1999 got £2,500 in addition to their pay. So, whatever £2,500 might be worth to a Senior Executive, to someone who is earning £16,000 a year it is huge money. There is a direct relationship between profits and what they get in their back pockets. It is amazing how often the question comes up 'What does that mean for our profit-sharing?' The profit-share is a way of making the whole thing real to them. So it has worked well.

A union representative also spoke favourably of the profit-share scheme:

We got £2,500 in 1999. It helped in keeping industrial peace in the place. It was a clever move on their part. The rest of the country is only now talking about introducing it. You get the idea that you are working for yourself when you are cutting glass. It is a system whereby you can get money. That is what drives all of us.

Efforts were also made to promote equal opportunities policies. The 'Group Corporate Code of Conduct' states:

Employment selection, promotion, payment and security of employment shall be based on suitability for the job and there shall be no discrimination on any grounds, regardless of sex, sexual orientation, creed, colour, marital status, age, nationality or disability.

There are a range of equal opportunities policies, such as anti-harassment and sex discrimination policies, provisions for maternity and parental leave, and an innovative initiative promoting employment opportunities for disabled workers, called the 'Horizon Project'.

Further, in 1999, the company launched a new corporate culture programme called the 'Waterford Way'. A new 'Group Code of Corporate Conduct' was issued to every employee in summer 1999. The Code contains a number of economic and social value statements under the headings of shareholders, business integrity, customers, suppliers, outsourcing, employees, and the wider community. The employee value statement incorporates issues such as equal opportunity, fair compensation, training and communication. A senior manager remarked:

We launched an initiative called the Waterford Way. It is about having a culture that supports things the company wants to do, and brings people along. It was sponsored by the Chief Executive. It comes from the very top. Every one of us has to meet with our people and take them through it in relatively small groups. Otherwise it wouldn't work. Also, people are more inclined to say what they think. And, as management, we are putting ourselves under much stricter criteria than before. When issues arise you ask yourself, 'is this consistent with what we said?' It works both ways, but the major onus for trust is on management to say 'look, we want to work with you, we want to explain the rules, we want your involvement in the creation of those rules, and we are saying we are prepared to be judged by them'.

But a senior union representative expressed a belief that management may use the Waterford Way to try to marginalise the union to try and win the 'hearts and minds' of the workforce. Nevertheless, the union decided that it was best to engage with it from the inside, rather than remaining on the outside:

That kind of approach is a more cynical way of marginalising the union than approaching it on the basis of we want to do things in partnership with you. I think the strategy of employers in developing philosophies like that is about winning the minds of their employees away from the union. We will look after your welfare because we have this philosophy. But, they knew that if the union took up a position of we are not having anything to do with this, what good would it have been to them? At the same time, there wasn't much point in us saying that is a load of nonsense; we are not having anything to do with it. If there were issues that we could see as being of tangible benefit to our members then why not go along with it.

The union focused on the obligations in the Waterford Way to raise various issues with management, notably a concern that it contained inequalities:

The Waterford Way, up to now, has built in a number of inequalities, injustices and discriminatory practices between how union members and staff members are treated. Here are some examples. The sickness scheme. When a member of staff is out of work sick they are paid their full wages every week, yet when a member of the union is out sick they suffer a 25 per cent reduction in their wages. The policy of non-recognition for staff.

Employees who are told that they are being put on staff are told
that they are not entitled to union recognition. Why?

Management Controls

Despite the fact that management was concerned with moving towards a
more cooperative relationship, this did not mean that it loosened its
control – far from it. Levels of direct supervision are high (though the
style is now more facilitative than coercive); formal rules are applied
more vigorously; workers are more exposed to market pressures, notably
the threat of outsourcing; and management has also introduced technical
controls such as industrial engineering techniques to tighten work
standards, and new computer and monitoring systems.

i) Threat of outsourcing/production re-location: From the early 1990s
onwards, management has used the coercive threat of outsourcing to
force change. This factor, probably more than any other, has shaped IR
since the 1990 strike. In stark contrast to the pre-1990 situation, the
Waterford manufacturing base is no longer the only source of
production, and the fear of production relocation has ensured
union/worker compliance with change. A crucial factor is that the
production process is fragmented and comprised of distinct stages, which
do not need to be carried out in one location. Outsourcing was
instrumental in reducing union power. A union representative said
resistance to outsourcing could potentially result in job losses:

> It will always be there as an issue. It will always be their trump
> card, particularly if there is a downturn. Anytime we raise an issue
> that is going to have a cost implication for the company, they say
> that is going to have an impact on jobs. It will become more of an
> issue if you have a downturn in the company. We are trying to hold
> on to what we have, they will always be able to use that as a big
> stick to push agreements and cut costs here and there.

Similarly, another union representative remarked:

> For years we were brought up thinking the Waterford brand name
> was something wonderful. We sold a lot of glass in America.
> This company was like a family-run company. But then they
> were suddenly saying that we could make Waterford in

Czechoslovakia, stamp Waterford on the glass on the boxes, and put it on the shelves in America. We were then left with the choice of how far these people could diminish the brand name if they were pushed to the pinnacle. It got to the stage where we were saying 'do they want to close the factory?'

An engineer also summarised the outsourcing threat:

The management has said that they are never going to make any item of glass at a loss ever again, and that directly impacts upon the workers – because if there was a loss, glass would be outsourced. And we are now an outsourcing company rather than a homogenous company, which we used to be pre-strike days. So, if we are not able to produce the glass at the price the market requires, the company is in a position to brand it strongly enough that it could be made in Portugal or wherever, and as the volume goes out of the plant, then obviously jobs will also go out of the plant. I think that really is the biggest thing facing the company and the workforce. There is a constant threat to jobs.

Management also increased its use of temporary contract labour and sub-contracted non-core functions, such as canteen, transport, security, and cleaning operations. At the time of the research fieldwork, there were approximately 160 short-term contract workers at WC. These contract staff can be hired or fired in accordance with fluctuations in product market demand.

These developments at WC correlate with Burawoy's (1985) argument that the globalisation of production and capital is increasingly creating employment relations regimes under which workers are coerced into complying with management objectives, largely because of the fear of production re-location, plant disinvestment and job displacement.

ii) Technical control: Management have also used various forms of technical control over workers' activities, such as industrial engineering techniques to tighten work standards, and advanced computer technologies, which can be used to monitor workers' performance.

Prior to the introduction of industrial engineering, a joint management-union piece rate committee negotiated piece rate standards. However, the committee has gone, and management now largely controls piece rate standards unilaterally. Standards are determined by the Industrial Engineering Department, and industrial engineers can go down on the shopfloor almost at will to set new piece rate standards, or to maximise the efficiency of the production process. Industrial engineers use various work-study techniques to set standards for the piece rate system, as well as to maximise machine utilisation or plant layout. The procedures that govern the work-study practices associated with industrial engineering are contained in the 1990 collective agreement:

> Management has the right to assign, establish, examine, review and implement methods, work standards and bonus systems on an ongoing and regular basis. This applies to both existing and future arrangements. Standards will be reviewed where there are changes to either the method, layout, plant, equipment or manpower level, or established and implemented where none exist. This will be conducted by the Industrial Engineering Department in conjunction with managerial staff in the area and in accordance with internationally accepted I.L.O. standards and principles.

There is no negotiation with the union as such, although it is consulted about the methods used and can dispute any standards after they are set. An industrial engineer described the process of setting standards for piece rate payments and machine efficiency:

> If you were looking at wages, you would use a computer-based system called Techtime. It is an electronic study board and it replaces the old stopwatch system. It is much more accurate, and what we do is go down and study the item somewhere on the shopfloor. And you would do a number of cycles and get an average time across that. You then apply standards like rest allowance to come up with a minute value, and that minute value also has a monetary value. And by setting a certain output per day it allows the person to earn their wages and some bonus on top. If you were looking at machine optimisation, you would look at how long the machines run for, the down time for the machine, the loading and unloading of machines.

A union representative remarked:

> It is a necessary evil. It is so subjective. It is not an exact science and it can cause problems. The company puts in a system and we

get it checked out. We are allowed to check it and do restudies. Usually the studying and timing is not the issue, it is the rating and the allowances that are the key things that need to be negotiated. But all the systems that have been put in we haven't had a huge problem with, because people have been able to earn a bonus on them. The problem is going to come when the company see that they are paying out bonuses when they could be getting more production for less money. They will use the methods to try and reduce the bonus payments, or at least increase productivity for the same payment.

Another union representative observed how industrial engineering techniques are used to tighten work standards:

We work a British Standard Industrial System (BSI). We are paid according to how long it takes to cut a glass. If you change a wheel or something, that is built into the system. But it is a much tighter structure. They might say, 'look there is a looseness in that system, the next few glasses, tighten it a bit more'.

As well as industrial engineering, advanced computer-based information technologies with sophisticated software packages have been introduced, which generate detailed information on various aspects of production, such as how much product is being made, whether it is of the right quality, how much product has been lost, and so on. This information is quickly accessible from personal computers. A manager commented on the nature of the computer-based control system:

We have a shopfloor control system that will tell you the results at any one time on some of the higher volume automatic lines that we've got here. It is a computerised software system that talks effectively to our automatic stemware blowing machines, and it talks to all the machines along the entire line, from the start of the process to the end. And it gives you real information on how many you make, how many were good, whether they were lost, and so on. And it is available at the machine; it is available throughout the process. There are two stem lines, and for each stem line there are three different screens where you can access information. Plus you can access it on your PC. It is PC based.

iii) Performance management control: Since a terms and conditions of employment agreement was implemented in 1992, the workforce has been governed by a dense framework of formal rules covering issues such as time-keeping, work roles, pay, and discipline. These rules are quite strictly enforced, although there are differences across the factory. A union representative mentioned that 'in terms of disciplinary issues, the method of discipline has become much stricter in comparison to the past'.

The workforce is now much more subject to performance controls. By implementing performance controls, management has established a systematic link between individual productivity and performance targets. Performance management control has been facilitated by information technologies capable of producing complex performance data and delineating performance standards and targets. There are four key performance indicators (KPI): production costs, product quality, customer service and plant efficiency. A manager emphasised the importance of performance management control:

> You must have information and data, which you use to control the process. Now as part of that you are controlling people, of course you are. What we try to do is instead of making the controls overt, they are covert and less visible. The problem you have is translating that data into useful information, 4 or 5 key performance indicators.

These KPI are linked to budgetary control processes in each area, which come under the jurisdiction of the manager in charge of that area. Each individual function head has to ensure that KPI are met, and has to operate within certain budgetary constraints. In turn, these local budgetary control processes are linked to the overall annual budget, which is set following negotiations between the Waterford Wedgwood Board and Waterford Crystal senior management.

This dual approach to the regulation of the employment relationship at WC (which is illustrated in the table below) constitutes a particular balance between generating cooperation and maintaining control in a particular context at a particular point in time, and is much more complex than portrayed by optimists and critics in the literature. A senior manager lucidly described the balance between control and consensus at WC during the pragmatic partnership period:

> Gurus who write books saying that command and control is over and it is all about consensus management – that is bullshit. There is a boss, a leader. The answer is trying to work together to get the biggest form of consensus agreement. There is always control. Rather than command, it is now facilitator control. Workers can have increased autonomy over certain aspects of work, but there has got to be control. What I call soft control, rather than really overt in your face control. Control comes from parameters – these are the parameters within which you can work. But, the big dilemma is that the machinery and the process are bringing those parameters tighter and tighter, and yet we are trying to expand peoples' participation. One way round that is to introduce what used to be called multi-skilling or multi-tasking where people move round a different number of jobs. So, although you have got to have a consensus, the consensus has got to be lead by what the technical structure of the business is.

Another manager remarked:

> Overall, we are moving from control to commitment, and from manager to leader/facilitator. We are moving that way. We are on the continuum. We are only moving. We are not remotely at this approach across the company.

Table 3.3: 'Pragmatic Partnership': Combining Cooperation and Control

Cooperative 'Partnership' Practices	Management Control Practices
- Management-union task group - Management-union IR monitoring group - Information and consultation - Profit-share scheme - Extensive training - Two-way communications - Equal opportunities policies	- Outsourcing, threat of production re-location - Performance management/ measurement - Technical controls – e.g. industrial engineering - Direct supervision (facilitation)

The Balance of Mutual Gains (and Costs) for Management, Union and Workers

We now turn to the balance of mutual gains outcomes for management, the union and workers.

Gains and Costs for Management

Management secured a number of gains, notably greater workforce effort, increased productivity, lower costs, lower conflict (no major strike since 1990), reduced accident claims (down from 60 accident claims per year before 1993 to less than 10 after 1993), less absenteeism (down from 7.5 per cent in 1993 to average of 3–5 per cent), and improved product quality and innovation. While this could not all be attributed to partnership, it played its part. Partnership had an impact on the bottom line, with significant increases in profitability during the partnership phase.

The company-union task force, especially, was practically significant in generating mutual gains, dispelling the conclusion by critics that cooperation between management and unions is largely illusionary.

i) Productivity and innovation: Levels of productivity and innovative behaviour from workers and union representatives clearly increased during the pragmatic partnership phase. The management view is that the task group played a vital role in the companies' revival and undoubtedly helped boost competitiveness and productivity. To this end, a manager remarked:

> I do believe that it influenced a lot of items that would have otherwise been outsourced. We were able to prove that they could be produced here just as competitively.

The task group facilitated not only increased profitability of existing products, but also the winning of new products, and even winning back products that had already been outsourced. Crucially, the task group was very instrumental in facilitating the introduction of the new tank furnace. The extensive information and consultation that took place in the task group was vital for boosting productivity and innovation. But although increased innovation was also evident to some extent at task level, worker innovation at the point of production has been circumscribed by limited opportunities for direct job participation. This was not just attributable to management. The union opposed management-sponsored direct employee involvement, fearing it could undermine union influence.

ii) Industrial action: The level of overt industrial conflict has reduced significantly since the 14-week strike in 1990, although there have been a number of unofficial stoppages by small groups of workers. For instance, a group of twenty-four furnace workers engaged in four days of unofficial action in September 1995. Moreover, although binding arbitration (which lasted from 1993-1999) contributed to industrial peace, the union did not welcome it and there was tension over its operation. Overall, there has been less recourse to IR third parties than during the adversarial period.

iii) Absenteeism and labour turnover: Absence levels have decreased significantly since 1993. Absenteeism levels were approximately 7.5 per cent in some sections in 1993, whereas since 1993 they have averaged 3 to 5 per cent. Before 1993, management didn't really keep close track of absenteeism. Since then, management has imposed much greater control over attendance and time-keeping. Levels of labour turnover, aside from redundancy programmes, also decreased.

iv) Accidents: There has been a significant reduction in accident levels since 1994, as well as in compensation claims. Before 1994, there was an average of sixty accident compensation claims per year, and insurance costs relating to compensation claims between 1990 and 1994 amounted to IEP 640,000. Since 1994, there have been less than ten accident compensation claims per year, and the cost of accident insurance has reduced dramatically.

Despite the gains accruing to WC management above, partnership also entailed costs for the employer. In particular, it takes a lot of vigilance, effort and resources to sustain partnership.

Gains and Costs for Union

The union also held a favourable view of the task group, the implication being that it generated mutual gains – a key yardstick of genuine partnership in the literature (Kochan and Osterman, 1994). In particular, the union felt that the task group was important for increasing participation, and gaining access to important information on strategic issues facing the company:

> We went through a period when the company froze us out of any information, and there is certain information that you need to have. You need to have future plans that the company is thinking of implementing. You need to know what they see down the line as the future for the workforce so you can respond. You can be prepared, as against a crisis situation when you find out suddenly. What they held out was the possibility of that information being given under the umbrella of what they call the task group. We got guarantees and parameters going into it. We really went in to milk any information we could get on all aspects of the company. It has delivered in that sense. We can have the financial director in the task group at our request. We can get the Manufacturing Director to give us his immediate plans, we can get a handle on the latest technology in the glass industry, and the whole business of information technology is something that we have been tracking within the task group.

In a similar vein, another union representative remarked:

> In the task group he (Manufacturing Director) gives us information and feeds it out in a non-confrontational committee. You leave your union hat outside the door. It works for him, but it also works for us as well, because we are told a long time before things happen, so we have time to prepare. It is win-win for the union and management. An awful lot of problems have been solved at that forum. It was a great idea. Maybe he should patent it.

Crucially, the task group was strongly driven and championed by senior management, particularly the Manufacturing Director, Michael Wilcock, who chaired the meetings. Union representatives respected the Manufacturing Director:

> I found him very honest, with common sense. He treated people with courtesy and was excellent at his job. I would actually put a lot of what happened in here down to him. There could have been problems in here that he diverted by having some common sense.

Although the Manufacturing Director built up considerable credibility and gained a certain degree of respect from the union, this did not mean, however, as we noted earlier, that the union perceived its participation in the task group as constituting partnership with management. Rather, the union perceived it as a means of boosting their independent influence beyond traditional industrial relations channels. The union was concerned with maintaining its independence from management, being of the view that it is best to proactively work on the inside than be on the outside. A senior union representative remarked:

> There isn't a partnership model in Waterford Crystal in my view. We have approached things, and have always approached things, on the basis of getting the best deal for members. The structure of industrial relations has changed, but it hasn't changed on the basis that the union has now decided that we want to become partners with the company, or the company has decided they want to become partners with the union. It was a structure that was strategically thought out. There were policy changes from ourselves, such as becoming involved in the task group to get access to information. The management had a different approach based on being more open to us about decisions they were making and the implications for our members, and managing the problem with the union. I don't consider that partnership. I consider it to be progressive management thinking as opposed to trying to impose something.

Another union representative emphasised the importance of maintaining an independent stance:

> I think the important thing that we have maintained is the independence of the trade union here. If I was advising anyone in similar situations, the advice I would give is to stay independent. As part of the changes they continuously seek to invite the union into what they call partnership. What we said was we think we are strong enough to get involved in this without diluting our independence, so we got an agreement from the company that only elected union representatives would be involved from our side in the task group. I think the agreement we achieved prior to going in protected our independence. The company wanted to set up a workers council, worker participation, partnership – they wanted to call it everything.

In a similar vein, a manager remarked:

> The union doesn't like the word partnership. They would say it is in
> our interests to be part of this task group. They don't like the word
> co-operation. They are co-operating in their own interests. They
> hold on to their independence. They get all the information they
> need so they can be better prepared to influence the decisions being
> made. They can get in at the development stage to shape it to their
> own advantage. It is not because they are in it because they want to
> be in with management or think partnership is a wonderful idea.

In other ways, however, partnership was a double-edged sword for the
union, in terms of a weakening of traditional collective bargaining
power. But this was not because of partnership per se, it was already a
factor because the union had less power to mobilize after the 1990 strike.
Furthermore, its new cooperative role meant it was less visible to the
workforce than under its traditional defensive adversarial role.

Gains and Costs for Workers

Outcomes for workers from pragmatic partnership' were mixed. To a
significant extent, the findings correspond with the contingency literature
(cf. Edwards, 2003; Geary and Dobbins, 2001) in the sense that it is clear
that WC workers experienced a mix of benefits and costs as a result of
managerial practices – in terms the balance between involvement and
rewards, on the one hand, and management control and intensity of work
effort on the other. The main gains included stakeholding through the
profit share scheme; far more communication, information/consultation;
better relations with front line managers; and substantially more
training/education. The main downsides were employment insecurity,
outsourcing, work intensification, industrial engineering (resulting in
tighter work standards), shiftwork, and limited direct job participation.
Overall, the gains accruing to employees from 'pragmatic partnership'
were less than those accruing to management.

Employee experiences of 'pragmatic partnership' shaped the state of
their 'psychological contract' with management, which will be discussed
below under the headings of worker perceptions of management
competence, trust and fairness. In turn, the state of the psychological
contract has influenced worker attitudes on issues such as job

satisfaction, loyalty to the company, commitment to management aims, and views on the changed role of the union.

In the next part of the discussion, we consider worker views on the gains and costs of 'pragmatic partnership' in more detail. In terms of worker experiences of changes in work organisation, a number of workers felt there are too many FLMs. However, most employees saw a big improvement in the style of front line supervision, in terms of more facilitation and less aggression. An engraver stated, 'I am given a job to do by the FLM. The supervision would be quite relaxed. I work as an individual and would have quite a lot of discretion'. A cutter commented 'You don't need the supervisor over your shoulder. They are more relaxed now'. A machine operator in the auto-cutting section remarked, 'the auto-cutting teams are working o.k. You don't have the FLM breathing down your neck. He is not in your face telling you what to do. A general operator commented, 'FLMs are fine. Supervision is quite relaxed'. Against this, a number of workers felt that the level of supervision was still quite intense in their area. A blower remarked, 'There is definitely a strong level of supervision there, no question about it', while a general operator commented 'Supervision in some areas of the factory is tight'. Overall, however, the irritant of tight supervision is not as widespread as during the adversarial phase.

The majority of employees said they do not exercise much autonomy or discretion over work organisation, either individually or as part of a team – certainly compared with the indulgency period. Front line managers now control the majority of issues relating to how work is organised, and by implication, workers believe that they do not have many opportunities to directly participate in decision-making over day-to-day work tasks. Many employees – particularly craft – had far more autonomy over work organisation during the indulgency phase. A cutter remarked:

> We have less discretion now. We are a market driven company. We have a chain of people in different areas. I am only part of that cog. I do what I have to do. I don't have any real decisions outside my areas. When it comes into my area, the only say I have is possibly over the quality I produce. I can make suggestions to FLMs, but sometimes they may be a bit slow to take them up. But, overall, you are just part of a cog in a very large wheel.

Employees on continuous shiftwork have generally found it difficult to adjust to the new system. Many complained about the physical and mental stress and strain associated with shiftworking, and the problems of trying to reconcile work duties and responsibilities outside. The comments of a worker in the repair shop illustrate these tensions: 'many people are pissed off with shiftworking', while a machine operator remarked, 'They would want to start looking at shiftworking much more because I don't think they give a damn. They don't take into account what effect it has on family life. It is bad for you'.

In sum, the findings on work organisation and direct worker participation illustrate that, having experienced considerable autonomy during the indulgency phase, employees felt that they had little autonomy and direct involvement at the point of production. Supervision was more relaxed, but FLMs were present in large numbers. Given that the literature informs us that autonomous teamwork/advanced direct participation at the point of production are one of the key requisites for successful mutual gains partnership (cf. Kochan and Osterman, 1994), the absence of such initiatives at WC placed limits on partnership. Partnership was restricted to the apex level and had not percolated down to the factory floor.

In terms of worker experiences of management control, there was a widespread perception that the utilisation of controls has resulted in an intensification of work. Many workers perceived work effort and pressure to be quite relaxed during the indulgency phase. Traditionally, they had considerable autonomy over the pace of work. However, most employees across all grades suggest that effort levels have intensified in recent years. Many employees feel they are now working harder all the time, and have little respite. An operator observed, 'we are under more pressure now than ever. It couldn't get any harder'. A cutter commented, 'work pressure is now much harder. They are tightening the process up'. A blower said: 'They are looking for more and more. It has become so scientific. It is all about costs'. But employees in some areas found work somewhat less demanding. For instance, an engraver, who was formerly a cutter, remarked: 'they seem to work harder in the cutting shop now. Engraving is physically not as hard. Effort levels are acceptable, though you now have less time to do the job'. A worker in the repair shop felt that 'the job is not hard in the repair shop'.

A number of employees objected to work intensification and the factors behind it. The main reason they felt they are working harder is because management has tightened the production system to increase efficiency. Management has reduced production downtime, introduced industrial engineering, and raised performance standards. For instance, a number of workers expressed the view that industrial engineers are continually tightening the piece rate system. As a result, workers are discovering that they have to work harder to earn the same money. A number of workers objected:

> The piece rate system is totally inhumane. It is just not normal the way we work. Management cannot tighten the system anymore. It is not a fair system. It is a joke. They have tightened the system so much, you hardly have time to go the washroom. Another problem is that we are all getting older (cutter).

Another cutter remarked:

> Work has got much harder. Under the piece rate system, the clock is boss. The industrial engineers tighten up the system. You have to stay on the wheel all day to make it worthwhile.

The ageing workforce was also clearly a factor. Many workers suggested that because they are getting older, they are finding it more difficult to deal with work tasks that are quite physically demanding. In particular, blowing and cutting is very arduous work. Many employees have been at the company for about thirty years, and are not finding the work any easier. There are concerns that the pressure and stress will become intolerable if they are pushed any harder. For instance, a female general operator commented, 'the lines below are fit for younger women, but it is hard for the older women'.

Some workers didn't necessarily object to increased work effort if kept them in a job. They were more concerned about inconsistencies in the production process. That is, they were calling for greater certainty and stability in the production process, which they felt, was not always there; though it was seen as an improvement on the adversarial pattern. For instance a blower remarked, 'The work load has increased. I don't object, but there is not enough consistency. Every day there is chopping and changing. That increases pressure'. In addition, a general operator commented, 'Work effort and pressure has definitely increased. I don't mind as long as everything flows freely. Sometimes it can get congested'.

Employee experiences of work have shaped the psychological contract, in terms of how workers view management competence, trust and fairness, which has, in turn, influenced attitudes on job satisfaction, loyalty to the company, commitment to management, views on the role of the union.

i) Management competence: From 1993 onwards, management tried to rebuild cooperation by attempting to tackle some of the major irritants that had been a source of conflict during the adversarial phase. The most fundamental irritant was the workforce perception of general management incompetence, and a sense of no clear direction or stability for the business. Management set about constructing strategic direction by introducing new products, new technology, and improving the organisation of production. It also introduced new cooperative practices linked to business strategy, notably the management-union task group.

There is a perception that overall, management competence has improved since the adversarial phase, although there are still tensions. The following quotes illustrate employee perceptions of management. An operator said she was 'more than happy with management' and that 'work is better organised'. An engraver felt that 'management seem to know what they are doing'. A blower remarked 'they are very professional in their particular areas of expertise. They are better at their jobs'. A cutter expressed the view that 'top management are very good. They turned the company around'.

But alongside this positive view of management, some employees were critical of what they perceived as a profit-driven agenda, which conflicted with their own values. A cutter remarked: 'I wouldn't have anything against any of them, but they are quite detached. The bottom line is that they are money merchants'. A repair's worker said:

> I have no problem with FLMs, but there are problems from plant manager upwards. I would like to see senior managers listen to the workforce more. They never come back to you with answers.

A general operator commented:

> They are making profits, so you can't knock them for that. But, saying that, they are doing away with jobs with the cutbacks, and the machinery. So, it is good and bad.

Some employees expressed reservations about changes at senior management level. All but one of the core senior management team responsible for developing partnership, and who the workforce respected as competent managers, had departed WC by 2002. The workforce were wary of some of the new managers who came in after 2002, who were seen as exhibiting less inclination to pursue partnership.

ii) Trust: Although trust levels improved after the dark days of adversarial IR, they were not very high at WC at the time of the fieldwork, although this could vary; depending on the individual manager. The quotes below illustrate this. One general operator said that she 'trusted management to keep promises', but two other operators were less sanguine. One operator commented:

> Trust is not great. You would wonder are they going to close the place altogether. They can make the glass cheaper elsewhere. None of us know what the top management are planning at the end of the day.

Another remarked, 'I don't trust top management. They don't deliver on their promises'. A machine operator commented, 'You can never trust management. They are like the government. They will say one thing and do another'. Trust in management amongst other grades also appeared to be quite low. A cutter stated, 'I trust some managers, but not others. HR is very weak, while sales and marketing is excellent', while a worker from repairs commented 'management see the company as a brand to make profit. Management is often breaking its promises'. A blower remarked, 'I don't trust management. They don't fulfil their promises. I only believe them if they actually put something into practice', while another blower felt that trust was 'not very high'. This distrust reflects a commonly held view that management sometimes breaks promises. Moreover, distrust reflects the fact that job insecurity is a big concern, and that employees are subject to management controls and have little autonomy at the point of production.

iii) Fairness: A number of employees felt that there was no sense of fairness, notably in terms of the distribution of pay and rewards. This was heightened by the fact that many employees were accustomed to high pay during the indulgency phase. There was a common perception that, while senior management had received substantial financial benefits during the most profitable years in the companies' history, employees had not received their fair share. The fact that workers were expected to bear the brunt of cost cutting added to this grievance. A blower said: 'rewards are not being distributed fairly. The financial incentives are not good enough. They could solve a lot more problems if workers received more financial benefit', while another blower commented:

> It is totally immoral. The amount of money they (certain senior managers) receive is obscene. They are getting performance-related bonuses of between half a million and a million pounds at a time when there is a huge emphasis in here on cutting costs on the shopfloor.

A worker in repairs remarked:

> The Performance Related Bonus for management is a bone of contention amongst people in this factory. The whole idea of the profit share was to share the money equally with everybody. But, nobody knew that management was getting this PRB until about a year ago. Everybody said, Christ, they are getting two profit shares. A lot of people resented that.

In turn, employee views on management competence, trust, and fairness have fed through to attitudes on job satisfaction, loyalty to the company, commitment to management, and attitudes towards the union.

i) Job satisfaction: Many employees felt management has made little attempt to design jobs that are intrinsically satisfying, or to develop employee participation schemes. Further, there are few opportunities for promotion. This has placed limits on job satisfaction. Instead, extrinsic financial rewards have historically been the key means of satisfying workers. In recent years, however, substantial investment in training and education, and a degree of job rotation, has contributed to some increase in intrinsic job satisfaction, though there were limits to this. A general operator found her job to be 'quite challenging', while another operator remarked 'I find my job interesting. I have a certain amount of job satisfaction'. Another general operator was more critical suggesting that her job was simply a case of 'coming in and getting out. I don't find it interesting. As long as I get paid'. A machine operator commented, 'I enjoy where I am working'. An engraver – who now spends quite a lot of time working with information technology in the Learning Centre – remarked that he found his job to be 'very interesting and diverse'. A blower commented, 'I am content in my own job, but there are no doors opening to progress. I like coming into work, but they could give more opportunities'.

ii) Commitment and loyalty: In terms of the extent of commitment and loyalty, commitment levels are undoubtedly higher than during the adversarial phase. But, it is important to distinguish between commitment to management aims and loyalty to *the company* as a broader entity. On balance, the majority of employees, having devoted their working life to the company – which in many cases amounts to thirty years or more – expressed relatively high levels of organisational commitment and loyalty. They have a great sense of pride in the company. This is despite the fact that trust levels are quite low, 'them and us' attitudes are still prevalent, and there are differences between the interests and values of employees and senior management. In workers' eyes, management and the company are two different things. That is, managers come and go, but the company has always been part of their lives.

The quotes below illustrate employee attachment and loyalty to *the company*. A general operator commented, 'I am very committed to the company', while another general operator suggested 'my loyalty and commitment is 100 per cent. I have never been off in seventeen years'. A cutter remarked:

> I have absolute commitment. I have criticised the company to the management. But if I walked out of here and met a thousand Americans in a pub I would sell this company hand over fist. Most of us came here straight from school. I have a great standard of living.

Another cutter stated, 'I would have 100 per cent loyalty and commitment. It is a great employer. I have a decent living'. An engraver commented, 'I am committed to the company. I feel loyal'. A worker in the repair shop remarked, 'I could have gone many times, but I have a high degree of loyalty to the company'. A blower suggested, 'my loyalty and commitment would be very strong. I have no intention of leaving', while another blower commented 'my loyalty has accelerated since 1998 when the company funded my education. I was always committed to the job and I am now committed to the company'.

A number of employees expressed lower levels of commitment, and there are definite limits to the diffusion of commitment across the factory. A general operator suggested 'I have been here nineteen years, but basically I just look it as a job'. An engraver remarked, 'I don't really have loyalty. As long as I get my wages'. A machine operator, who used to be a blower, remarked, 'When I was blowing I had pride in the company. I am now in the auto-cutting section, and do my days work and go home'. A cutter commented:

> I am very proud of working for Waterford Crystal. I have given my whole life to the bloody place. But it is hard to say, overall, how committed I am. There is a feeling now that you are just a number in here. I do the work to the best of my ability and then leave. I want the money to live, I am not here for the love of Waterford Crystal.

iii) Views on role of union: Employees felt that relations between management and the union had become more cooperative. But workers from all felt that the power and influence of the union have decreased, and a number of workers expressed dissatisfaction with the effectiveness of union representation. The quotes below illustrate this:

> I wouldn't be pleased at all with union representation now. In the past we were well represented, but now the union don't seem to have the same clout. We are not well represented in the general section. The structure is not geared towards the lower paid (general operator).

> The union got a wallop. It is still there, but it is not really communicating with the workforce. Sometimes, you would have

little faith in them at the moment, I am sorry to say. They seem to be in the background (general operator).

In relation to issues, which I have brought up, which I thought were genuine issues, I would score them two out of ten, and that is probably being generous. I had specific grievances. I brought them to my shop stewards attention, and they then went to the convenor. But, they just died. They were never resolved. It has got to the stage now, where I won't even bother going to them (blower).

The union is not doing a good job, even though people are being wronged. In the old days it was very strong, but now its bite or fight has gone (cutter).

The union is no longer a kind of hands-on organisation. They are caught up in a web of meetings and task forces. That takes them away from the every day running of the area. They were probably too much in control before. But it has turned full circle now. They have less power now. They haven't really progressed. They are from the old school of thinking. Nobody goes to union meetings, because they are after being taken over by the SWM (Socialist Workers' Movement) (cutter).

The decline in union influence appears to be connected to a number of issues related to the fact that the union is both less powerful and less visible. First, there is a perception that the union had become quite detached from the membership, and had not been as proactive as they perhaps could be, in terms of addressing worker interests. Second, there was much less conflict and more management-union cooperation. The union spent far less time visibly fighting management over traditional adversarial bargaining issues, and more time engaging with management at a strategic level, but the flipside is they were less visible. Third, overall, management was deemed to be more competent at managing employment relations than in the adversarial years, so there was less need for union intervention. Fourth, the power balance shifted heavily towards management, who had the 'trump card' of outsourcing. Finally, wages have largely been set by national partnership agreements since 1987, so the role of the local Joint Negotiating Committee has diminished.

Despite the widespread perception that union visibility and influence has waned, the vast majority of employees retain some distrust of, and distance from, management, and still perceive the protective independent role of the unions to be important. This is influenced by the strong collective traditions at WC, and indicated enduring 'them and us' attitudes. The quotes below illustrate this. A general operator stated:

> I wouldn't like to see the union go. They are still needed. The union are o.k. at the level they are at now because I feel they haven't got as much power. Before, I felt they had too much power.

An engraver commented:

> I think everybody should have representation. I think a union is vital, even for getting management's message across to workers. You also need the union to keep management in check, because to them profit is god.

A blower remarked:

> There is still a need for a union to protect worker rights. I feel that if there were no union or unified voice, there would be more exploitation and intimidation of workers. I support the union as a body and a structure. I would be seriously concerned about what would happen if they were not there.

In terms of what they see as the most appropriate role for unions, a sizeable number of workers felt that management-union co-operation was a more preferable route to adversarialism. The overriding perception was that employee interests can best be served by collaboration with management over common interests. For instance, a general operator felt that 'the union and management are better off working together', while an engraver commented, 'The union's role in the past was get, get, get, but now they have a new role, which involves working with management as well as against'. Many workers knew little, however, about the activities of the union-management task group, which indicates a common problem facing partnership experiments not connected to the shopfloor. A cutter remarked, 'The task group is a talking shop. I don't know what is happening. We are not informed by the union', while another cutter stated, 'I don't know too much about the task group, but it is a good idea. If management and the union could work in harmony it would be a better system'. A blower remarked: 'We don't get feedback from the union about issues arising from the task group. I go to the union meetings, but I have never heard a report or minutes on task group meetings.'

The table below summarizes the gains and losses accruing to the various stakeholders at WC and illustrates what is deemed to be an unequal balance of mutuality.

Table 3.4: Unequal Balance of Mutuality at Waterford Crystal

	Management	**Unions**	**Workers**
Gains	Higher productivity, effort, creativity, lower costs, higher quality, innovation, lower conflict, reduced accidents, less absenteeism.	Input into operational and some strategic business decision-making, notably product strategy. Much more information and consultation.	Much better training, profit sharing, better relations with line managers.
Losses	Takes a lot of vigilance, effort and resources to sustain partnership.	Less power, less visible. Decline of traditional collective bargaining.	Threat of outsourcing, job insecurity, work intensification, industrial engineering, little direct participation.

Conditions Underpinning Pragmatic Partnership

Finally, the main contextual conditions promoting a (partial) balance of mutuality were top management support; efforts by all parties to add value to achieve higher performance and management partially implementing workplace stakeholding by adopting new IR/HR practices (notably strategic management-union partnership, profit share, training, better communications). But there were limits to mutual gains because WP was truncated and offset by competing pressures. Despite some tinkering, traditional hierarchical structures largely remained intact and key partnership elements were missing (notably employment security and job participation). The lack of direct involvement, especially, meant participation was largely confined to representative partnership and information provision. Workers also perceived that financial rewards were too heavily skewed towards top management, raising the issue of fairness. In short, WP was not sufficiently institutionalised and vertically aligned. Also, management control policies, notably the threat of outsourcing/production relocation, generated workforce insecurity and constrained the balance of mutuality.

Conclusion

In this chapter, we have attempted to address the central aim of this book: whether pluralist workplace partnership can deliver mutual gains and, more specifically, to examine the following three questions:

- How have employers tried to move towards partnership, and has it displaced management control?

- Does workplace partnership deliver mutual gains for workers, unions and employers, and what is the balance of mutuality?

- How do external and internal contextual conditions influence the adoption and sustainability of partnership?

In terms of the first question, an attempt has been made to illustrate how the relative balance between different approaches to employment regulation, in terms of management's concern to maintain control and generate consent, has been periodically redefined at WC over the last fifty years or so. Attempts to introduce partnership did not constitute a fundamental break with past practice or displace management control. Yet elements of partnership were new. Three distinct historical phases are evident, where different patterns of securing control and cooperation from employees have been adopted: the 'indulgency', 'adversarial' and 'pragmatic partnership' phases. During these phases, particular methods for regulating work relations became the dominant tendency for a time (collective bargaining and direct worker autonomy during the indulgency phase), before different methods came to the fore during the adversarial phase (unilateral management control and concession bargaining), and then during the pragmatic partnership phase (management-union partnership and a re-casting of management control). Since about 2003 (after the fieldwork was complete), as competitive conditions deteriorated again, there has been a move back towards unilateral management prerogative and concession bargaining, with partnership in retreat. Therefore, we can see why and how tendencies towards different managerial IR practices have occurred at certain times and under particular contextual conditions.

The 'indulgency pattern' lasted from 1947 to 1985, and laid the benchmark for what followed. For much of the indulgency phase, a context of continuously high product demand and profitability meant management bought consent from the workforce by offering the carrot of very high pay. Management largely abdicated control of the shopfloor to the union, which, in the vacuum created, grew increasingly powerful, securing successive concessions from management through collective bargaining. The benefits of the indulgency pattern outweighed the costs. The indulgency phase was characterised by over thirty years of industrial peace, with very little conflict. But the indulgency pattern proved to be unsustainable, as the company's cost base spiralled out of kilter at the same time as competitive pressures intensified from the 1980s.

The 'adversarial pattern' lasted from 1986 to 1993. During this period of competitive crisis and intense market pressures, management was prompted to tighten its unilateral control over the workforce and the union to secure massive cost cuts. Management forced compliance by initiating redundancies, implementing successive rounds of 'concession bargaining', utilising coercive threats of outsourcing or closure, and tightening direct control on the shopfloor. In terms of how employees and union representatives experienced this, the costs far outweighed the benefits. There was significant distrust and conflict, culminating in a bitter 14-week strike in 1990. Management took on the union and 'won' the battle, but this was at a cost, in the sense that management lost the 'hearts and minds' of the workforce, and were widely perceived to be incompetent. Conflict was rampant, there was very little consensus, and performance and profitability were poor.

The third phase ('pragmatic partnership) began in late 1993 and lasted until 2003. Boosted by more buoyant external conditions, and enabled by a more competent senior management team, moves towards co-operative IR were promoted by the strategic coordination of a new product market strategy based on product customisation, quality and innovation, and advanced technology. The new business strategy meant worker inputs of adaptability, innovation and skill were vital for promoting competitive advantage for WC, because it could not emulate low labour cost producers.

Union marginalisation was not a viable option. Management introduced a company-union task group, which gave the union a joint decision-making input, notably in product strategy. The task group was practically very significant in generating mutual gains, dispelling the conclusion by critics that cooperation between management and unions can not 'work'. Various complementary HR practices were also introduced.

As noted above, moves towards partnership did not mean management abandoned control. Rather, in response to product market pressures, management utilised a variety of controls – notably threats of outsourcing – alongside partnership practices. These controls placed limits on mutual gains.

In terms of the second question, relating to outcomes, there were elements of mutual gains, but the balance of gains clearly favoured management. The move towards pragmatic partnership enabled management to introduce workplace change more effectively, and at a faster pace than was possible under the adversarial pattern. The cooperative task group was particularly important in boosting innovation, problem-solving activity and productivity – proving the practical benefits when management introduce genuine cooperative arrangements. Industrial relations also improved dramatically. The union also secured gains from the task group through joint decision-making, consultation and participation, notably at a strategic-level in relation to product strategy. But partnership was something of a double-edged sword because the union was less visible and its traditional collective bargaining role diminished.

Workers experienced fewer gains from partnership than management. Their experiences were much more upbeat then under the adversarial period, with various benefits derived from partnership being reported, but workers also experienced a number of negative elements arising from management controls and intense market pressures. The main benefits cited included overall perceptions of more competent management, better relations with front line managers, much more information and consultation, and upskilling through significant training/education. The main costs experienced were a widespread perception of employment insecurity, and concerns about outsourcing, work intensification, industrial engineering, shiftwork, limited direct participation, and some dissatisfaction with pay and rewards.

The result was a higher level of mutual gains consensus than under the adversarial phase, but within definite limits. The main conditions driving these outcomes were greater management competence, and, at a more indirect level, new employment relations policies, notably strategic management-union partnership via the task group; a more buoyant external climate; and the pragmatic acceptance by a more 'disciplined workforce' of new competitive realities. Mutual gains were limited because control practices were common, traditional organisational structures remained intact, and key parts of the partnership 'bundle' were missing (notably employment security, single status conditions and opportunities for task participation). Partnership was distant from shopfloor employees, being largely confined to representative participation. Trust levels were not that high, and many employees cited unfairness, in terms of the unequal distribution of status and rewards between management and themselves. And although the union was weaker, most employees said a union was necessary to protect their interests – an indication of continued 'them and us'. In addition, although a more 'disciplined' workforce had pragmatically accepted the need to cooperate with management in very difficult competitive circumstances, this did not translate into active commitment to management. It more accurately amounted to pragmatic worker consent to specific aspects of workplace change in difficult times.

In terms of the third issue, the main conditions underpinning a (partial) balance of mutuality were top management support, efforts by all parties to add value to achieve higher performance, and management partially implementing workplace stakeholding by adopting new partnership practices (notably strategic management-union partnership, profit share, training, better communications).

The Waterford Glass partnership 'worked', but, ultimately, it was not sustained, though it lasted nearly ten years. WP was a victim of various external and internal pressures. Since 2003, there has been a move back towards unilateral management control and concession bargaining, influenced by a 'new crisis'. Crucially, partnership's demise was caused by acute deterioration in the company's competitiveness and an unfavourable dollar-euro rate, culminating in job losses, cost-cutting, pay freezes, and outsourcing. The company has faced severe competition from Eastern Europe, especially after EU enlargement. In 2005, 480 jobs were lost after the closure of the Dungarvan plant. Most recently, in spring 2008, a voluntary redundancy programme providing for up to 490 employees to apply for an agreed severance package was negotiated (IRN 13/2008). The company then announced in October 2008 that it plans to make a further 280 people redundant, which, if it goes ahead, would mean the end of large-scale manufacturing at the plant. Most production would be relocated overseas to central and eastern Europe, where costs are lower. The company has informed workers it would continue to make some hand-crafted crystal products in Waterford, and would also keep its on-site tourist trail/visitor centre. But this would leave just 70 production staff in the plant, mainly making luxury hand-crafted glass for the tourist centre. Two hundred employees would remain in total, including sales and marketing, maintenance and administrative staff. This compares with a high of 3,300 in the 1970s, a dramatic decline in fortunes for one of Ireland's flagship indigenous companies. Another factor influencing partnership's demise was that the senior managers responsible for its operation had left by 2002, and some new managers seemed less inclined to maintain partnership when confronted by serious competitive difficulties. This raises the issue that, without succession planning, voluntary WP is vulnerable to collapse when key management (or union) supporters leave. A third factor was that WP was not sufficiently institutionalised to survive 'pivotal events' in relation to a new crisis and senior management turnover. In short, the conditions supporting partnership were too weak to counteract the pressures undermining it. It illustrates the difficulty of sustaining voluntary WP in the face of environmental turbulence and weak institutional supports.

Figure 3.1 on the next page summarises historical IR patterns at Waterford Crystal. The next chapter examines attempts to move towards partnership at the second case study site, Aughinish Alumina.

Figure 3.1: Summary of Patterns of Workplace IR at Waterford Crystal: 1947-2008

Indulgency Pattern (1947–1985)	Adversarial Pattern (1985–1993)	Pragmatic Partnership Pattern (1993–2003)	Unilateral Management Pattern (2003–??)
IR pattern: indulgency	*IR pattern: adversarial*	*IR pattern: cooperation and control*	*IR pattern: unilateral management*
- union power	- concession bargaining	- cooperative relations	- concession bargaining
- worker autonomy	- management coercion	- management controls	- management controls
Outcomes	*Outcomes*	*Outcomes*	*Outcomes*
- 35 years of peaceful IR	- frequent conflict, big strike	-partial (unequal) mutual gains	- resigned acceptance of crises
- mutual gains	- no mutual gains	- pragmatic cooperation	- partnership gone
	- very little trust, cooperation	- still conflicts of interest	- no mutual gains
Contextual conditions	*Contextual conditions*	*Contextual conditions*	*Contextual conditions*
Supportive:	Negative:	Supportive:	Negative:
- very good external context	- severe crisis	- improved competitiveness	- competitive crises
- stable work organisation	- exchange rate problems	- better exchange rate	- poor exchange rate
- financial indulgency	- mismanagement	- new technology	- EU enlargement – more competition

Workplace Partnership in Practice

Supportive (cont'd):	Negative (cont'd):	Supportive: (cont'd)	Negative: (cont'd)
- union-manager distance	- poor work organisation	- willingness to cooperate	partnership gone
- employment security	- management coercion	- profit share scheme	Intensification of management control
- paternalism	- cuts in pay and conditions	- much better training	acute employment insecurity
- union job controls	- redundancies, insecurity	- communication, information and consultation	
		But also negative conditions:	
	- outsourcing	- outsourcing	
	- erosion of indulgency	- industrial engineering and technical controls	
		- work intensification	
		- shiftwork	
		- employment insecurity	
		- very little direct employee participation	

Chapter 4

MANAGING CONFLICT AND COOPERATION AT AUGHINISH ALUMINA

Introduction

This chapter examines historical patterns of industrial relations at Aughinish Alumina (AAL), Askeaton, County Limerick, and then considers why management attempted to move away from adversarial IR towards workplace partnership with employees and union representatives, the nature of partnership practices, the balance of mutual gains (and costs) accruing to employers, workers and unions, and the conditions underpinning partnership.

Addressing the first research issue, the chapter will first consider how AAL management attempted to break away from adversarial IR and move towards partnership from 1993. To this end, the motives behind, and the nature of, new partnership practices will be described. A related issue is whether partnership practices constituted a fundamental break from traditional IR at the plant, and displaced management control practices. With regard to the second research issue, the balance of mutual gains (and costs) for management, workers, and the unions, are considered. We examine whether partnership has benefited management, in terms of contributing to higher productivity, greater innovation, lower conflict, and so forth. The impact of partnership on the role of unions at AAL is also considered. For employees, we consider various gains and costs, in terms of experience of the balance between management control and worker participation, work effort and reward, employment security/insecurity. Finally, the external and internal conditions underpinning workplace partnership at AAL are considered. The chapter finishes with a conclusion summarizing the findings.

The chapter begins with background information on AAL in terms of ownership, financial position, business strategy, organisational structure, structure of production, technology, and work organisation, and industrial relations structures.

Background Information

Aughinish Alumina Limited (AAL) is a single site alumina refinery producing 1.5 million tonnes of alumina (aluminium oxide) annually. The alumina is extracted from the raw material, bauxite, which is imported by ship from West Africa. The alumina is then exported overseas to aluminium smelters. AAL was established on a greenfield site, with production commencing in 1983. The construction of the site began in 1978, and total investment amounted to one billion US dollars. AAL is situated on Aughinish Island in the Shannon estuary in the south west of Ireland, approximately eighteen miles from Limerick City. The plant lies on a 1,000 acre site. It currently employs 435 people in comparison to 800 when production commenced in 1983. There are also 20 apprentices, 25 temporary workers and approximately 100 contractors.

Ownership

When production began in 1983, ownership of AAL was shared between three companies: Alcan, Billiton, and Anaconda. The majority shareholder was the Canadian multinational aluminium manufacturer, Alcan, which had a 40 per cent share. Alcan had most control over operations when production commenced in 1983. For instance, Alcan always appointed the Managing Director. Alcan chose Ireland as a location primarily because it was within the European Union, and was perceived to offer economic and political stability. However, because it could not fund the project alone, Alcan sought collaboration with other companies. The second largest owner, with a 35 per cent share, was Billiton, a subsidiary of the Dutch multinational Shell. In addition, Anaconda, a subsidiary of the American multinational Atlantic Ridgefield, held a 25 per cent share. In 1985, however, Atlantic Ridgefield sold this share to Alcan for a small sum because it perceived that the plant was losing too much money. Consequentially, Alcan owned 65 per cent of the plant, with Billiton owning the remaining 35 per cent. This left Alcan with more control over how the plant operated.

In the mid-1990s, Billiton announced that it wanted to sell its 35 per cent share, but there were no takers. The reason for this was that AAL was not seen as a financially viable investment – it was viewed as 'a white elephant'. Alcan eventually bought Billiton's share, and, thus, had become the sole owner by 1995. In 1999, however, Alcan sold AAL to Swiss multinational Glencore, a diversified natural resources group with world-wide interests in mining, smelting and refining. Significantly, the AAL senior management team became wholly Irish, and had more autonomy from centralised control, because Glencore took a much more hands-off approach, so long as the plant was profitable. In contrast, for much of the time when Alcan was the owner, AAL senior management were mainly Canadian, and the plant operated within a context of relatively tight centralised control imposed by Alcan HQ. Since March 2007, AAL (and Glencore) have been owned by Russian multinational, United Company RUSAL, which is now the world's largest manufacturer of alumina and aluminium.

Financial Position

After experiencing severe financial difficulties for a number of years, AAL has been operating at a profit since 1994. In the financial year 1996/7, its turnover was IE£130 million, while total costs incurred stood at IE£115 million, leaving a profit of IE£15 million. Since then profits have risen significantly. The profit on a tonne of alumina is determined by the margin between the sale price and the unit cost of production in $ per tonne. The sale price of alumina is linked to the price of aluminium (in US dollars) on the London Metal Exchange. Thus, the price of alumina changes according to fluctuations in the market price of aluminium, as well as fluctuations in the US dollar.

Business Strategy

AAL manufactures a single product, alumina. International competition is quite intense in the alumina industry, with AAL's main competitors located in Australia, South America, Canada and Jamaica. Cost containment/reduction, product quality, technological innovation, and the development of human resources are deemed by management to be crucial issues for the plant's competitiveness. To a significant extent, AAL's competitive advantage is derived from producing more alumina with less staff than comparable alumina plants elsewhere.

Cost containment and reduction is a key aspect of AAL business strategy. Economies of scale are crucial, as the more alumina that is produced the more efficient the plant is in terms of unit costs per tonne produced. The company has no influence over external factors such as the market price of aluminium or changes in the value of the US dollar, so costs may fluctuate. In addition to these 'non controllable variable costs', the plant was, and still is to an extent, burdened by various 'non-controllable fixed cost' disadvantages in comparison to competitors. It has high-energy costs relative to producers in other countries, although this situation has improved following the construction of a new power plant. The company also has high freight costs as the raw material has to be shipped from West Africa, and the final product then has to be shipped overseas: there are no aluminium smelters in Ireland. This can be contrasted to competitor plants in places such as Australia and South America, where the whole process of mining bauxite, refining alumina and smelting aluminium is self-contained. That is, the alumina refinery is situated right next to the bauxite mine, with a coal-fired power station producing power for the aluminium smelter beside it. Concomitantly, AAL management can only influence 'controllable costs', such as labour costs and production/technical costs, which, together, determine the unit cost of production per tonne. In terms of overall 'non-controllable' and 'controllable' costs, AAL would currently be near the industry average. Its total costs per tonne of alumina produced are lower than Canadian plants, on a par or slightly higher than Jamaican plants, but higher than South American and Australian plants.

Continuous improvement of alumina quality is another important aspect of business strategy. There are rigorous quality standards and targets in place at the plant. Furthermore, AAL has also invested in advanced technology in recent years, which has been important for improving the business. Finally, in recent years, investment in human resources has been a crucial aspect of business strategy. To compete with less staff,

AAL has had to improve its people management capability. The company has invested in training, and has introduced semi-autonomous teamwork to secure greater involvement from workers to tap into their skill and knowledge of the production process. Management has also attempted to build co-operative relations with its trade unions. These new HRM and IR practices are strategically integrated with business strategy and advanced technology.

Organisational and Occupational Structure

In the early years, AAL had a highly bureaucratic and hierarchical organisational structure, which was largely modelled on the Canadian owner Alcan. The complex system of formal bureaucratic rules promoted a highly mechanistic approach to personnel management and industrial relations. There were nine organisational layers, compared to three today. Significantly, there used to be two separate departments dealing with employment relations: an industrial relations department dealing with the unionised industrial workforce, and a personnel department for non-union staff.

Starting from 1986, however, the organisation was gradually restructured to make it flatter and less hierarchical. Alcan and Shell decided that they needed to do something about AAL's mounting costs at a time when the aluminium industry was entering a difficult period. Two layers of management were removed, who were mainly Canadian and Dutch expatriates, and a smaller seven-member senior management team was established. Five local small management units (SMUs) were also created in 1987, which were accountable for their own budgets, costs, operations, maintenance and staffing. The changes also involved bringing operations and maintenance together, which occurred in September 1987, with managers reporting to a single plant manager. Previously they were separate entities with competing interests, and were under the control of two different senior managers. During this period, a number of able young Irish employees were promoted into management positions in operations and maintenance. They were primarily engineers who had been at the plant from the beginning. They were put through a management development programme, and became quite a cohesive group. Then, in 1988, forty redundancies occurred amongst the industrial workforce.

Despite these changes, the organisation structure was still quite bureaucratic and hierarchical. This changed radically in 1993, however,
following an extensive re-structuring and rationalisation programme involving the removal of further layers of management, as well as 150 redundancies among staff and industrial workers. The old IR department
was disbanded, leaving a single personnel department. There were also
moves to devolve responsibility over work organisation by establishing
semi-autonomous teams at the point of production. As a result, the organisational structure is now much flatter. The apex of the organisation
structure is comprised of the senior management team, which is comprised of the Managing Director and three senior managers. The senior
managers are the plant manager, the technical and commercial manager,
and the human resource and public affairs manager. In contrast to the
past, when ex-pats were in the senior positions, the senior management
team is now wholly Irish. Below the senior management team, there is a
stratum of 12 coordinators/facilitators. There is one shift plant facilitator
in a management role on days, who is responsible for supporting the
teams across the whole plant. At the level of the five local production
areas there is a staff presence on days in the form of co-ordinators, operations facilitators, maintenance facilitators, planners, and engineers.
Co-ordinators are there to provide a leadership role and to support decision-making by the teams and their local facilitators. As well as their
local role, co-ordinators also have plant wide functions in areas such as
maintenance, process control, and contractor safety, so that co-ordination
is promoted across the plant. The role of the local team facilitator is to
coach and support the teams, rather than closely direct them, which was
traditionally the case.

In terms of the occupational structure of industrial workers and staff,
there are a variety of trades and skills across the plant. There are approximately one hundred skilled craft workers (instrument and electrical
(E/I) workers and maintenance fitters), who primarily work in the central
workshops. In addition, there are over 160 operators working in the five
local production areas. There are also a number of other general workers
across the plant, such as in the central stores. Finally, there is a number
of support staff, such as clerical workers, technologists, and laboratory
analysts. Ninety three per cent of the workforce is male, and seven per

cent female. Ninety seven per cent work full-time, and three per cent are temporary workers.

The Structure of Production, Technology and Work Organisation

The production process is organised round advanced continuous process technology. The plant runs 24 hours a day, 365 days a year, and produces over 4,000 tonnes of alumina per day. The production process is known as the 'Bayer Process', which involves the purification of bauxite into alumina by dissolving the impurities in alkali solution. The process is named after the German scientist who invented it in 1889, K. J. Bayer. The Bayer production process consists of five stages, under which the alkali solution, or so-called 'mother liquor', continuously circulates round the plant. The raw material, bauxite, is then added to this liquor, and the final product, a fine white powder called alumina, is eventually extracted for export to aluminium smelters.

The plant has some of the most advanced technology in the industry. There has been significant ongoing investment in advanced quality control technology – a Honeywell 3000 quality control system was introduced in 1991. This has provided a platform for further automation and contributed to reduced costs and improvements in quality and productivity. Continuous chemical analysis is required at various stages of the production process to ensure quality control. The raw materials coming in, the various waste products, the final alumina product, and samples from the intermediate stages of the process, all have to be monitored using advanced microelectronic technology. The advanced technology helps to contain costs and improve productivity by ensuring that the maximum amount of alumina can be extracted.

Work organisation in the five local production areas is based round semi-autonomous teams with team members having responsibility over many aspects of decision-making at the point of production. There are about fifty teams across the plant's industrial workforce, each with an average of six to eight team members, although there are larger teams in some of the craft areas. Teamwork is not present in non-union staff areas such as HR and Finance. Teams are either purely operations- or craft-based, rather than being multi-occupational in composition. In a typical operations teamwork set-up, there would be a continuous 12-hour 4-shift system rotating day and night. There would be one operations facilitator on days – but not nights and weekends – responsible for the operating teams. The operations facilitator would, therefore, have little direct contact with each operations shift. Teamwork in craft areas differs from operations in the sense that the facilitator would see their teams more often, because craft workers typically work a day-based system. There would be one maintenance facilitator in each craft area responsible for a team of fitters and a team of electrical/instrumentation (E/I) craft workers. The nature of teamwork is dealt with in more detail later.

The main task of the skilled craftspeople is to improve the reliability of plant equipment, and minimise and repair breakdowns. The work of semi-skilled and general operative workers is more routine, and incorporates tasks such as de-scaling pipes and vessels; cleaning tanks; collecting, transporting and packaging all sample types; and receiving and issuing all material requirements.

Trade Union Representation

AAL has recognised trade unions from the outset. Approximately 70 per cent of the workforce is unionised, which constitutes the whole industrial workforce. Union membership is confined to the industrial workforce, with management and staff being non-union. The breakdown is roughly 300 unionised industrial workers and 130 non-unionised staff and management. There is a multi-union structure, with three unions. Instrument/electrical technicians are represented by the Technical Engineering and Electrical Union (TEEU). Fitters are represented by the TEEU, as well as the Amalgamated Engineering and Electrical Union (AEEU), which is now part of UNITE. Finally, operators are represented by the Services Industrial Professional and Technical Union (SIPTU). Negotiations take place through single-table bargaining. There are twelve shop stewards on site, six from SIPTU, four from the TEEU, and two from UNITE. There is a ratio of one shop steward for every 25 union members.

The 'Adversarial IR Pattern': 1983–1993

This section considers how management attempted to move away from adversarial IR towards workplace partnership at AAL. Two distinct patterns of employment regulation can be identified. The first phase, which can be called the 'adversarial pattern', lasted between 1983 and 1993. This period was characterised by adversarial IR and management was concerned with securing minimal compliance from the workforce and the unions – primarily by buying it through collective bargaining and high levels of overtime. The period between 1992 and 1993 was crunch time, because the costs incurred through buying compliance became unsustainable. Consequentially, management then set about forcing change by significantly tightening its control over the deployment of the workforce, and forcing the unions to engage in concession bargaining. Once it had overcome resistance and reasserted its authority, management began to move towards fostering more co-operative employment relations. This second phase, which commenced in late 1993, can be called the 'pragmatic partnership pattern'. Under this pattern, management have combined various new workplace partnership practices with indirect management control practices.

The industrial relations history of the plant dates back to 1978 when site construction commenced. Industrial relations were extremely adversarial during the construction phase, and this carried over when production commenced in 1983. At the time, AAL was structured round the hierarchical, bureaucratic rule-based model that was operational in Alcan HQ in Canada. This model was directly transferred to AAL by Alcan senior management. Alcan HQ did, however, allow AAL management an element of freedom to develop personnel and industrial relations practices without interference. This was partly because Alcan was not the sole owner at the outset. Significantly, Alcan and Billiton had some different preferences in terms of personnel management practices. For instance, there were two different sets of rules governing ex-patriot managers from the respective companies. In addition, Alcan HQ recognised that it would be advisable to take Irish IR traditions into account. At the time, it was a key policy of the Irish Government and the Industrial Development Agency (IDA) to encourage incoming multinationals to recognise trade unions, though this is no longer the case. Concomitantly, unions were recognised from the outset at AAL.

The Nature of Adversarialism

We now consider the main features of the adversarial pattern of IR, and then the negative outcomes it generated for all workplace stakeholders.

i) Financial indulgency – buying compliance: The employment relationship during the adversarial period at AAL was centred round exchanging financial rewards in return for worker compliance with continued production. Significantly, this took place within a broader climate of 'financial indulgency' throughout the company, in the sense that management made little attempt to control costs. 'Financial indulgency' at AAL occurred via collectively negotiated pay agreements and extremely high overtime levels. Management would buy the compliance of the unionised workforce during pay negotiations with trade union representatives. Negotiations were adversarial and based on a 'distributive' mode of collective bargaining (Walton, Cutcher-Gershenfeld and McKersie, 1994), in the sense that a gain for one party constituted a loss to the other. But this is what both parties were accustomed to, and all they knew. Management and the unions concluded an extremely complex 'Comprehensive Agreement' in 1987 governing pay and working conditions, which became known as the 'little grey book'. This arms length accommodation was based on management conceding the right of unions to represent their members' interests relating to pay and conditions, and the union's conceding that governance of business issues should be solely the prerogative of management.

The unions were perceived to be quite powerful and to possess a degree of control over the economic wage-effort bargain. But it was a narrow form of economic control, in the sense that they used their collective power to maximise pay for their members. A union representative put it thus:

> It was very adversarial. We went in and asked for something and they automatically said no, so we applied a bit more pressure. Basically it was strong-arm tactics from either side that tended to win the day.... We would have been fairly well organised. We tended to act as a fairly coherent group, which I suppose gave us some semblance of power.

As a result of this collective power, pay rates at AAL compared quite favourably (and still do) with other companies in the Limerick area, particularly when overtime was added. Basic pay rates (in Irish punts) for the various grades as of 1 April 1987 are shown in the table below:

Table 4.1: AAL Pay Rates in April 1987

Grade	Basic Rate per Hour	Basic Rate per 40 Hour Week
5 – craft workers	£6.26	£250.40
4 – control room operators	£5.96	£238.40
3 – process room operator, storeman	£5.36	£214.40
4 – Maintenance serviceman, plant and wharf serviceman, sampleman	£4.77	£190.80
5 – utilityman	£4.17	£166.80

Source: Comprehensive Agreement (1987: 78).

In comparison, according to data provided by Ireland's Central Statistics Office (CSO), average weekly earnings in manufacturing industries in 1987 stood at £196.55 (and £201.68 for all industries).

The unions also used their power to secure various shopfloor 'job controls'. The shop stewards were widely perceived to have the power to prevent line managers doing certain things they didn't agree with. If they didn't like something, the stewards used to often go to the IR department. The unions also had veto power to prevent contracting out of work: no job could be contracted out until a shop steward agreed. The main purpose of this, from a union perspective, was to maximise overtime opportunities for the workforce. For its part, management was prepared to indulge the unions and the workforce by paying overtime, so long as production was maintained. As a result, an endemic overtime culture developed, and there was a desire amongst many workers to secure as much overtime as possible to top up basic pay. It was evident that workers would deliberately engineer overtime by storing up work for evenings and weekends. The work system actually encouraged manufacture of overtime, because the worse the plant ran the more money workers could make. Thus, it was in workers' interests to be inefficient be-

cause they could derive substantial financial reward. This was emphasised by a trade union official:

> Things that people realistically could do on a Monday the thing
> would be shelved until Saturday for overtime purposes. So
> you've lost production – if it had anything to do with production.
> If an employer say's to one of my members be inefficient and I
> will double your wages I know what my guys are going to do. If
> they want to do extra things for their family they'll do it.

A facilitator remarked:

> There was a huge overtime culture because of the monetary
> rewards and certainly overtime was engineered. We had overtime
> of maybe twenty to twenty-four per cent in some instances. The
> unions' wouldn't allow the company to contract out work to
> alleviate that situation.

As a result of these job controls, workers had some control over, and
space within which to define their own level of work effort and reward.
However, there were definite limits to these job controls, in the sense
that workers were subject to intense supervision and were expected to
comply with strict formal rules.

ii) Direct control: Direct supervision was very intense across the plant
up until radical re-structuring in 1993. Prior to the re-organisation, there
were approximately 55 supervisors for about 400 plus industrial workers,
which constituted a ratio of about one supervisor to seven workers. There
was a supervisor for every shift in each local area. As a result, although
unions and employees had certain job controls, the autonomy and discretion afforded to workers over day-to-day work tasks was very tightly
constrained. There were rigid job demarcations and very strict controls
over timekeeping. Workers were expected to rigidly adhere to their own
specific job tasks – nothing more, nothing less. One ex-supervisor, currently in a facilitator position, described the traditional structure of supervision:

> There was very direct supervision at the time … I couldn't
> believe that you would have to go out and tell qualified people
> what piece of equipment they required to do a specific job rather

than allowing that person the opportunity to choose himself. You as a supervisor had to tell them what was required right down to the last spanner. It was a totalitarian type of structure. It was horrible. It was very close policing from the time they arrived in to the time they were at their workstation.

Similarly, a union representative remarked:

I would class it (supervision) as quite poor. It was very much the old fashioned way. A guy coming round telling you what to do, when to do it. In a lot of cases he couldn't tell you how to do it because he didn't have as much experience in a line of work as the people he was supervising. That could lead to conflict because you might have someone telling you how to do your job when they didn't understand that job. There would have been a lot of personal conflict, people not getting on at a personal level.

The control of timekeeping was particularly strict, with one shop steward observing:

It reminded me of a military model of organisation. We were dealing with codes like absent without leave. They were very strict on timekeeping and rules were pushed down your throat. They would watch you coming back from tea breaks.

This conflict between supervisors and workers was further exacerbated because supervisors were non-union and sometimes earned less than the unionised workers they were supervising.

iii) Bureaucratic control: The plant was traditionally very bureaucratic and hierarchical. Management attempts to secure compliance on the shopfloor through direct supervision were reinforced by a dense framework of rules covering issues such as work roles and demarcations, pay and grading, promotion, timekeeping, discipline, general standards of conduct, safety and hygiene, and grievance procedures. All of the rules affecting the industrial workforce were contained within the 1987 Comprehensive Agreement. Paragraph 1.2 in the Work Rules Section states:

All employees, as part of their contracts of employment, must observe the Work Rules and should make themselves thoroughly

familiar with these Rules as lack of knowledge will not be
accepted as an excuse for their infringement or non-observance.

For instance, if an operator wanted assistance from a craft worker they
had to go through a highly bureaucratic procedure. They first had to go
and ask their immediate supervisor, who then had to go and ask the other
worker's supervisor, who then had to tell the worker concerned to provide assistance.

The complex web of formal rules contained within the Comprehensive Agreement were interpreted in different ways by management and
the workforce, which took up a considerable amount of time and created
many difficulties. Management tended to apply the rules strictly to the
letter, which tended to breed resentment amongst the workforce. As a
result, it was extremely difficult for management to generate informal
co-operation and flexibility from workers. A facilitator observed that:

> Most people tried to work the grey book on both sides to the
> letter of the law and that was a huge hindrance. It didn't allow
> any type of individual flexibility.

iv) Coercive comparisons: From the mid-1980s, management placed
increased emphasis on the fragility of the plant's future in the face of
external competition and cost pressures. Accordingly, there was an element of coercive comparison with rival plants. Initially, this had little
effect, as trust levels were very low. The workforce simply did not believe that management were telling the truth. The workforce only began
to realise that management might be serious about the precarious situation facing the plant when small rounds of redundancies occurred in
1988 (42 industrial workers) and 1992 (20 staff).

From the late 1980s, it became increasingly apparent to Alcan HQ
and AAL senior management that – in the context of the extremely poor
IR climate – the costs incurred at the plant had become untenable. The
plant was now about to confront a serious crisis in the marketplace, as
external economic pressures and contradictions intensified. This crisis
had been gaining momentum since the mid-1980s, as product market
pressures began to bite. First, there was an overproduction of aluminium,
with new producers entering the market in places such as South America.
Second, following the implosion of communism, there was a flood of

cheap metals from Eastern Europe and former Soviet Union at a time when western economies were already affected by overproduction. Third, as a result of the over-accumulation of aluminium, the price of aluminium fell from a record high of US$2,427 per tonne in 1988, to a record low of US$1,043 per tonne in 1993. This 57 per cent fall in aluminium prices was much more pronounced than previous fluctuations and cycles: prices were relatively stable during the thirty-year period of economic boom that followed World War Two.

Although AAL's competitors also experienced these product market pressures, AAL had a number of 'non-controllable' and 'controllable' cost disadvantages in comparison to many competitors. In what amounted to a major abdication of responsibility, AAL management had made little attempt to contain costs since production commenced. The cost of producing alumina at AAL was significantly above most competitors. The industry average cost of alumina production in 1987/88 was US$130-140 per tonne. While Australian plants produced at an average of US$80-100 per tonne, AAL was producing at over US$170 per tonne. There was a real fear among senior management that if the efficiency and cost position of the plant did not improve rapidly, Alcan might lose patience and close the plant. At the time, AAL was Alcan's second most expensive plant. It was well known that Alcan had already re-structured and streamlined some of its international operations in response to over-capacity. Alcan had also brought in an external consultant (Henry Porter) from the University of Harvard in the United States to conduct a viability study of AAL. Porter basically informed Alcan that AAL was not viable. Therefore, the predicament facing AAL was extremely serious, and it seemed very possible the plant could close.

The situation came to a head in 1992, and it became starkly apparent to AAL management that they would have to devise a solution internally to rescue the plant from crisis. Previously, problems were dealt with externally, through Alcan. This time, however, Alcan had no solution to AAL's problems, bar implementing Porter's recommendations, which appeared to spell closure. Therefore, AAL senior management set up a strategy team to develop a solution. Significantly, a new Managing Director was appointed during this period; who was to prove much more decisive than previous MDs. He was determined to assert his authority and to bring the plant out of crisis. Although he was regarded as tough, he commanded more respect than previous MDs. A union representative made the following observation:

> Things started to change when we had a new MD here. He was very much a no nonsense guy. He put it on the table and said this is it. He didn't want to hear any bullshit. Once we had got over the shock of hearing that, he started to make changes and turn things round. We would have had a grudging respect for him. He wouldn't have been the most likeable person, but we could look at him and say there is a better hand in charge than in the past. He seemed to understand the business a bit better and have a genuine interest in improving things.

The new MD and his management team set about tightening control over the workforce by exposing it to the coercive forces of the marketplace. In this way, management announced a comprehensive five-year 'business plan', entailing significant job losses and radical re-structuring. The MD announced the plan to the workforce in a general meeting in October 1993. Following the announcement, he continually hammered home to the workforce at monthly communications meetings that the plant was in serious trouble and required radical surgery. He was determined to communicate directly with the workforce, rather than through the unions, and he went as far as sending every worker a video to convey this message, and what he and his team proposed to do to turn the company around. The business plan was quickly and unilaterally implemented during October/November 1993, after eventually being approved by Alcan Head Office. Alcan had initially refused to finance the plan.

The business plan incorporated substantial unit cost reductions amounting to US$25 per tonne of product produced. These 'controllable' cost reductions were achieved by various improvements in the technical efficiency of the production process (which constituted unit cost savings of US$19 per tonne) and by reducing labour costs through redundancies at all levels of the company (which constituted unit cost savings of US$6 per tonne). The production improvements consisted of increasing plant capacity from 1 million tonnes to 1.3 million tonnes, as well as enhancing the efficiency of production, particularly through removing bottlenecks and implementing semi-autonomous teamwork.

The redundancy policy, which took place in October/November 1993, was the first major change. It involved 150 'voluntary' redundancies, including the cutting of 27 management positions, so the workforce was reduced from 580 to 430. Although, on the surface, the redundancies were voluntary, there was a perception that senior management deliberately targeted individuals – at all levels, including management – who were perceived not to fit the profile of the 'new organisation'. A plant wide appraisal and interview process was conducted. Management used this process to identify the people they wanted to weed out and the people they wanted to stay. In some instances, the individuals targeted were given attractive severance packages intended to be 'very difficult to refuse'. The overall redundancy package was comprised of five weeks pay per year of service plus statutory entitlements, and a lump sum of £2,000. The company also set aside £500,000 for an enterprise support scheme to assist those leaving to set up their own businesses, or to help people who wanted to pursue further education and training. There was a general perception that the people who remained chose to stay, and wanted to make a go of improving AAL.

Significantly, the trade unions had very little input into the business plan. It was introduced speedily and unilaterally in the midst of a crisis and was presented as a fait accompli. There was no negotiation and little consultation. In the months preceding the re-structuring, union officials had been briefed about the crisis facing the plant, but they were only informed about the true severity of the changes a short time before their members. Management was determined to assert its prerogative to manage the plant. The message to the unions was basically, 'take it or leave it'. The unions were left with little choice but to comply. Resistance to management appeared futile at the time. If they engaged in industrial action the unions risked precipitating plant closure. In the end, the unions were concerned with company survived and securing the jobs of the remaining workforce. The capacity of the workforce and the unions to resist unilateral change was also weakened by the fact that unemployment across the country was high at the time. Moreover, the unions and employees had by now realised that change was unavoidable. A union representative noted:

At that stage your options are limited. You can do the normal adversarial thing of industrial action to prevent it. But people realised that yes we do have to change. They (management) also made it attractive enough with regards redundancy packages and helping people to set up businesses, that it wasn't too bitter a pill to swallow. In the end there were more people who wanted to leave than there were places. At the time, given the nature of the economy, it was a good package. As good as you would have got anywhere in the country.

Outcomes of Adversarial Pattern

Turning to the outcomes of adversarial IR, the costs outweighed the benefits for all stakeholders. The overwhelming perception from workers was that, although their pay was good, the costs of the adversarial pattern outweighed the benefits. Their experience of work relations tended to be very negative, and this applied to union representatives as well. For management, meanwhile, the adversarial pattern generated a number of negative IR outcomes, such as poor productivity, soaring costs, frequent conflict and grievances, and a serious trust deficit. This meant that any attempt to introduce change was very slow and protracted. For example, it took four years to negotiate a flexibility agreement during the 1980s. Industrial relations were so poor that trade union officials often had to visit the plant a few times a week to deal with grievances. The company had to process approximately 100 formally written grievances a year, and sometimes up to 150. Most grievances were over issues such as supervision, overtime, and meal vouchers. Some were very petty, and a failure by management to deal with them internally meant some went all the way to the Labour Court. A facilitator described the cold IR climate at the time:

> I couldn't believe the friction that existed over very small issues. We had one particular petty issue, which was a meal voucher which people were entitled to if they worked overtime. And that went to the Labour Court. So that's how bad it was.

A shop steward implied that management weakness encouraged workers and their unions to pursue grievances:

> If we had grievances that weren't resolved, we had nothing to lose by going to the Labour Court. I think it was a failure on their

part to see that they should have tried to resolve it...It was a weak management. The hole started getting deeper and deeper. Grievances were mounting. Instead of dealing with them internally, they sought outside help all the time.

Furthermore, there were incidences of industrial action: an unofficial strike in February 1986, and unofficial picketing occurred on 24 November 1986 and 1 April 1987. There was an infamous incident involving people chaining themselves to cattle grids, and a number of workers were eventually dismissed in April 1987 because of serious bullying of colleagues. It took a very long time for management to act on this, which again, was seen as another sign of weakness. Management eventually dismissed certain individuals.

The prevalence of conflict pre-1993 was confirmed by workers in interviews and informal discussions. One worker described the operation of the plant as being 'very dogmatic. It was control from the top. It was very rigid and bureaucratic'. A fitter felt that a lot of problems emanated from the managers who worked in the old industrial relations department, who have since left the company:

> There were two people here in IR and they were constantly looking to put you down. They would never be looking to do you a favour or give you a break. Those two guys were responsible for a lot of the grief here. They would stir up trouble, and stir up shit to keep themselves in their jobs. But they were the first people to go out the gate during the re-organisation. If they hadn't got rid of those guys I don't think things could have changed, because there was so much history and bad feeling.

The majority of workers suggested that they were closely monitored and supervised under the old regime, and they resented this intrusion. They classed the quality of supervision as being 'very poor'. Workers said supervisors would come down hard on them over issues such as 'coming back a few minutes late from tea break'.

In the later stages of the adversarial period, and prompted by new market pressures and uncertainties, management coercively imposed its authority, engaging in concession bargaining and cost-cutting. In terms of how employees and union representatives experienced managerial practices, the perception was a far cry from mutual gains, the overwhelming feeling being that the costs far outweighed the benefits. In particular, management significantly tightened unilateral control, work effort intensified, and employment became more insecure. There were considerable costs for the unions, who were by-passed and saw much of their power base diluted. For management, although the balance of power shifted strongly in its favour, deep-rooted conflict of interests meant it was only able to force compliance at best from workers and the unions. This reassertion of unilateral management prerogative corresponds with what Streeck (1987) calls a 'return to contract' – driven by new market contradictions and uncertainties, management concluded that it had to stamp its authority on the employment relationship. However, while this coercive period was all about hard-line management, it paved the way for the moves towards partnership that followed immediately after. Plus, the new MD and his team had begun to gain some respect from the workforce, a vital ingredient in any recipe for managing employment relations that previous senior management had not been able to find.

Conditions Influencing the Adversarial Pattern

The main conditions underpinning adversarial IR were firstly, and most fundamentally, the deterioration in the company's external competitive position and falling profits – culminating in a crisis situation – persuaded a new senior management team to enhance 'efficiency' by cutting labour costs, after previous managers had let costs spiral unchecked. Employees perceived this attack as a violation of existing workplace customs and norms that management had previously 'allowed' to develop. Secondly, and crucially, management at all levels was generally deemed to be directionless and incompetent for much of the adversarial period. It was only when a new MD came in and applied shock therapy and began to communicate with the workforce that this started to change. The general chaos in the plant at the time constituted a violation of worker expectations of predictability and stability, and the importance of production continuity for maintaining workplace order is highlighted in a long-line of industrial relations literature (cf. Batstone, 1986; Hodson, 1999, 2005; Edwards and Wright, 2001; Nolan and O' Donnell, 2003). Thirdly, very intrusive supervision at the point of production and the strict imposition of formal rules were significant irritants that generated conflict time after time. Fourthly, employment became more insecure as management forced redundancies.

The 'Pragmatic Partnership Pattern': 1993+

Having unilaterally forced the workforce and the unions to acquiesce, management then decided to attempt to move towards partnership. Therefore, immediately after the re-structuring in late 1993, management set about fostering more co-operative workplace relations. This coopera- tive approach was accompanied, however, by more indirect forms of control, notably performance management controls and advanced techni- cal controls. This section will examine why there was a move towards partnership, how this occurred in practice, and finally, how new indirect forms of control exist alongside attempts to mobilise consensus. It will then examine the balance of mutual gains accruing to management, un- ions and workers. It will be concluded that the balance of gains were shared relatively equally and fairly between the various stakeholders. Finally, conditions influencing partnership are considered.

Why the Move Towards Partnership?

Three reasons can be identified for moving towards partnership: the co- ercive backdrop of crisis and mass redundancy, the strong union pres- ence, and the existence of capital intensive continuous process technol- ogy. First, the backdrop of crisis made people at all levels realise that the adversarial approach was no longer viable in a context where interna- tional product market pressures had intensified. After initially respond- ing to the crisis by coercively asserting its control over the workforce, cutting costs, and forcing acceptance of change without any negotiation, management strategically set about moving towards partnership. The capital-intensive nature of the plant meant 'sweating' labour was not vi- able. In order to secure the plant's future, management realised there was an urgent requirement to enhance production efficiency by tapping into the knowledge and skill of the workforce and securing ongoing co- operation with change. Traditionally, the knowledge of the workforce had remained largely untapped, resulting in substantial inefficiencies. For their part, exposure to a serious crisis promoted pragmatic acceptance of change from the remaining workforce and the unions – giving rise to a more 'disciplined' workforce.

Secondly, the strong trade union presence was an important condition influencing the move towards partnership, a fact also identified in the literature (cf. Edwards and Wright, 1998; Geary and Dobbins, 2001; Oxenbridge and Brown, 2004). Once it had asserted its prerogative to manage, management was concerned with building co-operative relations with the unions to promote acceptance of change among the wider workforce. There was a realisation that attempts to marginalise the unions would have had a negative impact on generating consent from the wider workforce. A senior manager remarked:

> The challenge facing this plant was how to create a culture and climate and system of work where people feel that they can contribute to their full potential. And that's what we set about doing since 1993. We saw that the adversarial way couldn't continue. Unions represent 65 per cent of the workforce, so there is no way the plant could thrive where 65 per cent of the workforce operated under adversarialism. So it was seen that the way forward was in partnership.

The third main condition promoting the move towards partnership was continuous process technology, which was particularly suited to the introduction of semi-autonomous teamwork. The nature of the continuous process technology meant that it made practical sense for management to remove direct supervision and provide workers with the time and space to operate in teams in order to tap into their discretionary knowledge of the production process. Moreover, the capital-intensive nature of the technology meant that the pressure to closely control workers and cut labour costs was far less acute than in more labour intensive industries.

The Nature of Partnership Practices

The first real steps towards developing partnership occurred when the plant manager (at the time the research for this book was conducted) was sent out in the early 1990s to conduct a study of best practice in a range of Alcan and non-Alcan sites across the UK. He came back with a number of best practice ideas; such as mutual gains bargaining, semi-autonomous teamwork, annual hours, and single status conditions. Senior management then set about putting some of these ideas into practice.

Management-Union Cooperation

Management realised adversarial IR was no longer viable, and set about fostering co-operative relations with the unions. Management was concerned with promoting a joint problem-solving approach with unions over issues of mutual concern. It was evident that management-union partnership took place largely on an informal basis. There was not a permanent formal partnership forum in place at the time of the research – like the Waterford Crystal 'task group', for instance. Partnership had not been given institutional expression at AAL, in terms of formalizing union co-decision-making powers over employment and business issues. Instead, a series of informal joint issue-based partnership teams have been set up as and when required to examine significant issues. The partnership arrangements mainly consist of joint consultation, but also contain some elements of joint governance, both over operational and strategic-level issues, but mainly the former. The new management/union cooperative processes operate in parallel with traditional collective bargaining structures. But traditional collective bargaining now tends to play a less prominent role than years gone by, particularly given that, since 1987, pay levels have been set centrally through successive national partnership deals; though local bargaining still takes place around this pay floor. The evolution of management-union partnership at AAL is described below.

Union representatives were generally tired of adversarial IR, and were ready for an alternative, though it took some time for distrust of management to dissipate. The framework for management-union partnership was first set out in the 'Future' document (1993: 33):

> We see a partnership role for the trade union in the new AAL. Our objective is to create a climate of trust where this partnership can develop to ensure that AAL remains competitive. Our common interests allow for a significant trade union role in shaping AAL's future. We believe that the new culture and the change in management style will allow the trade unions to respond with a flexible and supportive approach. The use of the

'Getting to Yes' principles will support and facilitate the new style and culture.

The first major step towards co-operative relations with unions, which occurred in September/October 1993 – a few weeks before the mass re-dundancies – was the 'getting to yes' training programme. The timing appears paradoxical, in the sense that management ran a joint training course promoting 'principled negotiation' a few weeks before unilater-ally implementing mass redundancies. Management's intention was to create awareness among union representatives of an alternative approach to industrial relations, as well as to shape attitudes and help promote pragmatic acceptance of the necessity of change, and prevent further conflict. A senior manager commented on the timing of the 'getting to yes' programme:

> We had a choice of going through this change the old way, which probably would have led to a strike and the shut down of the plant. Our owners didn't believe 100 per cent at the time that what we were presenting would work. So we had a choice of saying let's go through this change programme the old way, or let's look at another, more constructive, way of doing this. That was management's view at the time.

The 'getting to yes' concept had already been used at Alcan's Lyne-mouth plant in the UK, and therefore, because it was quite familiar, it was much easier to gain acceptance from Alcan HQ. The concept of 'getting to yes' was originally developed by Roger Fisher and William Ury (1999) from Harvard University in the US. It is closely associated with 'mutual gains bargaining' or principled negotiation, which is seen as an alternative to 'hard' positional adversarial bargaining. Fisher and Ury's (1999: 11-12) model of mutual gains bargaining, adopted by AAL senior management and key union representatives, incorporates four ba-sic principles. The first principle involves separating the people from the problem in the sense that 'the participants should come to see themselves as working side by side, attacking the problem, not each other'. The sec-ond principle involves focusing on interests rather than positions, the purpose being to 'overcome the drawback of focusing on people's stated positions when the object of a negotiation is to satisfy their underlying interests'. The third principle is inventing options for mutual gain that 'advance shared interests and creatively reconcile differing interests'. The fourth principle involves an insistence that the results be based on some objective criteria, in the sense that 'the agreement must reflect some fair standard independent of the naked will of either side'.

The external consultants who ran the AAL 'getting to yes' training programme incorporated these mutual gains principles into the course. The breakdown of participants was comprised of 23 staff and 28 industrial workers from across the plant. Senior management, union officials and shop stewards also took part. The training programme was held off-site in a hotel in an attempt to build informal relations between management and workers in a more relaxed and different environment. The purpose of the training was to attempt to equip course participants with the ongoing skills to improve trust in working relationships, reduce conflict, and jointly come up with mutual gains solutions to joint problems. Therefore, management was attempting to provide an alternative to adversarial collective bargaining, and was hoping that the unions would buy in to this alternative. Many of the participants felt that the programme was quite a useful exercise. A union representative commented:

> It was certainly helpful. It opened the door to a new way of doing things. It demonstrated that you don't have to follow the adversarial approach. Most of us followed the adversarial approach because as shop stewards we had never seen an alternative and that was the way things were done, so you just fall in. But having been shown an alternative we were certainly ready to try it. The trust was then gradually built.

Management first began to set out a 'co-operative' agenda with the unions in practical terms – based round the bargaining principles of 'getting to yes' – during the first meeting with unions after the redundancies. The shop stewards felt quite positive about the behaviour of senior management during this meeting, although the link between the 'getting to yes' training programme and a new IR strategy was not immediately evident to them. After years of adversarial bargaining, it was difficult for them to grasp that management was trying to set out a cooperative agenda based round mutual gains bargaining. Management said to the unions at the meeting: 'Here is what we want, now what do you want?' According to one shop steward, this was 'the first time that management had asked what they wanted'. During the meeting, management set out a number of short and long-term partnership issues. A joint sick pay scheme and a new grievance procedure were two short-term issues on the partnership agenda (the intention being to get some quick wins to kick-start partnership), while annual hours was one of the longer-term issues. A jointly monitored sick pay scheme was introduced in July 1994, while management attempted to implement annual hours during 1995/96 through collaboration with the unions. The unions were quite reticent about collaborating on annual hours, however, and told management to go away and develop a proposal on its own. Thus, it took some time for unions to buy into mutual gains bargaining, and management was largely driving the partnership agenda during this time. The concept of mutual gains bargaining was new to both sides, and there was still a degree of mistrust from the adversarial legacy, which took some time to heal.

However, the unions gradually became more involved in various informal issue-based partnership initiatives. The emphasis on workplace partnership in Chapter 9 of the Partnership 2000 national agreement provided an added impetus to partnership at AAL. Management and unions took stock of what had happened on the partnership front since 1993 and assessed how to take the process forward. Thereafter, various informal issue-based partnership teams were formed. These teams can be distinguished from teamwork at the point of production. Rather, they consist of management and union/staff representatives, and meet on an ad hoc basis to solve issues of joint concern. Teams are established on a needs basis and meet at intervals as required and disband when the issue has been dealt with. For example, a plant wide issue would require a team with representatives from all areas of the organisation, while a more localised issue would entail a team of specific people.

For instance, a Joint Pension Committee was formed to consider how improvements could be made to the pension scheme. Membership was comprised of the plant manager, two shop stewards, and two staff representatives. It successfully established arrangements to provide options for retirement from age 50, based on employees transferring part of their national wage agreement increases to the pension fund, together with a commensurate company contribution.

The most significant and innovative collaborative initiative was the establishment of a Joint Steering Committee known as a 'Business Performance Improvement' (BPI) Team, to examine a number of strategic issues facing the company. The BPI Team has provided unions with an input into high-level strategic decision-making, particularly in relation to the formulation of five-year business plans. To this end, a senior manager remarked:

> Every couple of years we do a five-year business strategy plan. Up until the BPI initiative started that would have been done by management. The challenge for us was how do we do that jointly? How do we look at the future in terms of the next five years jointly? That is where the BPI came from. It is joint involvement in strategic planning. The challenge for the BPI now is how to get everyone involved. You don't want the managers and the unions now on it to become an elite group. That group can't be making decisions for everybody else.

Although it was still at an early stage of development at the time of this research, and meetings were quite sporadic, the BPI team provides unions with a scope of involvement someway beyond engaging with management over lower-level operational issues such as sick pay and pensions. The unions have some input into strategic decision-making, which would have previously been controlled by senior management alone. The overall objective set for the BPI team is to find ways of increasing company margins through revenue creation, cost containment and cost reduction. To achieve this, the team has been involved in the following broad tasks: reviewing current business performance against best practice, creating and reviewing options to improve performance, and prioritising proposals for implementation. More specifically, the BPT Team examines production targets, safety targets, technical issues, and means of improving margins through value-added people development. Membership of the BPI team is comprised of shop stewards, management, engineers and staff. Unions appoint their own representatives.

An additional initiative was the setting up of two sub-groups of the BPI. One sub-group is a 'joint incentives group' examining new forms of reward such as gainsharing linked to performance and productivity measures. The group was set up to devise appropriate incentives promoting an ownership or stakeholding culture, facilitate performance and productivity increases, and allow workers to share in gains. A gainsharing scheme was subsequently introduced. A second sub-group is a joint 'key performance indicators' group, whose remit is to come up with appropriate performance indicators in each of AAL's five business units.

Another initiative aimed at moving partnership forward was the commencement of facilitation for partnership training in October 2000 for union representatives, management, facilitators, and staff. The training was provided by external training facilitators from Education & Training Services (ETS) (a trade union sponsored research and training agency). It took place for two days off-site every month, for a period of six months. The idea for the initiative came from a union official from the TEEU. The training was partly designed to increase awareness and knowledge of business issues amongst union and staff representatives. To this end, a senior manager remarked: 'it is difficult to have partnership if people haven't got the knowledge to contribute'. Another purpose of the training is to ensure people involved have sufficient knowledge to facilitate and promote partnership.

As at Waterford Crystal, both management and the unions were generally reticent to describe the moves towards co-operation at AAL as constituting partnership. Moreover, there was a perception that partnership is a vague and unhelpful term. A senior manager stated:

> We set up a group to look at partnership and to find out where we are on the partnership scale, and to define partnership. That became an impossible task because talk to one company and teamwork is partnership. Talk to another and annual hours is partnership. Really, partnership is a state of mind. It is really about sharing power with another stakeholder. We are still working towards that. The Business Performance Improvement team – that is really a partnership initiative at a strategic level.

Another manager remarked:

> Me and my wife have a lot in common and I think we are partners. A union official and me have a lot in common, but we have some issues that we do not have in common and that makes it probably impossible for me to view partnership with my wife the same as work partnership. A good healthy co-operation may

be a fairer phrase.... The 'Getting to Yes' approach would say well you have got your needs, I have my needs, and they are not always the same. It would be carved out, maybe on a board, that maybe 80 per cent of the items are common, but the other 20 are divergent.

A union representative came to a similar conclusion:

I think we could be kicking it up in the air for the next ten years and we still wouldn't know what partnership is. Management don't know what partnership is, and unions don't know what it is. When you think of partnership you think of husband and wife or something like that. If it is a partnership that is the way it should be. But that's not the case here, and its not the case anywhere to be honest. They should be using a different word rather than partnership and define it.

It was apparent that management wanted to avoid what they see as 'top-heavy' structural arrangements, and preferred the flexibility afforded by the fact that partnership remains on a largely informal footing. But, from a union perspective, the absence of formal structures means there is less institutional protection and security for partnership. However, as depicted in the last chapter, the fact management-union partnership was more formalised at Waterford Crystal did not prevent its demise.

It is often suggested in the literature that partnership requires an effective long-term permanent and formalized structure providing independent employee voice (cf. Gunnigle, 1998; Roche and Turner, 1998, Oxenbridge and Brown, 2004). However, Roche and Turner (1998: 90) enter an important caveat with regard to informal partnerships such as at AAL:

The international literature on partnership might be disposed to describe such a consultation-focused model as a relatively weak version of partnership in that it relies primarily on the active maintenance of co-operative relations with trade unions through information exchange and consultation and stops short of structures or arrangements which accord unions a more active voice in company decision-making, other than perhaps on an ad-hoc basis. For the companies involved, however, the model provides a viable and highly effective basis for winning both employee and trade union acceptance of HRM policies, flexible working arrangements and high levels of staff involvement in work. Several companies adopting this model are viewed as exemplary cases of highly effective employee relations in which harmonious relations with trade unions are seen to benefit both the company and employees.

The Removal of the Old IR Department

Another important step towards a cooperative approach was the dismantling in 1993 of the old industrial relations department, which had been so closely associated with adversarial IR. Senior management made a conscious decision to dismantle the IR department, as part of the attempt to remove the IR history. From that point, there was a single personnel department, with a new personnel manager, dealing with all employment relations issues for the whole workforce. As well as dealing with a new personnel manager, the unions and the workforce were also now dealing with other new management faces. Significantly, the dismantling of the IR department was as much about the re-assertion of management authority and order within management as about improving relations with the workforce and the unions. There was a perception that the old IR department had grown too powerful. A union representative believed unions responded to the removal of the IR department quite positively:

> We were dealing with new people, new faces. The old IR department that dealt with the industrial workforce had gone. Its members had left the company. It was new people across the table. That helped a lot. We could start afresh. There was no way we could continue to deal with people who for years and years we had poor relations with.

Management also decided to clear outstanding grievances in 1993. Both management and the unions were concerned with 'clearing the decks' where grievances where concerned, regardless of who was right or wrong. In the event, the grievances were settled within the space of a week or so.

Teamwork and Direct Worker Participation

Although management did not formally introduce teamwork until late 1993, a number of developments dating back to the early 1980s helped pave the way. First, many workers had worked in informal groups before management formally introduced teamwork, so they had some prior experience of group work. Second, many managers and front line supervisors had intermittently participated in leadership training and team oriented training from the early 1980s onwards. A third development was the removal of organisational layers and the establishment of five small management units (SMUs), which occurred during the first re-structuring of 1987. A fourth development was the flexibility agreement concluded in June 1993.

The flexibility provisions in the 1993 agreement were first proposed in 1989, but due to the adversarial IR climate at the time, the deal was not finalised until 1993. Management was concerned with increasing flexibility between craft workers and operators by removing what they perceived as inefficient job demarcations and restrictive practices by implementing a grading/flexibility deal. The agreement incorporated the integration of the previously separate electrical and instrumentation crafts, flexibility between crafts (E/I workers and fitters), and flexibility between craft workers and operators, and removing some operator grades (IRN 9, 17, 25, 1993). Therefore, there has been some increase in cross-functional flexibility since 1993.

Following the conclusion of the flexibility deal in June 1993, management then set about removing close supervision and implementing semi-autonomous work teams across the industrial workforce. Teamwork was introduced unilaterally by management at a time of crisis, and this occurred from November 1993 onwards. Teamwork at AAL is of an advanced type in the sense that workers possess a high degree of autonomy and discretion over work organisation. Accordingly, it corresponds with the advanced forms of teamwork identified in the literature, which are seen as a crucial component of partnership (Proctor and Mueller, 2000; Geary 2003). Management objectives for introducing teamwork are set out in 'The Future' document (1993: 5), which outlined the new form of work organisation:

> We believe there is a large amount of untapped potential in our
> people. It is crucial to the success of the Business Plan that this
> potential is fully utilised. Teamwork and the empowerment of the
> individual are the principal ways we will achieve this. For the
> organisation, teamwork increases the available pool of skills and
> knowledge, and facilitates rapid responses to change.

Therefore, management was concerned with devolving responsibility for
decision-making to the lowest possible level to tap into worker knowledge and to harness it to promote continuous adaptability to change.
With regard to the nature of teamwork, there was no strict blueprint de-
termining the form that teamwork should take. The teams were generally
left to their own devices, and teamwork gradually evolved. There was an
ambitious definition of teamwork included in the 'The Future' document
(1993: 5):

> By teamwork we mean individuals with a variety of talents, skills
> and knowledge, working together in group's to achieve agreed
> outcomes and taking full responsibility and accountability for
> their actions. Teamwork moves away from dependency on direct
> supervision to become more self-managed, self-motivated with
> more control over the planning and organising of work.

It was mentioned earlier that teams are made up of people from the same
skill categories. That is, operators, fitters or E/I craft. Although there has
been an element of increased flexibility at the lower levels of each craft,
there is no significant multi-skilling within the teams themselves. This is
because the continuous process technology largely dictates the nature of
work that is to be done, so work tasks are generally quite routine – particularly for operators. The people who are currently in teams are, by and
large, working in the same places and doing the same jobs as they were
under traditional work organisation. But within these confines, they exercise considerably more autonomy over how work is organised.

The most radical changes, in terms of the move towards a participative mode of production, have involved the removal of direct supervision, the development of a more indirect facilitator role, and devolving
extensive decision-making responsibility to employees at the point of
production. Whereas traditionally there were 55 supervisors in a direct
controlling role, there are now 12 facilitators in an indirect coaching role.

As a result, the ratio of supervisor/facilitator to employee has gone from about one to seven to one to 25. The primary role of the facilitator is to support the teams and help them solve problems. The facilitator acts as a trouble-shooter and coach, rather than a controller. Management deliberately concerned itself with ensuring that the staff placed into facilitator positions had the appropriate management style and personal skills to fit the new form of work organisation. On the whole, there appears to have been significant moves away from direct supervision to indirect facilitation, although a facilitator said the transition was not easy:

> The transition from any traditional type of structure – direct supervision or policing – is very difficult for some people. The transitional period is one that takes a lot of hard work because there is a lot of fear. There are a lot of unknowns. People have been used to being told what to do, when to go to the toilet … now they have to manage all that themselves.

In a similar vein, a union representative commented:

> We didn't really know a whole lot about teamwork. The company made the change and said from now on we are going to work in self-managed teams. We didn't really know what that meant day-to-day. It could have quite easily turned out to be one of those American ideas that's really only an idea in name and doesn't make any real difference. You change the supervisor's name and do exactly what you were doing before. We would have been a bit sceptical. There wasn't a master plan to say we'll develop along these lines, it was largely left to the teams. It has developed and it has worked very well in a lot of ways. Where I work, the supervisor became a facilitator and he immediately moved office completely to a different part of the building. He is not sitting in the office overlooking your work desk. When he moved it gave us much more confidence, that maybe they are serious about it, let's give it a go.

It would be erroneous to suggest, however, that direct supervision no longer exists. There are still occasions, albeit far less so than the past, where direct supervision is used, particular in relation to a few problem teams. A manager remarked:

> I don't have any problem in saying that facilitation, which is really the basis of this organisation, carries with it a responsibility that sometimes you have to supervise. You have to judge what is appropriate. If teams are developing and you have a collaborative approach you have to let them go out and make decisions and accept that sometimes they make mistakes. But sometimes you have to step in and say this is not right.

In addition, a facilitator commented:

> There have been a few occasions in the past where direct supervision had to take place because the team itself was discarded in a sense that people were taking all kinds of different directions. There was conflict within the team itself, and that happened on a few occasions.

Teams possess a significant degree of autonomy over local decision-making, which can be measured according to the frequency, scope, and intensity of involvement (Marchington and Wilkinson, 2000). In terms of frequency of involvement, teamwork affords workers continuous participation in the organisation of work. The scope of involvement ranges from fairly minor issues, such as the scheduling of holidays, right the way through to issues such as budgets and discipline, which would have traditionally been solely controlled by supervisors. The intensity of involvement ranges from joint decision-making with facilitators to full autonomy and self-control. Decisions about whether to have a team leader are controlled by individual teams. Most teams would not have a formal team leader, although some teams would have an informal leader. A facilitator remarked:

> There is no clear formality on this one at all. There is nothing written in stone. Some teams have team representatives, some of them don't. Some teams feel that they are all equal representatives, and there is no one progressing through the ranks as being a team leader. In some cases, teams have team leaders, but they rotate it.

Although the nature of work tasks has largely stayed the same, crucially, the manner in which work is scheduled, allocated and paced – the actual process of work – has changed substantially. Teams now have significant control over the scheduling, allocation, and pace of work. Work schedules in each local are drawn up during a weekly team meeting between the planner, a maintenance person and operators. Sometimes a facilitator would attend these meetings. The operator then communicates work schedules to other team members, and teams are then free to decide how the schedule is to be allocated amongst each member. A union representative suggested that 'the difference now is we decide how we can best carry out the work, we decide the work process'. Similarly, a manager commented:

> Within the teams they will allocate tasks based on individual competence and preferences and what they are good at. Whereas before supervisors would just pick someone to do something.

In terms of conducting the actual work, teams decide the pace at which they work. Operators now also have the authority to go directly to a craft worker if assistance is required, whereas traditionally they had to follow a complex bureaucratic procedure of going through supervisors. Team members are now responsible for their own attendance and time-keeping, which is a significant break with the past, when there was very strict control over timekeeping:

> People now fill in their own time returns. Traditionally you would have had clocking in. That's gone. The team now returns its own time returns. Each individual is responsible for putting in their own times.

Another significant feature of teamwork is that teams control their own budgets. Each team would have a budget for items such as safety supplies, tools, meal vouchers. Teams would be free to order supplies. A union representative commented:

> We didn't realise all these budgets were there for tool allowance, safety allowance, etc. The supervisor dealt with this in the past. You had to beg at times for things. Whereas now you see what you are entitled to and share it out.

Teams would also be responsible for interviewing and recruiting team members, although the facilitator also has some input. By and large, however, team members ultimately play the leading role in deciding whom to recruit and select if there is a vacancy on their team. Group dynamics are important here, in the sense that teams would often have some sense of whether an individual is or is not suitable for their team. Significantly, teams also possess an important element of control over team discipline. Teams are informally expected to be the first line of discipline, although the extent to which teams choose to use these interpersonal disciplinary powers varies. If the team is unwilling to take on this role, the facilitator steps in.

While there has been a significant shift from direct control to semi-autonomous teamwork across the plant, some teams would have more autonomy than others. In particular, teams that work on night shifts and at weekends generally have more autonomy than those on days, because the management presence is limited to one shift plant facilitator, whose job is to travel round the plant to solve problems. A senior manager remarked:

> It won't be a formalised acknowledgement of autonomy. It is more an informal thing. For instance, we have a team that takes out large transformers on their own basis. Its very complicated work with very low levels of facilitation.... For the night shift and the weekends there is one staff person here and the plant functions. The plant is five kilometres long and one kilometre wide, and there are ships coming in. The industrial workforce handles it. They are doing a lot of things now that under our old mindset we wouldn't have thought them capable of doing and let them do.

There was a fairly lengthy transition period between the removal of direct supervision and the move towards teamwork. It took a while for teamwork to bed in. There were, and still are, differences amongst teams, with some teams operating better than others. Teamwork continues to evolve.

New HRM Practices

i) Communication and information mechanisms: As part of the move towards partnership, management has been concerned with improving communication and information and consultation, both indirectly through representatives and directly to employees. There is a perception among shop stewards that workers are receiving a lot more information now than hitherto, and that management is much more open. Communication has been enhanced by the removal of organisational layers, and management has utilised a wide variety of mechanisms to communicate information, such as top-down team briefings and newsletters. Significantly, almost all information across the plant is available to workers, even sensitive financial information – with monthly financial reports issued to the workforce. A shop steward remarked: 'the company are quite open with their costs and financial statements'. There is also plant-wide communication sessions about two to three times a year, where senior management brief the workforce on how the company is performing. A manager commented:

> They have full business information now. They get the monthly costs now, the financial position. It is available to all employees. Ten years ago middle managers wouldn't have that information. They have a right to that information because their future and the future of the plant is dependent on it.

There is also a bottom-up suggestion scheme with monetary rewards being issued when workers come up with innovative ideas to improve production.

ii) Annual hours: A key partnership practice was the introduction of annual hours for the industrial workforce in 1996. Annual hours was introduced to improve productivity and working time efficiency and, in particular, to end the endemic overtime culture. A senior manager commented:

> The annual hour's system was brought in to be a win-win system. We didn't believe that high levels of overtime were justified. We believed that people were doing it to earn money. We came up with an intermediary position. We paid people for a certain amount of hours and expected that they wouldn't have to work many of those hours to get the work done, and that has transpired. We paid a bit over the odds for it. What we want is to have the plant in good shape. The more tonnes that are produced the better

> it is for everybody. We don't have an agenda – as long as the job
> gets done to the right standard, with the right safety.

Management first signalled its intention to implement annual hours back in 1993, but perceived at the time that it would be too big a challenge to bring it in immediately. Management eventually brought it back on the agenda in 1994/95, after other changes such as teamwork had been introduced. Although it didn't know that much about annual hours at the time, management put it to the unions that it could generate mutual gains, and that they should both go away and jointly learn about it. In calling for a joint learning exercise, management was concerned to tackle the issue collaboratively based on the principles of 'getting to yes'. The unions were quite sceptical at the time, however, and told management to go away and come up with a proposal and that they would then examine it. Management duly went away to develop a package and came back and presented it to the unions. The presentation took place over a period of five days in a hotel off-site. Management was determined to take the time, in a neutral environment, to develop at least some understanding of what annual hours would entail. The unions then tried to sell the proposal to their members, who then voted on it in a ballot.

Initially, there was quite a lot of resistance and suspicion among the workforce, particularly amongst operators. This was because employees knew very little about annual hours, and were fearful they would lose out financially if it was introduced, because of substantial reductions in overtime pay – overtime then accounted for up to 15 per cent of total operator earnings. Ballot results were mixed. While craft workers accepted the proposal in May 1995, operators rejected it by two to one. The major reason for the operators' rejection was their concern over the loss of overtime and the number of reserve hours they would work. In the event, despite the operator's rejection, management decided to press ahead with an annual hours scheme for craft workers, which was implemented in April 1996. A union representative said operators eventually came on board after seeing how well the system worked for crafts:

> It took 12 months for the craft groups and another 9 months on
> top for the operators. The operators then saw how it worked with
> the craft and they came on then. There was still a bit of mistrust

there. They thought that they would be made to work reserve hours.

Annual hours at AAL is based on payment of a fixed basic salary incorporating payment for extra hours (reserve hours) that may have to be worked in unpredictable circumstances, emergencies, and extra training and meetings. Employees are contracted to work approximately 200 reserve hours, which has meant that the traditional overtime system has gone. Reserve hours are paid upfront, whether they are worked are not. In practice, the level of reserve hour's usage is quite low at about 20 hours per worker, which is of significant benefit to employees. The acceptance of annual hours by the workforce was heavily influenced by the very attractive increases in guaranteed basic pay, which helped compensate for overtime losses. Operators and craft workers on days and two-shift working received a 20 per cent increase in basic pay, while general and craft workers on four-shift working received a 25 per cent increase. There was also a significant increase in pension entitlement, because pension benefits are linked to much higher levels of basic pay than under the old overtime system. Therefore, workers earnings and pension entitlements are much more stable than under the overtime system. There has also been a significant reduction in working time, with a standard working week of 39 hours. People now have considerably more time to pursue their interests and responsibilities outside work. Annual hours also provides for the harmonisation of terms and conditions with staff, such as Voluntary Health Insurance, and a guaranteed minimum of five training days per worker. A union representative remarked:

> Our earnings are more stable, and if we go off sick we can get paid for six months, and then we go on long-term disability, and you have got more time off.

A senior manager confirmed this:

> The average amount of overtime (reserve hours) worked by a man might be 20 hours and he is paid for 200. So he has got 180 hours free. He has got more time off, which as people age, becomes more valuable. And he has got a guaranteed payment, which is linked to his pension entitlement. The company's gain is

on a well-run plant, which in our case makes for more production because of the continuous nature of our process.

In relation to efficiency considerations, concern among employees to avoid having to work reserve hour's means it is now in their interests to be efficient and get the job done as fast as possible. Moreover, employees are now far less willing to call colleagues in to work reserve hours. A real alignment between annual hours and teamwork has also been created, which has helped to encourage creative suggestions from workers to improve the production process, which, by implication, reduces the necessity to work reserve hours. A shop steward observed, 'people are looking every day to see how they can improve their own area and come up with ideas and suggestions'. In stark contrast, under the traditional overtime system, it paid workers to be inefficient: the more inefficient the plant ran the more overtime they could generate. A manager commented:

> It (annual hours) is a more effective way because at least the person's remuneration is linked to the plant's performance, whereas before it was directly converse to the plant's performance. In our case, because it is a continuous process, when the plant was shut down you needed people to fix it to get it going again. The overtime was highest when the plant was in the worst condition, so the incentive was completely the wrong way.... Instead of wasting time on overtime, we now have more time to concentrate on value adding rather than damage limitation. It also gave the good worker more of the lead than the poor worker.

A union representative reiterated this:

> They (management) have flipped the coin. Whereas in the past people were paid to be inefficient, they are now paid to be efficient. It is now more beneficial to do what you are supposed to be doing when you are there as efficiently as possible so you can piddle off. The motivation is there.

The traditionally thorny issue of using outside contractors under the overtime system has also been turned on its head, as a senior manager observed:

The wheel has turned from the old organisation to the new organisation. Under the old organisation it was always difficult to get contractors in to do maintenance work. Now with the annual hours it is different. You have to stop core maintenance work going out to contractors. In the past we wanted to bring in contractors to reduce costs, now under annual hours, we don't want to do that because we've already paid up-front for it.

iii) Employment security clause: The literature points to the importance of employment security for stable workplace partnerships (Collinson et al., 1997; Geary and Dobbins, 2001). After the redundancy programme had been concluded at AAL in November 1993, management gave a five-year employment security guarantee to the remaining workforce in return for co-operation with change. A manager commented:

Employment would be secure. When we changed in 1993 we guaranteed peoples' jobs for as far as we could. We said five years. That's clearly stated. If you are going to ask people to improve, generally people will not improve if you are going to do away with their jobs. Ideally everybody that is here, we would prefer to see them well trained, well educated and adding value.

Although this five-year mark elapsed in 1998, management is still committed to employment security:

It is a fact of business life today that jobs and roles continuously change and indeed need to change for organisations to perform effectively and remain competitive. While jobs and roles will continue to change at Aughinish we are committed to our workforce retaining their permanent, individual employment status (BPI team minutes).

A key emphasis has been placed at Aughinish on further plant expansion and investment, and tapping into the skills of the workforce to add value, rather than competing through further rationalisation and redundancy. Moreover, there is a feeling that further rationalisation would not be viable given how flat and lean the organisation now is, even in the event of a downturn in the market. The accounting co-ordinator felt that, even if there is a downturn, the company would not be in a position to 'run the plant with a significantly lower number of people'.

For their part, the unions believe that employment is secure, and there is a concern to work with management to enhance this security. One steward remarked:

> Employment looks very secure. We have just got planning permission for a coking plant. That should secure this plant a lot more and bring down the costs again and make it more efficient.

iv) Training: There has been a substantial increase in investment in training and development in recent years, which has supported teamwork and employment security. AAL first achieved the FAS Excellence Through People training quality award in 1997, an indication of the high standard of training. Every year, training plans are developed for each employee in consultation with their facilitator. Each employee receives an average 5.6 days training per year. Training can take many forms, including on-site courses, off-site courses, night classes, multimedia, local mentoring, and distance learning. Training is generally closely related to the following areas: occupational skills, mobile equipment, safety, quality, process training, and personal development. There is a learning centre on-site, which is open 24 hours a day for use by employees and their families.

v) Single status conditions: Another major HR initiative was the introduction of common conditions of employment for industrial workers and staff. Management decided to harmonise conditions and break down the status divide between industrial workers and staff. Traditionally, there had been a 'them and us' divide between the two groups, exacerbated by the superior status benefits enjoyed by staff. The accounting co-ordinator remarked:

> In the past we would rarely have contact with industrial people or even talk to industrial people, because they wouldn't talk to us and that has all changed. I mean, we are now all seen as one, and that is a big difference. There has been a harmonisation of conditions. They don't perceive themselves as getting less preferential treatment.

The first major step towards removing status differentials was the introduction of a sick pay scheme for industrial workers in July 1994, jointly monitored by management and unions. A previous sick pay scheme for industrial workers had been discontinued after consistent abuse. In addition, a 39-hour week was introduced for everybody, as well as a common canteen that senior management also use.

v) 'Other' HR practices: Various equal opportunity and family friendly initiatives have also been introduced. Management implemented an Equal Opportunities and Sexual Harassment/Bullying policy in August 1994. There are a number of formal and informal 'family-friendly' provisions. A senior manager commented:

> We've looked at how we can flex the organisation. In the last couple of years we would have some individuals on a four-day week for family reasons. By and large we would be fairly flexible for time off for family reasons. We don't operate to rigid rules.

Finally, AAL's traditional organisational culture was autocratic and adversarial. Management has attempted to underpin its new approach to employment relations with a new organisational culture that advocates five central values of 'integrity', 'performance', 'accountability', 'recognition' and 'teamwork' (Future Document, 1993: 25-30). 'Integrity': 'An AAL employee needs to complete tasks unsupervised, respect the opinions of others and admit mistakes when they occur'. 'Performance': 'An AAL employee needs to complete tasks to a high standard, and on time. 'Accountability': 'An AAL employee needs to take the initiative and accept responsibility for their own actions'. 'Recognition': 'An AAL Facilitator/Co-ordinator/Manager needs to encourage and promote high performance for all his or her employees. 'Teamwork': 'An AAL employee needs to be able to work effectively as part of a team'.

Management Controls

Even though management has fostered cooperative work relations, this does not mean it has relinquished control. Rather, management controls have become more indirect and sophisticated, whereas traditionally they were often direct and unsubtle.

i) Market pressures: The most acute control continually in the background at AAL is market pressures. Comparisons are often made with the performance of rival plants round the world, and management communicates with the workforce about the challenges of international competition. Thus, elements of coercion are still present. Employees are more aware of this threat, which influences their attitudes and behaviour. This was emphasised by a shop steward: 'people realise if they don't produce their jobs are at stake'.

ii) Technical control: Management has increasingly utilised the sophisticated technology at its disposal to increase control over workforce productivity. An advanced technical control system called the Honeywell TDP 3000 was introduced in 1991. This provided a platform for further automation and advanced control procedures. Another form of technical control is a 'pie system' which management can tap into using personal computers to collate data from the Honeywell control system on all facets of plant performance. The information technology allows management to quickly pinpoint any performance problems. A senior manager commented:

> I can look at it (the pie system) from my desk here or from home. Within a couple of seconds I can find out how the plant is performing. I can see how the craft is performing. A negative way of looking at that is that people know big brother is looking at the highest level of the organisation. But people have got over that.

The company is looking to continue to introduce advanced technical controls, although a senior manager said this might reduce employee involvement:

> Advanced controls take the involvement of the people out because it will take the best of the peoples' knowledge and implement the changes in the process without people knowing it. They are just looking at things happening in front of them that are happening automatically. We are spending a fair amount of money on advanced controls, but this won't necessarily involve people more in the business. We are trying to struggle with that.

iii) Performance management control: Work organisation is less bureaucratic, and management place less emphasis on using formal rules to discipline workers on issues like time-keeping. Formal rules are still there, however, and there have been some disciplinary issues over time-keeping. This was emphasised by a co-ordinator:

> We have had a few cases where the integrity with which we try to run the plant has been breached. It has happened in cases where the teams perhaps haven't been the most effective team. We have had a few issues with time returns. This year a person was dismissed for being absent from work and working outside. That was a difficult team.

One area where rules are always strictly enforced, given the nature of the plant, is health and safety. A senior manager stressed this:

> We don't operate to rigid rules, with the exception of health and safety. Health and safety is one area where we need compliance. We want commitment and try to get commitment to health and safety but compliance is non-negotiable. You have to have that for the small minority that will take short cuts from time to time. Our strongest control would be on health and safety.

In recent years, new more indirect controls have emerged, in the form of performance measurement. These performance controls ultimately derive from the overall cost budget decided by senior management at AAL's parent company, following negotiations with senior management at AAL about a feasible annual budget. The budget is essentially based on how much it costs to process x tonnes of bauxite and convert it into alumina. A senior manager commented:

> If you look at control in the wider sense, the single biggest control over all of us are the objectives we have to meet on an annual basis. In other words in the year 2001, this plant will produce 1.5 million tonnes at x dollars per tonne. That is a control that is built in over the years. We also have safety and environmental license requirements that we have to meet. So they are external controls as well. We also have to control our costs as well. Internally, we have budgets, which are a form of control for teams. It is a form of control, but it also gives people control as

well because they have an agreed budget – say for safety supplies and maintenance – and they operate within that.

The business units across the plant are responsible for controlling their own budgetary and performance standards and targets. The budgetary process would start at the lowest level, with teams in each of the five local business units accountable for budgets and performance targets. Each team is held accountable for a number of performance targets – known as key performance indicators (KPI) – set in their local areas and teams. The first line of accountability is the team facilitator, and then the plant manager, who is responsible for the overall plant budget. The performance indicators include productivity levels, safety, quality, efficiencies. If an individual consistently transgresses performance targets they may be dealt with informally by their team, or if this is not feasible, through the formal disciplinary process. A manager remarked:

> If there is someone consistently not doing their job than that is addressed as a performance issue with that individual. It can go through the formal disciplinary process or it might be addressed informally through the team. If the team cannot address it, it has to fall to management to address it.

iv) **Self-discipline/peer control**: Another form of control that has emerged at AAL is informal self-discipline within teams. There are occasions when teams would act as the first line of discipline, so issues may be solved before reaching a formal level. There was one particular instance during the early stages of teamwork, when one team used the disciplinary powers devolved to them to the full by suspending a team member repeatedly warned about misbehaviour. The manager who was involved in this case commented:

> I was the manager involved in that. It was pushed and it was far more cutting edge than anything that I have been involved in. I think they got it to a level that we would never have got. If we tried in the old organisation to suspend a person with suspended pay there would have been a collection on site for him. They put in a stipulation that he was suspended without pay and that there would be no collection, and he had to sign it. That was more exacting than anything we would have been able to achieve.

A union representative who was also involved in the case remarked:

> Part of the teamwork thing was that the team would decide what disciplines would apply. A couple of guys took this seriously and there was somebody messing and they were given all the opportunities not to mess, and they continued, and they were fired. That used to be a management prerogative. The group of people who did this were challenged on the basis that they were acting like management. Everybody learnt a lesson. If you are misbehaving with your peers and not listening, there is a sanction that they have to have, because if you are not doing your work they have to do it for you. It only happened the once though.

The case above was an isolated incident, and it would appear that use of self-discipline is not common practice across the plant. Some teams would be more willing than others to resolve their own disciplinary issues. A manager remarked that the company would like self-discipline to go further, and the fact that this had not happened yet could be interpreted as:

> An indication that we are not as mature as we would like to be, because ideally disciplinary problems would be dealt with by the team itself in a really mature teamwork organisation. But that is a long journey before that takes place I would say.

Accordingly, rather than control being displaced, moves towards partnership have coincided with the evolution of new indirect means of control, with employees much more accountable for performance. A senior manager commented on the current balance between autonomy and control at AAL:

> I think we had a lot of control and supervision traditionally. In 1993, when it went to a teamwork organisation a lot of people misunderstood that to be no control. So we have had to comeback and I think people sometimes saw the coming back. They might even see me today as coming back – he is far more into control. But I see it more as a balance. If you have all control it won't work. If you have no control it won't work. It is important to know what to intervene on and what not to intervene on, and that is what separates a good manager, co-ordinator, facilitator from a bad one. In our case people have the right to enter their own

times, but we do spot checks, and two people have resigned this year relating to time checks. Our basic premise is that we trust the employee. We don't have heavy supervision. But what goes with that is a certain accountability and responsibility.

Table 4.2: 'Pragmatic Partnership': Combining Cooperation and Control

Cooperative 'Partnership' Practices	Management Control Practices
- Management-union BPI group	- Performance management/ measurement
- Semi-autonomous teamwork	
- Information & consultation	- Technical controls
- Annual hours	- Facilitation
- Gainsharing	- Peer control, self-discipline
- Extensive training	
- Two-way communications	
- Equal opportunities policies	
- Employment security clause	
- Single status conditions	

The Balance of Mutual Gains (and Costs) for Management, Union and Workers

We now consider the balance of mutual gains outcomes for management, the union and employees.

Gains and Costs for Management

Management have secured numerous gains from partnership, notably greater legitimacy, increased productivity and innovative behaviour, lower costs, much less conflict, reduced accidents, and less absenteeism. Perhaps the greatest overall dividend for management arising from cooperative relations (the same dividend applies to employers from social partnership at national level) is *stability*, which is a vital commodity and advantage in a context of uncertainty.

i) Labour productivity: Labour productivity has increased dramatically at the plant since the re-organisation in 1993. In output per person terms, the workforce has been reduced from 650 to 435, but a much greater volume of alumina is being produced (from 1 million tonnes per year pre

1993 to 1.5 million tonnes in 2001). Much of the increased output is due to technical improvements in the production process – such as de-bottlenecking the plant and extracting more from the continuously flowing liquor – but changes in people management have also had significant effects. In a continuous process plant it is difficult to disentangle the impact of improved technical efficiency from the less tangible impact of changes in people management, but it is certainly the case that cooperative work relations have greatly enhanced labour productivity. Productivity improvements stem from the fact that employees are working harder and effort levels have intensified. However, employees are also working much smarter. The personnel manager confirmed this:

> Generally it is in workers' interests for the plant flow to stay stable, because if there are problems there is more work. They are working harder if productivity is down almost. Looking at the level of reward people have now, it is much higher than say ten years ago. We have done that through de-bottlenecking, technological advances, and through people working smarter and making a contribution in terms of their own intelligence and creativity: through making suggestions and being more proactive. We have broken production records in this plant virtually every year. You don't do that unless people are contributing. There is no doubt about it that peoples' contribution has moved us forward and kept us competitive.

Annual hours has generated labour efficiencies because it is now in employees' interests to get the job done in less time to avoid having to work reserve hours, which they are paid for upfront. For the company, this has helped to align employee interests and rewards with company goals, and has resulted in greater stability in the production process and significantly less equipment downtime, the eradication of overtime, significant cost reductions, and more predictable annual labour budgets. Therefore, annual hours has improved the efficiency and productivity of working time. Some efficiency problems are evident from a management perspective, however, because the use of reserve hours is quite low, and people are less willing to respond to call-outs when at home. But overall annual hours has generated very positive productivity outcomes.

Teamwork has contributed to superior labour productivity, because employees are now more willing to release their discretionary effort and knowledge of the production process, and to solve problems. The removal of the old 'irritant' of direct supervision has contributed to this change in behaviour. Workers have more autonomy to make their own decisions, whereas before they would have to wait until a supervisor told them what to do. As a result, there is much greater process continuity and less equipment downtime. Workers are more likely to utilise the various competencies and experiences accrued within teams to solve problems, and complete tasks faster and more efficiently than in the past. Employees were clearly working smarter and more collaboratively, which has boosted productivity.

ii) Grievances and industrial action: The industrial relations climate is much better. There have been no strikes or other form of collective industrial action in recent years, and a significant reduction in individual grievances. In the adversarial days there was anything up to 150 grievances per year, whereas now there are only three or four.

iii) Accident rates: Accident rates have also fallen considerably. Lost time accidents (LTAs) – resulting in workers taking time off due to injury – have decreased. The personnel manager commented:

> There would have been an improvement in LTA's. We have about one LTA per year, and we could go two years without a LTA. Then there are also recordable cases where people have to have medical treatment. We have maybe 8-12 recordable cases. We used to have huge numbers of LTA's – maybe 20 or 30.

iv) Absenteeism/labour turnover: In relation to absenteeism trends, the personnel manager said it is not really feasible to directly compare past and present data:

> It wouldn't be a direct comparison because in the past they wouldn't be paid sick pay. They were out unpaid. We introduced annual hours and they are now on full sick pay from day one. At the moment absenteeism varies. It generally goes up in winter. Generally it is about 3 to 4 per cent. When we put in a sick pay

> scheme we expected absence to go up. Not because people were taking advantage of the system, but because now if they are sick they receive sick pay. There would be very little abuse of the sick pay scheme.

Since the mass redundancies of 1993, labour turnover levels have been very low at the plant. They are less than one per cent for the industrial workforce. The vast majority of people who chose to stay rather than take voluntary redundancy are still there.

Despite the gains accruing to AAL management, as at Waterford Crystal, partnership also entails costs. In particular, it takes a lot of vigilance, effort and resources to sustain partnership. But the benefits for management clearly outweigh costs.

Gains and Costs for Trade Unions

Unions also gained from partnership. In particular, the BPI representative team provides unions with a welcome input into strategic decision-making. A shop steward gave his opinion on the BPI team:

> The BPI Team was an opportunity to get involved at a strategic level. It is at the early stages of its development. It is certainly something that is not going to happen overnight. I can't honestly put my hand on my heart and say I now have a strategic say in the way the company is run. I have an input into it, and it is something that I would like to see develop into something much more than it is at the moment. But it is certainly a start, and it is a good start. It has been done very openly and I certainly didn't feel that we were there for show.

A union official provided the following commentary on partnership:

> There are lots of people with the perception that partnership operates at Aughinish. That is bullshit, it doesn't. They have a good teamwork basis. They have a mutual gain's basis for doing some of their business. It isn't totally embedded in the system. They have a good opportunity to have a serious partnership arrangement. They are beginning to understand that partnership can be a good thing at Aughinish, and at the moment they have their toe in the water. Hopefully they will go further.

Although reticent to call it partnership, unions generally acknowledge they have a more constructive and proactive influence over bigger company issues than during the adversarial phase, when they were defensively fire-fighting and dealing with grievances, working conditions and pay. One union representative remarked:

> It has definitely improved. In the past it was just adversarial. Now we are looking at broader issues. We are participating in the strategic plan for the next five or ten years. That's a huge change, the BPI long-term plan. Our brief was to look at profits through people, and it was a joint union-management team.

It is apparent that the unions do possess at least some right of veto over decision-making, which implies that the scope of their influence goes beyond joint consultation in certain areas, and extends to joint governance. To this end, a senior manager remarked:

> They always have the right of veto. If somebody doesn't want to do something, they are not going to do it. If the union people on the BPI are not happy that something is going to work for them or the people they represent, they are not going to go ahead with it. Ideally the objective would be to try and get consensus, rather than management making the decisions.

There are important differences in the position of the respective unions with regard to the new approach to industrial relations. On the whole, there is a perception that the officials and stewards from the two craft unions tend to be more proactive in their approach than their SIPTU counterparts, some of whom still operate in a more traditional mode. Some trade union representatives, particularly on the craft side, are keen for joint decision-making at a strategic level to go further and be progressed by management at a faster pace. There is an element of uncertainty, however, in relation to how far union influence at a strategic level, as opposed to operational level (lower-level issues such as pensions), will extend in future. The BPI team affords an element of strategic partnership, but, overall, partnership at AAL is still most prevalent at operational level. Certainly, the unions are aware of practical limits to involvement in strategic decisions. When talking about the BPI team, for instance, a union representative observed:

> It was joint, but what we came up with still had to go back to top
> management here for approval. Well maybe that is as high as you
> can go. Ultimately I suppose the owner makes the decisions, and
> the representatives of the owner would always want to keep that.

Another union representative commented:

> I wouldn't really like to have too much influence over
> management. Management is there to manage and that is a huge
> grey area. How far do you go? What is the point in having the
> management team if they are not allowed to manage.

In some ways, as at Waterford Crystal, partnership was a double-edged
sword for unions. The unions were less powerful than before the 'defeat'
by management in the early 1990s, and in some ways less influential.
Furthermore, their new cooperative role meant they were less visible to
the workforce than under their traditional defensive adversarial collective
bargaining role.

Gains and Costs for Workers

Employees generally responded very positively to partnership, a finding
at odds with critics in the literature. Overall, workers have had positive
experiences of teamwork, with the benefits far outweighing costs. Many
workers had worked in informal groups before management formally
introduced semi-autonomous teams in 1993. Many workers are still
working in the same areas, with the same people, and doing the same
jobs as before. Accordingly, they had some prior experience of group
work:

> With the old system we were here in teams beforehand, and you
> had direct supervision. So, it wasn't that difficult to go into
> teamwork. The teams were already there. Nearly all the same
> people are here (operator).

The majority of employees were very satisfied with teamwork. The new
work structures were seen as a significant improvement on traditional
work organisation centred on direct supervision. Workers reported increased interest in their jobs, and experienced more freedom to take deci-

sions and solve problems. Significantly, no worker said they wanted to revert to old ways of working.

Most employees said they have much more autonomy over day-to-day work processes than in the past. Workers feel that they have quite a high degree of discretionary input over many aspects of work organisation, including: allocating how the team is to do work, pace of work, taking breaks, timekeeping, rotating between jobs, holidays, team budgets, safety, whether to appoint a team leader, recruiting team members. In the past, all these issues were controlled by supervisors. The following comments from a fitter are reflective of a general perception of increased autonomy:

> We have a team rep position that rotates once a month. We all do it. We have good freedom. Now if I need any clothing or equipment I don't have to go through the supervisor, I can just go and get it from stores. Likewise, with holidays we just have a board on the wall and we put up our holidays. We don't have to ask for holidays.

But some workers have found it more difficult to move away from the old system, having been conditioned to being told what to do by management.

Most employees perceive that supervision has been significantly relaxed, and they are generally happy with the new, more indirect, coaching and problem-solving role of facilitators. Most people resented being closely supervised and responded positively to the relaxation of direct supervision. For instance, people can go on their breaks without being watched, while operators welcome the fact they can ask a craft worker for assistance without prior authorisation from a supervisor. A number of workers said they wouldn't have much contact with their facilitator now unless there was a problem. Many workers feel that teamwork has significantly reduced traditional conflicts generated by personality clashes between supervisors and individual workers, although tensions remain in some areas. There is a feeling that some facilitators are better people managers than others are. A number of fitters stated that they are starting to see direct supervision creeping back in their area:

The supervision is creeping back. When we first started off, we were supposed to be self directed, autonomous work groups, but the supervision is just starting to creep in. I think it is being encouraged by management. But, it is in a nice way. It is not the same as in the past. I don't have a great problem with it. Sometimes we need a poke to get us to perform. It is not necessarily a bad thing. They have to be a little bit subtler in their approach now (fitter).

A criticism that I have of the system is that they say teams are autonomous, that we make decisions. That is not true. Not in our situation anyway. Our facilitator has not been onsite too long. He has come over here and he is dictating and shoving and pushing. He is acting like a supervisor. He is not fit for the job. The facilitator before we had no problem with (fitter).

In addition to greater job autonomy, many workers say there are now fewer job demarcations. There is evidence of enhanced flexibility and job rotation amongst many teams, and employees have responded positively to this. A process operator said team members on his team 'rotate every month between four different areas of responsibility'. The comments of an E/I worker illustrate, however, that there are limits to the extent job rotation and flexibility have been diffused and accepted:

On a team like mine, the old system tended to specialise people in areas. You had two guys who did valves all the time, a guy who did motors all the time, and so on. That has been difficult to change. People tend to want to stay in those roles and that would be causing problems. Within my team at the moment, we do need to be a bit more flexible. We are starting to change, but it is hard to persuade people if they want to stay on the work they are on. They know that they are not going to be caught for reserve hours because they are so used to doing the job. So, they wouldn't be that anxious to be more flexible within the team. That would be one of the problems.

Informal team briefings are held regularly, where team members are free to discuss issues relevant to their teams. Employees are generally satisfied with their input at these meetings. For instance, an operator commented: 'we have safety meetings and team meetings, and if someone wants to say something it is taken on board'.

Peer relations within teams appear very good on the whole. Employees are much more willing to help each other out and solve problems. Therefore, there is generally a good deal of cooperative behaviour among most teams. This co-operative behaviour is particularly pronounced in teams where roles and tasks are divided according to individual competencies and skills – some team members may be better at particular tasks, or more comfortable doing them. In contrast, under the old regime, the supervisor would just tell people to do something, regardless of whether individuals were comfortable with it. It would be wide of the mark, however, to claim team relations are totally harmonious. Some employees referred to problems within certain teams not being addressed. In particular, bullying and personality clashes are problematic in some teams. Also, some team members were seen to be abusing time-keeping and 'not pulling their weight'. A number of workers observed that some teams would deal with disciplinary issues within the team structure, and the issue would be resolved informally at an early stage. Other workers felt, however, that certain teams are unable or unwilling to confront abuses and discipline their colleagues, some of whom have 'domineering and strong personalities'. Disciplinary issues are still primarily seen to be management's responsibility, but there is a feeling that management is not doing enough to confront abuses within 'problem teams'. But such cases are in the minority. On the whole, team relations are very positive.

In terms of employee satisfaction with overall levels of direct worker involvement, there is a widespread perception that teamwork has enhanced participation in local decision-making, communication channels are much more open, and that people receive far more information and consultation on issues affecting the company. The most positive responses came from operators. On the whole, operators are very satisfied with their level of day-to-day involvement, and perceive that communication channels are much more open than in the past. One operator did say, however, that he would like to see involvement extend further:

> I know myself that I can get involved to a certain extent, but I know I can do more. But, it isn't myself that is stopping me. I suppose it is the management, and there is also a system here, and you have to work within that system.

E/I workers are also generally satisfied with their level of day-to-day involvement and perceive that communication is much better. Some concerns were evident though. In particular, some E/I workers expressed a desire for more influence over higher-level decision-making. One E/I worker stated that there are labour shortages in his area and that he would like 'some input over manning levels'. He added that 'management make the important decisions on manning', and that his concerns 'were not being listened to'. On the whole, fitters were less positive about their level of involvement compared to other groups. A couple of fitters stressed that poor facilitation in their local area is a significant barrier to day-to-day involvement. Also, in terms of direct involvement at a higher level, one fitter mentioned that the company still sometimes makes changes without consulting the workforce sufficiently.

Employee experiences of new HRM practices are also broadly positive. Workers are generally content with training, employment security, annual hours, gainsharing, and basic pay. Workers across all grades have had very positive experiences of annual hours, and would not want to go back to the traditional overtime system. No workers responded negatively to annual hours, although a few workers did refer to some apprehension and resistance when it was first introduced. As one worker observed, however, once bedded in annual hours reduced conflict:

> It made a big difference in reducing conflict. We used to have terrible conflict over overtime – about who was going to get the money for it.

Employees believe annual hours provides them with various benefits, including more free time, greater stability of earnings, and big improvements in pension and sick pay entitlements. Moreover, most employees do not have to work many of their reserve hours. An E/I worker commented positively on how annual hours operated:

> One guy might have 7/8 reserve hours done. He would be the lowest. The highest might have 40 hours. I think the majority are happy with annual hours and they have got used to the time off. They are getting reasonable pay without having to put in very high hours. You know what you are getting, you know what your salary is for the week. The only thing not guaranteed is how

many hours you work for it, and that is down to how efficiently we run our bit.

An operator was also very positive:

> Annual hours is working well. We have a higher salary, better pension, VHI, sick pay, more stable earnings. It is the exact opposite of overtime because you have reserve hours. You try to work smarter to get the job done while you are here, so you won't get called in.

A number of employees emphasised that annual hours has resulted in 'mutual gains for management and workers', and a 'win-win situation':

> It is a win-win for us because we get more money for what we were doing before and we spend less time here. That is the bonus for us. Now, the bonus for the company is they have less production losses. They are getting the equipment back much faster, so obviously they are making more money (fitter).

Further, most employees are very satisfied with basic pay, which is perceived to be very favourable in comparison to rates in the local labour market. One operator mentioned that because 'the money is so good', management have been able to 'buy industrial peace'. Another operator felt that satisfaction with pay is partly reflected by very low levels of labour turnover, while an E/I worker commented: 'in comparison to anywhere else in the region, we are well paid. We can't complain'. There is some evidence that partnership has contributed to higher and more stable earnings. On a less positive note, some employees felt they should be paid more for length of service and experience acquired over the years. In terms of other benefits, employees are very satisfied with the pension and sick pay schemes:

> If you were sick in the past you had to take holidays for it, whereas if you are sick now you get paid for it. So, it is certainly better.

Most workers see employment as still pretty secure. There is awareness, however, that management has not offered cast iron guarantees of employment security, and, by and large, they pragmatically accept this.

Workers are kept fully informed of business issues and external developments, and are much more aware of competitive issues than in the past. Perhaps as a result of this increased awareness, there is concern among the workforce as to what effect any downturn in product markets could have on employment levels. One worker commented:

> The only thing that is annoying about this company is they will never tell you now that your job is safe for five years. They are constantly talking about markets. But, the good thing about this place is you cannot move it (E/I worker).

This latter comment is crucial, because the continuous production process at AAL means it is impossible for production to be broken up and relocated elsewhere. In this regard, employment at AAL is more secure than in a factory like Waterford Crystal, where production can much more easily be relocated.

Turning to employee views on training and skill development, the 1993 flexibility deal has produced a small element of cross functional multi-skilling for operators, who can now undertake some lower level craft work, such as repairing blockages and replacing small valves:

> We work night shifts and weekends and there aren't fitters and electricians around. There is only one fitter and electrician for the site. So, if we need to get a job done, say a blockage, we go and do it ourselves. In the past you had to call a fitter (operator).

Responses were generally more positive amongst E/I workers and operators than amongst fitters, with regard to training and skills. E/I workers perceive that there are sufficient opportunities for them to utilise skills, though a few concerns are evident. One E/I worker was concerned that craft skills were not being 'topped up' at the plant at a sufficient rate. He felt that there were 'not enough apprenticeships' and that 'the skills being lost when experienced workers left are not being replenished'. Furthermore, an E/I worker believed annualised hours might act as a disincentive for employees to engage in training:

> The training is available. The problem with training is that it competes with your ability to avoid reserve hours. We see it as our job to avoid having to work the reserve hours. We have been

paid if we don't work them, and we have made a gain. If you are
involved in training that means there is work not being done. So,
people are more wary. It is more difficult to get people to do
training (E/I worker).

Operators are also generally satisfied with their level of skill utilisation
and training. However, one operator stressed that he 'likes a challenge',
and felt his skills and knowledge could be 'more fully utilised'. Fitters
had more concerns than other grades. A couple of fitters said promotion
opportunities are limited because the organisational structure is so flat.
Another fitter said 'there could be more training opportunities', and that
'the level of skills training has dropped off recently'.

Interestingly, employee experiences of management controls were
pragmatic. In particular, while the vast majority of workers across all
grades suggest that effort levels have intensified, most workers do not
object to this, and in some instances, welcomed it. Plus, workers acknowledged they are working smarter as well as harder:

> The workload has increased, but it does not bother me
> particularly. It would bother me if it kept increasing. It is not
> intense all the time, but the majority of the time (stores worker).

> There is more work now, but we are doing it in our own time and
> we are deciding how to do it. We have more to do, but we have
> more personal control. I prefer that (operator).

> We are working smarter rather than harder (fitter).

> Work pressure has increased, but I don't object to working
> harder. I like to stay busy and don't like being bored (E/I worker).

> There is more work pressure. But, it is now in workers' interests
> to get the work done. The planning is also better (E/I worker).

Crucially, these positive responses would appear to be linked to the fact
management is seen to be more competent at planning the production
process and organising work. In this regard, teamwork and annual hours
have been important drivers of greater work effort. Employees feel they
have more discretion and personal responsibility over work due to teamwork, which has made them more willing to release their discretionary

effort. Many employees believe that the new form of work organisation represents a 'win-win' situation for themselves and the company, and it is deemed to be more coherent and involve fewer surprises. Therefore, it makes more sense for workers to work harder if this advances their own interests and serves a clear purpose.

A number of other possible reasons why employees are working harder came to light during discussions. First, the working time reductions associated with annual hours means workers are working harder while they are at work than in the past. Second, there are far fewer people in the plant. Third, the capacity of the plant has expanded (from 800,000 tonnes per annum in 1983 to 1.5 million tonnes in 2001). Fourth, management is much more focused on increasing the efficiency of the production process, significantly reducing downtime, and holding the workforce accountable for performance indicators.

Although workers are generally quite positively predisposed towards increased work effort, some concerns are evident, even among those who do not object to working harder. First, some workers cited poor facilitation as a source of dissatisfaction with effort levels. A couple of fitters mentioned that 'we don't mind working harder, but the facilitator is being unrealistic when setting work priorities and schedules'. Second, there are concerns that an ageing workforce may experience too much pressure and stress if pushed harder. Third, there are concerns that manning levels in certain areas need to be increased. An E/I worker felt that there has been an increase in work pressure but no corresponding increase in manning: 'there are not enough people do to the work in my area, so we are under pressure'. Fourth, there is also a fairly common perception that some workers in 'problem teams' have a high workload because some colleagues are not pulling their weight.

To some extent extra work effort has been balanced by the fact that advances in technology have taken away some of the more physically demanding tasks, although certain work tasks are still very arduous and potentially dangerous. Despite this caveat, on balance, effort and pressure levels have increased.

Also, workers were aware of limits to autonomy, and that their performance is still controlled and monitored; albeit in a less arbitrary and more indirect manner than the past. There is a widespread belief that the administration of discipline has changed for the better. Disciplinary measures are seen as less crude and much fairer. To this end, one worker stated, 'management are strict when they need to be, but they are fair'. Another remarked:

> You have to be stupid to get sacked. This is not a sacking company. Management gives people plenty of warning. They are fair. I don't have a problem with discipline here.

The fact that monitoring is now more indirect has reduced friction and conflict between workers and managers, and made it much easier to generate day-to-day cooperation. This does not mean that there are no longer any tensions over the administration of discipline. One worker pointed to 'inconsistencies in the administering of discipline', saying that a colleague was targeted by management because 'his face didn't fit'.

Employees are also aware that continuous process technology dictates performance:

> It is a continuous process. It is not as though you are making nuts and bolts. It is just a whole lot of liquor, caustic and product pumped round the plant. And that influences your job, which is to keep the plant running. You never see the product.

Advanced information technologies are also perceived to have an important influence on workers' actions:

> At the end of the day the DCS computer system monitors everything you do anyway. It monitors the whole plant really. If anything happens it can be traced back through the DCS, and the PC's as well. But, it doesn't feel like direct monitoring. I think everyone knows that the targets are there, and if we don't meet them we don't get paid. We have other things as well, like the Standard Work Methods (SWMs) and ISO 9000 to control quality.

Finally, employees are acutely aware of product market pressures, which act as a control mechanism. If they do not perform, they know their jobs could be at risk:

> If we don't produce the minimum of 1.5 million tonnes this year, our jobs could be under threat. They always hold that against us.

> It is a vicious market as well. The fact that we have got new owners brings uncertainty as well (E/I worker).

Worker experiences of management practices have shaped the state of the psychological contract between employees and management, discussed below under the headings of worker perceptions of management competence, trust and fairness. In turn, the state of the psychological contract has influenced worker attitudes on issues like job satisfaction, loyalty to the company, commitment to management, and views on the changed role of unions.

i) Management competence: There is a widespread perception that the present senior management team is very competent and is generally well respected:

> I have great respect for the present management team. There is a more open policy. If you want to go up to talk to them you can. You will meet the managing director walking round the plant, and you can talk to him as well as talk to anybody else (operator).

> The management team is now more in tune with the workforce and are more prepared to listen to what they have to say. It is a better style of management than the confrontational approach. Before it was just them against us (operator).

> The new MD is the best thing that has happened here in years. He has a great grasp of what is going on here. He worked here in the bad days (fitter).

A number of employees observed that the production process is better managed and more stable than in the past, and this was seen to be very important. A fitter said: 'you don't get too many surprises now. You know what is coming', while an E/I worker felt that 'there is now greater work stability, which is important'. But there was some dissenting opinion about senior management, although this was uncommon. A fitter said the plant manager 'does his own thing and has his own agenda'.

Views on the competence of facilitators were also generally positive, though somewhat more ambivalent. A quite common remark was that 'some facilitators are better than others'. Fitters were the most vocal critics of the quality of facilitation. Overall, facilitators are generally much better respected than old style supervisors.

ii) Fairness and trust: Most employees perceive that management are fair and trust relations have improved significantly. Whether the issue was discipline, pay, or more generally, most people felt that management acted fairly in their dealings with workers. In terms of trust, the majority of workers feel that trust in senior management is now much higher than the past. In particular, there is a general perception that management delivers on its promises. An operator commented 'we believe what the management team tell us. There is a perception that they are telling the truth'. A fitter stated, 'I trust management more now. I trust them to run the plant and to keep their word'. This trust did not appear to be total, however. An E/I worker said he had personally experienced 'a breach of trust' by management, adding, 'you can trust management on some issues, but not others'.

In turn, employee perceptions of the state of the psychological contract (views on management competence, trust, and fairness) have influenced attitudinal outcomes like job satisfaction, loyalty to the company, commitment to management, and attitudes towards unions.

i) Job satisfaction: Most employees expressed a high degree of job satisfaction. Work is widely perceived as being 'less boring' and offering 'more variety' in comparison to the past. An E/I worker commented: 'there has been an improvement in job satisfaction. I am quite happy with my job now', while another E/I worker suggested that he had a 'varied and enjoyable job. I have the opportunity to use my skills. It is not boring'. Furthermore, a fitter stated: 'I am very happy in the job. I am working within the comfort zone.' Finally, an operator commented: 'I find my job interesting. We rotate between tasks every two months. There is quite a lot of variety.'

ii) **Loyalty and commitment:** In terms of loyalty and commitment to the organisation – an important measure of the intensity of consensus – a large number of workers were highly committed, and this applied across different grades and skills. Under the traditional system of close supervision, most workers only gave minimal compliance to management aims. Workers would sit around and wait to be told what to do by supervisors. In stark contrast, they are generally much more enthusiastic and proactive now. An operator commented, 'I am very loyal. It is a great company to work for. There are great benefits and we are well looked after. I now look forward to coming into work', while another operator stated that he is 'very loyal to the company. I rarely take sick leave'. An E/I worker commented that he would be 'fairly loyal. I wouldn't bad-mouth the company'. Commitment amongst fitters is perhaps not as intense as other grades, but is still generally quite high. Significantly, a fitter who expressed a number of reservations about management at all levels – particularly dissatisfaction with the personal style of his facilitator – still commented that he was very loyal to the organisation having 'spent the whole of my working life at the company'. Furthermore, another fitter commented: 'I would say I would be a loyal employee, and I would be highly committed to the company.'

A positive sign of high commitment was that many employees indicated they are sufficiently motivated to make an extra contribution where necessary. For instance, an operator said he is 'willing to stay behind if needed to do extra work'. Furthermore, he considered AAL to be 'a good company', and suggested that a 'mutual respect' exists. A fitter stated, 'I would be one of the more motivated in my group and would take on a bit extra, but only up to a point'.

Despite these positive findings, there were limits to the diffusion of commitment across the plant. The commitment of a minority of workers is not particularly intense. One operator admitted he was 'largely here for the money'. There is some evidence that fitters are maybe less committed than other grades. One fitter commented, 'from my point of view, I come in and do what I have to do, and I volunteer for nothing', while another fitter commented, 'I have no real loyalty as such. I do the job and get out of here'. A minority of traditionalists are unwilling to change, and do not want to get involved or take on extra responsibilities. Finally, there are factors external placing limits on the intensity of consensus. Even though the plant was performing very well at the time of the field-work, employees are acutely aware that the parent company could make changes that could have a negative impact on employment security if there was a serious downturn in product markets.

iii) Worker views on role of unions: Another sign of workers' distance from management is that the majority of union members feel there is still a need for a trade union to protect their interests – an indication of continued 'them and us'. The vast majority of workers believe that relations between management and unions are much better than the adversarial days, but said union influence at AAL has decreased. This was also the case at Waterford Crystal. A number of operators said they now have little contact with their union (SIPTU). One suggested that SIPTU 'don't have a great say. They do not have a major role in the plant now', while another said:

> I feel SIPTU are useless. I think they could be more vocal. If SIPTU were to disappear out of the plant I don't think it would make any difference. We have a good management team who are willing to communicate, and SIPTU have no part in the middle.

Members of other unions also felt that the activities of their respective unions, the TEEU and AEEU (now in UNITE), have decreased. One E/I worker (TEEU member) said, 'we don't see enough of the union. I would like to see more of the union', while another E/I worker (TEEU) stated that 'there are less union meetings now. There should be more union meetings to address important issues'. In addition, a fitter (TEEU member) suggested that he 'does not have much contact with the union'. Finally, another sign of declining union influence was emphasised by a fitter (AEEU member): 'There is no full-time shop steward on site. Even the Chairman of the Shop Steward's Committee is not full-time.'

The perceived decline in union influence seems to stem from a number of factors that cropped up during discussions. First, there is much less conflict across the plant. Therefore, unions are spending far less time on traditional defensive conflict-related issues, and so they are simply less visible. Second, management is now deemed to be much more competent at managing, so there is less need for union intervention. Third, the balance of power has shifted in favour of management. Fourth, wages are determined at national level through partnership agreements, so the distributive role of local collective bargaining has diminished. Fifth, there is a perception that unions (nationally and locally) have sometimes not been as proactive in developing an influence in new areas of worker interest as they perhaps could be.

As noted above, despite the perception that union activity and influence has declined, most employees still want independent union representation to protect their interests against any potential management abuse. An operator emphasized that he would want unions to retain some independence from management, and he commented that he 'still sees a role for unions to protect workers' interests'. A fitter commented, 'I wouldn't like to give up my union membership, and I would think twice before going for a promotion that would take me out of the union'. Furthermore, an E/I worker stated, 'there is still a need for trade unions here. Management could ride roughshod over workers if there were no unions', while another E/I worker commented that 'it is definitely worthwhile having a union card here. We need the union to look after our interests. We would be a lot more vulnerable without the union'.

Turning to the most appropriate role for unions, most employees felt that management-union co-operation is a more effective means of advancing their interests than traditional adversarial IR. Therefore, workers themselves had no truck with Kelly's (1998) view that workplace militancy is the best means of advancing workers' interests. An operator suggested that cooperation 'is the right way to go', while a fitter said he 'preferred the partnership approach'. There is a general feeling that more can be achieved by collaboration than by opposition. Nevertheless, some concerns were evident. As in Waterford Crystal, many workers knew relatively little about high-level management-union partnership, and there is a perception that management and unions could do more to communicate what partnership entails. In particular, little appears to be known about the AAL Business Performance Improvement (BPI) team. Being somewhat distant and in the dark about partnership, some employees are unsure of management's intentions and motives. For instance, an E/I worker commented, 'workers are not being made aware about partnership and its implications. I would like to be made more aware of what it actually is'. In addition, a fitter claimed unions have not had much genuine input in shaping partnership, adding that, to a certain extent, management is interested in 'cherry picking' those aspects of partnership that best promote its own interests:

> Any management will cherry pick to a certain degree. It is in their interests to get what they want out of it. My view is that if partnership is to work you have to take all of it. You have to take the unpalatable stuff as well. That works both ways. The unions have to get involved in management decision-making as well, which may be unpalatable to their members.

The table below summarizes the gains and losses accruing to the various stakeholders at AAL and illustrates what is deemed to be a relatively equal balance of mutuality.

Table 4.3: Equal Balance of Mutuality at Aughinish Alumina

	Management	**Unions**	**Workers**
Gains	Higher productivity, effort, creativity, lower costs, higher quality, innovation, lower conflict, reduced accidents, less absenteeism.	Input into operational and some strategic business decision-making. Much more information and consultation.	Considerable autonomy at point of production. Annualised hours, gainsharing, job security, single status. Good pay.
Losses	Takes a lot of vigilance, effort and resources to sustain partnership.	Less power, less visible.	Few promotion opportunities, disciplinary issues in some teams.

Conditions Underpinning Pragmatic Partnership

The main contextual conditions promoting an equal balance of mutuality at AAL were top management support; efforts by all parties to add value to achieve higher performance, combined with management striving for fairness; and management consciously implemented stakeholder governance by adopting new IR/HR practices.

Conclusion

During the course of this chapter, we have attempted to address the central aim of this book, of whether pluralist workplace partnership can deliver mutual gains and, more specifically, to examine the following three questions:

- How have employers tried to move towards partnership, and has it displaced management control?

- Does workplace partnership deliver mutual gains for workers, unions and employers, and what is the balance of mutuality?

- How do external and internal contextual conditions influence the adoption and sustainability of partnership?

In terms of the first question, this chapter has explored how AAL management has regulated the employment relationship, in terms of maintaining control and generating cooperation. Attempts to move away from adversarial IR by introducing partnership practices did not constitute a fundamental break with past practice or displace management control. Nevertheless, elements of partnership were novel.

During the adversarial period (1983-1993), industrial relations at AAL were highly antagonistic, and closely resembled pessimistic accounts in the literature. The highly bureaucratic and dictatorial management style meant that alienated workers were only prepared to offer minimal compliance to management aims. The costs incurred by this adversarial pattern eventually brought the plant to the brink of closure, and after initially acting in a very coercive manner to tackle the crisis, management set about constructing co-operative work relations.

In terms of how management sought to move away from adversarial IR towards cooperation, the pragmatic partnership pattern followed a radical re-organisation of the company in 1993. To align its new employment relations strategy with business strategy, management required cooperative relations with unions to make it easier to get the workforce to buy into ongoing change. Union marginalisation was not considered to viable, because though weaker, unions maintained a strong presence. Management proceeded to introduce a bundle of mutual gains practices.

In 1993, management rolled-out advanced teamwork, devolving considerable decision-making autonomy to employees at the point of production. Also, management developed cooperative relations with unions through various ad hoc informal partnership teams – notably the Business Performance Improvement (BPI) team, which affords union representatives with an element of joint decision-making powers. However, unions would like to see partnership formalised and given institutional expression in some kind of permanent structure. Without stronger institutional support, they are concerned that partnership could atrophy. In addition, management also introduced a range of new complementary HRM practices.

Crucially, however, contrary to the views of some advocates, the move towards partnership did not mean management loosened its control. Rather, management moved away from reliance on abrasive direct controls, such as close supervision, towards more indirect controls, such as performance targets. These control practices placed limits on mutual gains consensus – a factor underplayed by advocates in the literature. In essence, partnership was a new dynamic, but one located within the traditional contested terrain of management seeking to maintain control and generate consent.

In terms of the second question, relating to outcomes, it is concluded that management, unions and employees all gained from partnership and, significantly, the gains were distributed fairly equally. Management have secured many gains from partnership, notably greater legitimacy, increased productivity, innovative behaviour, lower costs, much less conflict, reduced accidents, and less absenteeism. Pragmatic partnership has enabled it to introduce workplace change more effectively, and at a faster pace than was possible under the adversarial pattern. Significantly, partnership has been vital for delivering stability and certainty to management, an ingredient that was absent during the adversarial years. Productivity has increased substantially, particularly in terms of significantly greater process continuity and reductions in production downtime, and employees are working smarter as well as harder. There has been no collective conflict for many years, and individual grievances have declined substantially. Recourse to external dispute resolution institutions has been rare. Labour turnover is very low, overtime has been replaced by reserve hours, and accidents have reduced.

Unions also gained from partnership. In particular, the BPI team provides them with some input into strategic decision-making. Union representatives would like to see partnership extend further and be given institutional expression through some form of permanent structure. Without stronger institutional support, unions are concerned that partnership could atrophy. As at WC, partnership is a double-edged sword for unions. They have less power than during the adversarial days, and in some ways are less influential. Also, their new cooperative role means they are less visible.

AAL employees generally responded very positively to workplace partnership, a finding at odds with critics in the literature. Worker experiences and responses were far more upbeat then during the adversarial period, with many benefits of the new pattern of employment relations reported. Workers were very satisfied with teamwork, found their jobs more interesting, and most claimed that relations with supervisors had improved dramatically. Employee experiences of new HR practices are also broadly positive. Management are perceived as more willing to share information and consult, and employees are content with training, employment security, and annualised hours. Satisfaction with pay levels was also high. Worker experiences of management controls were pragmatic. They responded positively to the relaxation of direct monitoring, and less arbitrary administration of discipline – factors provoking conflict in the past. However, they are aware of indirect performance controls: advanced technical controls, performance targets, and market pressures. Work effort has intensified, and some workers expressed concerns. But, overall, workers did not object to working 'harder and smarter', and in some instances even welcomed it. This was largely because management is perceived to be more competent at organising production, together with a desire by workers to avoid having to work reserve hours. In short, workers believe their interests are best served by working smarter. But workers also experienced some negative elements and, therefore, there are some costs for workers, even where partnership is quite advanced – a fact downplayed by advocates. First, some workers felt direct supervision was creeping back. Second, tensions existed in some teams over timekeeping abuses and certain people not 'pulling their weight' and there was a perception that management had not addressed this. Also, some workers referred to insufficient promotion in a flat structure.

Overall though, the gains for employees far outweighed any negativity, which fed through into their attitudes and behaviour. It is clear that attempts to inculcate partnership had a positive impact on management-employee relations. The overriding view is that management is competent, generally treats workers fairly, and the organisation of production is more coherent. Trust has risen substantially, though not everywhere. Most workers reported high job satisfaction, and many are motivated to make an extra contribution beyond that expected. However, a small minority of workers only offer minimal compliance, and still harbour reservations about management. Workers generally felt that union influence has decreased, but most felt they still need unions to prevent potential management exploitation. Thus, there is still some sense of 'them and us', and workers retain some distance from management. Despite this, when asked, workers expressed a definite preference for management-union partnership over militancy.

The main contextual conditions promoting an equal balance of mutuality were top management support; efforts by all parties to add value to achieve higher performance, combined with management striving for fairness; and management consciously implemented stakeholder governance by adopting new partnership practices (notably strategic management-union partnership, information and consultation, semi-autonomous teamwork, annualised hours, gainsharing, employment security, single status, training). The organisation was radically redesigned to facilitate this stakeholder model. Managerial control policies were not so pronounced as to undermine the balance of mutuality.

In terms of sustainability, the AAL partnership has now lasted fifteen years. The following external and internal conditions have underpinned the durability of partnership: relative insulation from market pressures; continuity in top management and union support; quite strong internal institutionalisation of WP; and capital intensive continuous process technology. First, AAL faces competitive challenges like most companies, but it enjoys relative insulation from market forces, and has not faced a crisis since before WP was adopted, which has enhanced sustainability of WP. Second, AAL has not faced a senior management (or union) succession crisis – most of the key supporters of partnership remain. Competent management choices have been crucial for sustaining partnership. Third, WP is quite strongly institutionalised and vertically aligned at AAL, though unions would like to see stronger protections for representative forums. Finally, continuous process technology enhanced the durability of WP. Put simply, management are unlikely to relocate such an expensive capital intensive continuous process plant. In sum, the conditions supporting WP at AAL were strong enough to sustain it.

The diagram on the next page summarises the adversarial and pragmatic partnership patterns at AAL. The final chapter presents a discussion and some conclusions, as well as some policy implications.

Figure 4.1: Summary of Patterns of Workplace IR at Aughinish Alumina: 1983-2008

Adversarial Pattern (1983-1993)	Pragmatic Partnership Pattern (1993+)
IR pattern: adversarial, coercion	*IR pattern: cooperation and control*
- adversarial collective bargaining (1983-1992) - followed by unilateral management coercion and concession bargaining (1992-93)	- cooperative relations - management controls, but more indirect, less 'frictional'
Outcomes:	*Outcomes:*
- frequent conflict, grievances - no mutual gains - very little trust or cooperation	- relatively equal share of mutual gains - high productivity and high participation - signs of high commitment, high trust - still conflicts of interest, but largely institutionalized
Contextual conditions:	*Contextual conditions:*
- spiralling of costs leading to eventual crisis - external pressures began to intensify - exchange rate problems - extensive mismanagement, neglect, and coercion - poor organisation of work - defensive unions	- external environment improved - more favourable exchange rate - much better management - unions/workforce pragmatic engagement in cooperation - semi-autonomous teamwork, annual hours, gainsharing - extensive communication, information & consultation - continuous process technology - relative employment security - much more training

CONCLUSION: WORKPLACE COOPERATION IN PRACTICE – CAN PLURALISM DELIVER MUTUAL GAINS?

Introduction

There is an emerging narrative in Ireland about the competitive imperatives of building a knowledge economy, improving company productivity and performance, engaging in workplace innovation and cooperation. But this is arguably yet to be persuasively articulated by Government and the social partners into a coherent and integrated account of what 'good' workplace relations should look like in practice.

The arguments and findings in this book amount to a rallying call for the 're-institutionalisation of pluralism'. It is clear that new democratic 'checks and balances' or 'positive shock effects' promoting 'good' work relations are necessary if workplace partnerships are to be adopted and sustained in greater quantities than at present. The case findings show that pluralism can 'work' but that the forces retarding partnership are currently stronger than those promoting it. This is not just a matter of employees having a 'democratic right' to workplace 'voice' and information and consultation. High performance cooperative work relations are vital for economic progress if Ireland is to construct a genuine competitive knowledge economy. Ireland cannot hope to compete by driving down labour costs. It can only follow the high productivity route, which requires collaborative work relations. It is by now a well-worn argument that the highly collaborative Nordic countries are the most competitive <u>and</u> participative economies in the world. They combine high innovation with high participation, encompassing nothing less than a national collective collaboration involving all stakeholders. The task of creating high performance workplaces is too big for employers alone. To revisit Flanders' (1970: 172) old dictum: the paradox may be that management can best 'regain control by sharing it'. This is as much about changing 'mindsets' as policies.

The initial rationale for this book was the continued polarisation between competing perspectives about the dynamics and nature of workplace partnership, the balance of mutual gains and costs accruing to employers, workers and unions, and the conditions sustaining or inhibiting partnership. Three perspectives in the mutual gains literature have been described: advocates, critics, and pragmatic contingency. Furthermore, it has been noted that polarised views on workplace partnership in the academic literature are accompanied by ambiguity about workplace partnership among employment relations practitioners and policy-makers. In short, the political economy of workplace cooperation is a contested terrain.

At the outset, after reviewing the existing literature, we outlined three important research issues/questions requiring clarification:

- How have employers tried to move towards partnership, and has it displaced management control?

- Does workplace partnership deliver mutual gains for workers, unions and employers, and what is the balance of mutuality?

- How do external and internal contextual conditions influence the balance of mutual gains and the sustainability of workplace partnership?

This final chapter compares and contrasts the main case findings in the two case studies (Waterford Crystal and Aughinish Alumina), and, in particular, synthesises the balance of mutual gains (and losses) for all workplace stakeholders and addresses the durability of partnership. To assess the wider generalisability and significance of this study, the findings are discussed and compared with the existing literature on workplace partnership outlined in Chapter Two. Finally, in the concluding section, key themes emerging from the study are summarily outlined. The practical and policy implications of the study are also explored, as are possibilities for future research.

'Contradiction': Cooperation Co-exists with Control

The first question we raised is how has management tried to move towards partnership, and has it displaced management control? In terms of its antecedents, partnership's emergence at WC and AAL was attributable to a 'complementary cluster' of conditions present in both firms. Crucially, while competitive crisis provided the initial 'shock effect', the subsequent emergence of WP was promoted by improving market conditions. Without this, it would have been very difficult for partnership to take root. Another key antecedent was that both firms implemented new business strategies emphasising quality (of product, workforce skill, etc.) not just cost, and both developed advanced technologies (continuous process technology at AAL was especially conducive to WP). Significantly, both companies had new senior management teams willing to risk cooperation with unions/workers. Strong unions were also a factor and unions ready to engage in a 'new' approach to IR. Given both plants were highly unionised, management pragmatically concluded that forcing change was not conducive to developing high-value added competitive strategy. Together, these conditions meant management and other stakeholders – including owners and shareholders – decided the potential of cooperation outweighed the risks. Continuation with adversarial IR probably spelled closure, so alternative avenues to WP were closed off.

Responding to acute competitive pressures, both companies introduced new representative partnership arrangements providing unions with inputs into operational decision-making and, in some instances, business strategy. A crucial difference is that the partnership bundle was more complete at AAL. AAL had advanced teamwork, reinforced by annualised hours, gainsharing, single status conditions, and an employment security clause. In contrast, key mutual gains practices were absent at WC, notably teamwork/scope for direct worker participation, and employment security. Also, AAL implemented a flatter organisational structure, dispensing with most management layers, whereas WC remained very hierarchical with traditional work organisation intact. Comparing the AAL partnership with the now defunct Aer Rianta 'Compact' (cf. Roche and Geary, 2006), representative partnership was more advanced at Aer Rianta, but the opposite applied to direct worker participation and HR practices, where the AAL bundle was more complete. Meanwhile, while WC had an innovative form of representative participation, it had weak direct participation. The findings support the argument that partnership purely restricted to representative-level is insufficient in isolation, illustrating the importance of implementing the full bundle of representative participation, direct participation and complementary HR practices if partnership is to take root and prosper (cf. Guest and Peccei, 2001; Kochan and Osterman, 1994).

Comparing AAL and WC with international examples of advanced voluntary workplace partnerships, it is clear that the American Saturn experiment outlined by Rubinstein (2000) and Rubinstein and Heckscher (2002) remains a benchmark, in terms of the far-reaching extent to which unions are involved in co-management initiatives from shopfloor level right up to corporate level, and, allied to this, the scope for direct worker participation through self-managed work teams. No example of workplace partnership to date in Ireland, including our two case studies, measures up to this standard, but such a benchmark may be raising the bar too high. Cooperation at AAL and WC was more about workplace stakeholders responding pragmatically to difficult competitive circumstances than about creating a new model of joint control over workplace governance. In short, it was all about 'pragmatic cooperation', and all parties, including managers, were reticent to call it partnership.

Pragmatic cooperation at WC and AAL constituted a new means of managing contradictions in the employment relationship and negotiating workplace order. But there was no transformative break with the past or a displacement of management control. Cooperation and control co-exist 'in contradiction' as Edwards (2003) argues, a fact neglected by many partnership advocates. The means of control have changed at both WC and AAL, in that they became more indirect, a finding evident in the contingency literature (Gallie et al., 1998). But management controls were still firmly embedded in both organisations, albeit in a less invasive and crude form than yesteryear. The requirement to exert control was less pressing at AAL, given that competitive pressures were not as acute as in WC. It was also significant that AAL employ capital-intensive continuous process technology, which is particularly conducive to worker autonomy and participation (cf. Edwards and Wright 1998). In contrast, the WC production system is not a continuous process, and is thus much more susceptible to outsourcing.

'Status' and 'Contract'

Therefore, our two case studies illustrate that employment relationships in Ireland, like other industrialised economies, are thus subject to contradictory pressures. Recent contradictory trends in employment relations can best be understood by using Streeck's (1987) distinction between 'contract' and 'status'. As noted in chapter two, Streeck (1987: 290) argues that moves away from traditional pluralist collective bargaining are prompted by pressures to increase efficiency and flexibility in response to an 'unprecedented degree of economic uncertainty'. This requirement has necessitated increasingly close integration of industrial relations and wider business strategy, whereas in the past the two were largely disconnected. This has resulted in the unravelling of traditional IR institutions such as collective bargaining, which have been insulated from efficiency considerations, and which are perceived by many employers as constituting rigidities obstructing flexible work organisation and labour deployment. If we apply this analysis to this study, the perceived inflexibility and inefficiency of traditional IR systems at both WC and AAL prompted management to unravel them.

Streeck (1987: 292-5) distinguishes between management by 'contract' and 'status' when analysing the decline of traditional pluralist collective bargaining. Streeck suggests that employers may utilise two distinct means to dismantle perceived workplace rigidities, and to secure the requisite degree of worker consent to the adjustments deemed necessary to respond to market pressures: a 'return to contract' (corresponds with unilateral management prerogative) or an 'extension of status' (corresponds with partnership). But, reflecting the need to manage external and internal contradictions and uncertainty, Streeck clearly emphasizes that management will tend to simultaneously combine elements of status and contract. This was the case at WC and AAL, where the requirement to balance contradictory pressures meant that management simultaneously combined elements of status (partnership practices) with contract (control practices), although there was a greater tendency towards status at AAL than at WC.

'Tendencies' and 'Cycles'

The implication of having to manage complex external and internal contradictions is that patterns of employment regulation are diverging rather than converging, what Roche (2005: 2) calls 'a series of parallel landscapes rather than with any singular and all-encompassing process of convergence towards one landscape with well-defined common features'. But within this emerging picture of diversity, this study has illustrated that there will be times and contexts when management may display a greater tendency towards certain practices over others. As Edwards (2003) has argued, it is possible to identify *tendencies* towards or away from control (contract) or partnership/cooperative (status) directions respectively. Ramsey's (1977) idea that tendencies towards management control and worker participation occur periodically in 'cycles' (rather than constituting a fundamental turning point) provides a useful way of conceptualising this fluidity. At Waterford Crystal, for instance, we have described three broad historical patterns or cycles of employment regulation with particular tendencies to the fore: first, there was the indulgency pattern (collective bargaining, worker autonomy and union 'job controls'); second, when the indulgency pattern became unsustainable, there was a move to an adversarial pattern (coercive unilateral management control and concession bargaining); third, when the adversarial pattern became unsustainable, there was a move towards a pragmatic partnership pattern (management-union partnership, but accompanied by management controls). Since 2003, there has been a move away from pragmatic partnership back towards stronger management prerogative and concession bargaining.

The Balance of Mutuality

The second question is does partnership deliver mutual gains for management, unions and workers, and what is the balance of mutuality?

The conclusion here is that pluralist partnership can 'work' and deliver gains for all stakeholders (through adopting proactive joint problem-solving principles for mutual gains purposes). But the balance of mutuality varies according to context. In our two case studies, the balance of mutuality at WC favoured management, and the union also secured notable gains. But while workers did experience some important gains, these were offset by various negative experiences of workplace change.

In comparison, the balance of mutual gains at AAL was more equally distributed between stakeholders. The bundle of partnership practices was more expansive at AAL, which had a bearing on outcomes. Plus, AAL management explicitly operated partnership on the basis of mutual gains bargaining principles (known as 'getting to yes'). Conflicting interests remained in both plants, especially WC, and this is to be expected given the contradictions and structured antagonism at the heart of the contested terrain of IR (cf. Edwards, 1986, 2003).

Benefits/Costs for Management

Management at both companies benefited from increased productivity and innovation, reduced costs, less conflict, fewer accidents, and so forth. While it is difficult to disentangle the impact of improved technical/production efficiency from sometimes less tangible people management inputs, partnership has undoubtedly contributed to productivity improvements. Workers are working harder, but, crucially, also smarter. In short, partnership contributed to the business bottom line.

At WC, management viewed the company-union task group as playing a key practical role in the company's revival and helping to boost innovation, productivity and competitiveness. At AAL, the BPI representative management-union team played a similar role. On top of this, AAL management also reaped many gains from advanced teamwork and annual hours. In contrast, innovation at task level at WC was circumscribed by limited scope for employee participation at the point of production. This was not just attributable to management. The union at WC opposed management-sponsored direct employee involvement, fearing it could undermine union influence. Perhaps most of all, management at both companies benefited from the certainty, confidence, order and stability that workplace partnership provided. As Hastings et al. (2007) note, the main reason why employers at national level have supported social partnership is the stability and confidence it provides. But there was certain costs associated with partnership for management at both WC and AAL. In particular, the sustainability of voluntarist partnerships requires ongoing dedication, resources, support and vigilance from senior management.

Benefits/Costs for Unions and Workers

Unions and workers at WC and AAL experienced a mix of benefits and costs from partnership, but with workers at AAL clearly experiencing more benefits than workers at WC. Our findings support and reflect contingency theories emphasising the duality of workplace cooperation and conflict. Many advocates of partnership suggest that workers are experiencing widespread benefits such as enhanced empowerment, skills, and job autonomy, a relaxation in management control, greater rewards; and, where they exist, employee representatives derive considerable benefits from partnership. At the other extremity, critics often point to widespread costs for workers such as pervasive management control, deskilling, insecurity, work intensification, stress, and union marginalisation. Both the advocates and the critics are partially correct. But the reality tends to be somewhere in the middle. Advocates and critics miss the central theoretical point in the contingency literature, by failing to acknowledge that the contradictions of the employment relationship – driven by the need for employers to maintain control at the same time as manufacture cooperation – will generate a variety of responses from employees and their representatives, who will tend to experience a variety of costs and benefits because of the duality of employer practices (Edwards, 2003). We have noted that the work of Streeck (1987) is important, because he argues that elements of status and contract will usually be assembled in combination – for instance, employees and their representatives may experience empowerment in work teams and representative forums (status) but at the same time be subject to tighter performance measurement, which may cause them to experience greater work pressure (contract). It is how management organises and balances this contradiction that matters on a day-to-day level.

Unions at both WC and AAL benefited from the real influence over business decisions that partnership brought about, and this did not involve union incorporation as critics like Kelly (1996, 2004) suggest. Unions at both companies emphasised their independence from management, and did not use the word partnership to describe what was happening – and nor did management. But it is what happens in practice that matters. The union at WC held a favourable view of the task group, and explicitly suggested that it generated mutual gains – a key yardstick of genuine partnership in the literature (Kochan and Osterman, 1994); and which dispels arguments by critics that management-union cooperation is largely illusionary. The union saw the task group as facilitating increased participation and access to important information on strategic issues. Likewise, at AAL, the BPI team provides unions with some input into strategic decision-making. However, some union representatives at AAL would like to see partnership given institutional expression through some form of permanent structure. Without stronger institutional support, unions are concerned that partnership could atrophy. Partnership was a double-edged sword for unions at both companies, in terms of coinciding with a weakening of traditional collective bargaining power (a process already in train before partnership 'arrived'). Advocates sometimes gloss over this 'double-edged sword'. The unions were clearly less powerful than before their respective 'defeats' by management in the early 1990's, and in some ways less influential. Furthermore, their new cooperative role meant they were less visible to the workforce than under their traditional defensive adversarial roles. Despite this, when asked, employees at both companies expressed a definite preference for management-union partnership over adversarial IR. Accordingly, employees expressed little appetite for Kelly's (1998) advocacy of workplace militancy over cooperation.

As for employees, the AAL workforce experienced more gains from partnership than those at WC. At WC, outcomes for employees were mixed. The main gains from partnership included financial involvement through the profit share scheme, better relations with front line managers and substantially more training/education. The main downsides were employment insecurity, outsourcing, work intensification, industrial engineering (generating tighter work standards), shiftwork, and limited direct participation. The threat of outsourcing was a particular concern for WC employees. More generally, employees experienced uncertainty in relation to the external economic context. This mixed experience of costs and benefits fed into worker attitudes and behaviour, resulting in greater worker engagement and cooperation than during the adversarial period, but with distinct limits to consensus. Trust levels were not high, and many workers cited unfairness in terms of the unequal distribution of rewards between management and themselves. While the union was weaker, most workers still wanted it to protect their interests – an indication of continued 'them and us' attitudes. The fact that little attempt had been made to redesign work placed limits on job satisfaction. Furthermore, although a more disciplined workforce pragmatically accepted the need to work harder and adapt to market realities, this did not translate into active commitment to management values. Many workers had spent thirty or more years with the company, and they saw it as 'theirs', and were loyal to 'the company', whereas they perceived managers as transitory. Loyalty to the company and commitment to management were two different things.

At AAL, employees responded more positively to partnership, a finding at odds with critics in the literature. Most fundamentally, they experienced a much more stable company than hitherto, with greater workplace order, and with management seen as much more competent than their predecessors. Employees were very satisfied with teamwork, found their jobs more interesting, and claimed that relations with supervisors had improved. Employee experiences of new HR practices were also broadly positive. Management are perceived as more willing to consult and share information, and workers are generally content with training, employment security, and annualised hours. Satisfaction with pay levels is also quite high. Interestingly, employee experiences of management controls at AAL were pragmatic. They responded positively to the relaxation of direct monitoring, and less arbitrary administration of discipline – factors provoking conflict in the past. However, they are aware of indirect performance controls: advanced technical controls, performance targets, and market pressures. Work effort has intensified, and some workers expressed concerns. But, overall, workers did not object to working 'harder and smarter', and in many instances even welcomed it. This was largely because management is perceived to be more competent at organising production. In short, workers believe their interests are best served by working smarter, a factor noted by Collinson et al. (1997) in their 'disciplined worker' thesis. But workers also experienced some negative elements and, therefore, there are some costs for workers, even where partnership is quite advanced – a fact downplayed by advocates. Costs cited included: direct supervision creeping back in some areas, teams having to carry certain people not 'pulling their weight', and insufficient promotion opportunities in a flat structure.

Overall, however, employee gains at AAL far outweighed costs, which fed through into employee attitudes and behaviour. It is clear that attempts to inculcate partnership had a positive impact on management-employee relations. The overriding view is that management is competent, generally treats workers fairly, and the organisation of production is more coherent. Trust has risen substantially, though not everywhere. Most employees reported high job satisfaction, display high commitment, and are motivated to make an extra contribution 'beyond contract' (cf. Fox, 1974). However, a small minority of employees only offer minimal compliance, and still harbour reservations about management. Workers generally felt that union influence has decreased, but most felt they still need unions to prevent potential management exploitation. Thus, there is still some sense of 'them and us', and workers retain some distance from management.

Conditions Supporting and Sustaining Mutual Gains

The third question is how do external and internal contextual conditions influence the balance of mutuality and the sustainability of WP? This links into our fourth question: if mutual gains partnership 'works', why do few employers introduce it? Relating the case findings to existing literature, it is concluded that the main conditions promoting an equal balance of mutuality are top management support, efforts by all parties enhance firm performance combined with management striving for fairness and internal institutionalisation of vertically-aligned stakeholder

206 Workplace Partnership in Practice

governance models supporting proactive worker/union contributions to company performance *and* accommodating worker interests (encompassing strategic management-union partnership, information and consultation, financial stakeholding, extensive employee participation, employment security, training). In this regard, the findings correspond with existing studies (Kochan and Rubinstein, 2000; Roche and Geary, 2006) exploring conditions promoting a balance of mutuality. Such conditions were more prevalent at AAL than WC. In particular, there was more evidence that WP at AAL was vertically aligned from top to bottom. Partnership at WC was too restricted to representative level to promote a symmetrical balance of mutuality. Moreover, competitive pressures and managerial control policies were more acute at WC, which were in contradiction to a balance of mutuality.

In terms of sustainability, the AAL partnership has now lasted fifteen years, but the WC partnership broke down after ten. It can be concluded that the following external and internal conditions underpin the durability of partnership: relative insulation from market pressures; continuity in top management and union support; internal institutionalisation of WP and capital intensive continuous process technology. Taking these conditions in turn, AAL faces competitive challenges, but it enjoys relative insulation from market forces and has not faced a crisis since before WP was adopted, which has enhanced the sustainability of WP. In contrast, WC was more exposed to market turbulence and the demise of WP was ultimately caused by acute deterioration in competitive conditions. This deterioration in market conditions at WC coincided with the fact that the senior managers responsible for partnership had all left by 2002, and new managers were less inclined to sustain WP. AAL has not faced a senior management (or union) succession crisis and most key supporters of partnership remain. This leads to the conclusion that without succession planning, WP is vulnerable to collapse when top management (or union) 'champions' leave. In addition, WP is quite strongly institutionalised and vertically aligned at AAL, though unions would like to see stronger protections for representative forums. In comparison, partnership at WC was largely restricted to representative level. Finally, AAL's continuous process plant rendered relocation unlikely. In contrast, it is easier to relocate production from Waterford Glass. In sum, conditions supporting partnership at AAL were strong enough to sustain it. But, at WC, the forces undermining partnership became stronger than those sustaining it, leading to its breakdown.

Competitive Postures

More generally, the findings illustrate that it requires quite special conditions for management to insulate workplace productivity coalitions from market turbulence and balance the contradictions of IR. Tendencies towards enduring partnerships are most likely to occur where business strategy is oriented towards competing on the basis of knowledge, innovation, quality, and adaptability; utilising advanced capital intensive technology (notably continuous process technology); and marrying this with 'bundles' of cooperative IR/HR practices, supported by employment security (cf. Locke et al., 1995; Regini, 1995; Cappelli et al., 1997; Crouch and Streeck, 1997; Roche and Geary, 2000; Godard, 2004). But competitive alternatives to partnership are heightened in historically permissive voluntarist IR systems like Ireland and the UK and many employers may not see a need for partnership, given the availability of less time-and money-consuming alternatives. In liberal market economies, as emphasized by Streeck (1995, 1997), so long as management can respond by restructuring towards alternative modes of production/service delivery that function profitably with less demanding or no labour co-operation, employment relations will take place largely on management's terms. Similarly, as Godard (2004) suggests, alternative unilateral management control or 'weak' employee involvement approaches requiring fewer resources are more likely in 'liberal market economies' where cost minimisation dominates.

Institutionalization

The findings in this book also point to the significance of institutional conditions and historical starting points for promoting or retarding moves towards workplace partnership: illustrating that change is, to some degree at least, dependent on institutional starting points and legacies (cf. Locke et al., 1995; Regini, 1995; Streeck, 1997; Roche and Geary, 2000; Hutton, 2002; Belanger and Edwards, 2007). In traditionally voluntarist institutional contexts such as the UK (Edwards,

2003), the US (Cappelli et al., 1997), and Ireland (Roche and Geary, 2000), institutional conditions and financial markets have historically tended to encourage adversarial IR, short-termism, cost competition and management prerogative, rather than quality competition, collaborative production, and long-term thinking. In view of this, the findings in this book support the argument posited by Belanger and Edwards (2007:713) that conditions generating sustainable workplace compromise in liberal market economies such as the UK, US and Ireland are feasible but rare, and that stronger 'beneficial constraints' are necessary if partnership is to increase and endure – in the form of stronger external institutional supports insulating it from market pressures. Some might argue that Ireland is different from the UK and US context, given its strongly institutionalised tripartite model of national social partnership since 1987, and the existence of a specific institution, the National Centre for Partnership and Performance (NCPP), to promote workplace partnership. In reality, this has not greatly increased the incidence of WP primarily – it appears – because of the permissive nature of the Irish IR system (there have been WP clauses in national agreements but they are 'broad brush' and voluntary, while the role of the NCPP is largely advisory and facilitative). The NCPP has been engaged in commendable initiatives, notably the introduction of a workplace innovation fund designed to assist companies seeking to boost productivity through enhancing employee participation. At the end of the day, the NCPP can only push and cajole, and much depends on the strategic choices of Government and individual management and employee representatives.

'Good' Management (and Unions)

Growth of mutual gains partnership would also require more proactive advocacy and leadership by employers and unions as a generality than presently exists. A dominant thread running throughout this book, supported by the case findings, is the crucial importance of management competence, in the form of strategies and structures for embedding workplace partnership and producing 'good' pluralist employment relations. Our findings add credence to existing IR literature emphasising the importance of management competence for facilitating workplace order. This is recognised in a long line of IR studies dating back to the

British Donovan Report in the late 1960s, transmitting the seemingly simple but crucial message that good leadership and management is ultimately what matters for the negotiation of order (cf. Donovan Commission, 1968; Batstone, 1986; Nichols, 1986; Lazonick, 1990; Hodson, 1999, 2005; Edwards and Wright, 2001; Nolan and O'Donnell, 2003). According to Hodson (1999), for example, the critical factor influencing the intensity of organisational consensus is not the impact of specific IR/HR practices (though this is clearly important), but whether management respects or violates workplace norms such as fairness and a workable system of production. Our case findings support these important arguments. Good management was a vital condition for successful partnership at both WC and AAL.

Furthermore, although this book has illustrated that it is ultimately down to what employers do (employers possess the sole authority to initiate workplace partnership), the success and sustainability of partnership also depends a great deal on proactive strategies by unions, which supports the evidence in the literature (cf. Bacon and Blyton, 1999, 2002). At both AAL and WC, the unions eventually arrived at the pragmatic view that partnership with management was their only viable option – though, in both cases, unions were keen to emphasise their independence from management, and the term partnership was avoided. These were the practical realities facing unions. The 'alternative' was to continue adversarial IR and precipitate company closure.

Issues for Practitioners and Policy-makers

This study raises a number of issues relating to workplace governance in Ireland for practitioners and policy-makers at national, sector and workplace level (see Coats, 2005 and Edwards, 2007 for similar UK debate).

Improving People Management and Leadership

Above all, given the complexity of the managerial function, the findings highlight the vital importance of enhancing management competence and leadership capabilities in balancing a range of external and internal pressures. There is a need to foster and improve progressive people management skills. For instance, more attention needs to be given to employee expectations/interests (what workers want from work relations), rather than just focusing on a managerialist agenda restricted to looking at how partnership and high commitment practices can be used to promote higher performance, which tends to be the case at present. This requires the 'return' of pluralism (a recognition that there are two sides in the employment relationship with distinct as well as common interests), rather than a unitarist one-sided agenda. If it is to 'work', partnership should not simply be a creature of the employer. In short, the employer competitiveness agenda should be combined with an employee rights agenda, the aim being to produce mutual gains for all stakeholders. Increased productivity and stronger employee voice rights are compatible. Indeed, the two are mutually reinforcing.

'Re-institutionalisation of Pluralism'

In relation to the above point, while the social partnership model of pluralist joint decision-making has evolved since 1987 at national level in Ireland between Government, unions and employers, there is little evidence of workplace partnership. In fact, far from increasing, workplace pluralism appears to be in retreat, with management increasingly exercising unilateral authority, rather than seeking legitimacy. In short, a paradox has emerged between national level pluralist joint decision-making and the apparent retreat of workplace pluralism. In comparison to years gone by, state policy in Ireland seems to have moved away from positive support for pluralism (for instance, it is no longer state policy to encourage incoming multinationals to recognise unions for collective bargaining purposes). But we also have to seriously consider Streeck's (1987) observation that traditional defensive collective bargaining may no longer 'work' under new economic conditions. Therefore, it is arguable that new forms of 'win-win' stakeholder pluralism are required that can produce mutual gains: productivity gains for management, while meeting employee demands for workplace voice/participation, and learning. As things stand, the evidence, backed by the findings in this study, indicates that pluralist workplace partnership can produce positive results, including high productivity. But – in terms of wider application and generalisability – the contextual conditions constraining partnership are stronger than those promoting and sustaining it.

Given that under prevailing economic and institutional conditions, only a relative minority of employers will be inclined to voluntarily introduce mutual gains partnership practices – with managerial unilateralism being the norm – there is a role for positive state intervention to promote the wider diffusion of partnership and pluralism. A 're-institutionalisation of pluralism' would be required, but in new forms, whereby the state would do more to construct 'positive shock effects' promoting proactive workplace engagement for mutual gains purposes. At present, state employment relations policy is too strongly geared towards securing minimal employer compliance with the complex web of employment law (for instance, the function of the new National Employment Rights Authority (NERA) is to enforce minimal compliance). More proactive and joined-up state employment relations policies are required; and, in fact, are vital if Ireland is to move towards a commonly stated policy goal of becoming a knowledge economy. Unions too, need to be ushered away from defensive agendas and mindsets towards proactively driving the agenda around issues like upskilling and new forms of employee voice. A few possible 'positive shock effect' policy measures are outlined below that could potentially improve company performance and produce mutual gains.

'Positive Shock Effects'

Information and consultation. There could be much more constructive engagement by the Government and social partners on information and consultation, and workplace dialogue in general. The EU Information and Consultation Directive provides the potential institutional architecture for promoting workplace cooperation, but, influenced by employer lobbying, the Irish Government is widely perceived to have enacted a piece of legislation (Employee (Provision of Information and Consultation) Act 2006) that equates to a minimalist interpretation of the Directive, in the sense that groups of workers have to apply to 'trigger' the information and consultation rights. However, the standard fallback rules in the Irish legislation do provide for elected employee representative forums. But unions seem caught in two minds about whether to view the ICD as a new opportunity to institutionalise worker voice, or as a threat to the traditional single channel of union representation based on collective bargaining (Dobbins, 2006). As things stand then, the IC Act 2006 is unlikely to propel a big push in the partnership direction. More likely is a trajectory more or less along current lines, characterised by divergent IR patterns, but with islands of excellence (Dobbins, 2006; Geary and Roche, 2005). But we cannot discount the possibility that the IC legislation could yet encourage some tendencies towards partnership in the future, particularly if successful companies set a benchmark which other firms seek to emulate. Much depends on what employers and employee representatives do as a generality. If IC is seen to 'work' for all workplace stakeholders, and produces genuine and sustainable gains, then such 'legislatively prompted' pluralist partnerships may increasingly take root.

Proactive advice on 'good' IR. State advice on employment relations could be made much more proactive, in terms of promoting best practice on issues like information and consultation, representative voice structures, teamwork, appropriate training, and so forth. The idea would be to do more to offer specialist but easy to follow advice and guidance to employers, unions and employees on what 'high quality' employment relations should look like in practice. Far too much focus is currently on basic compliance with employment law, rather than giving employers, in particular, practical solutions to follow best practice and reap positive performance outcomes.

A 'working template' for disseminating proactive advice on 'good' workplace IR already exists, in the form of the Labour Relations Commissions' Advisory Service. The LRC Advisory Services Division works with employers, employees and trade unions in non-dispute situations to develop effective industrial relations practices, procedures and structures that best meet their needs. The Advisory Service assists employers and employees to build and maintain positive working relationships and works with them to develop and implement on-going effective problem-solving mechanisms. The LRC Advisory Service offers 'Industrial Relations Audits' to organisations in circumstances where a broad range of problems are perceived to exist or where the parties wish to gain a greater understanding of the dynamics at play in an organisation. Typically, the audit is presented to the parties in the form of a confidential report containing findings, conclusions and recommendations. In some cases, however, there may be a focus on the change agenda and the parties are presented with a series of recommended improvements. The Advisory Division provides further support in terms of post-report monitoring and, where necessary, assistance with the implementation of required changes and improvements. The Advisory Service is free of charge.

Sector partnership forums. Sector partnership forums could be developed to promote best practice benchmarks across a sector, which may then percolate downwards. The various stakeholders in such partnership forums could engage in joint problem-solving over mutual gains issues like improving productivity and upskilling. Practical examples of sector partnership forums already exist in Ireland. In particular, a Print & Packaging Forum was established in 2004 to address the serious competitive problems facing the printing industry. It is the first example in Ireland of a sector-wide partnership initiative in the private sector encompassing the main stakeholders: employers, trade unions, state bodies, and educational institutions. Since its inception, the Forum has generated a number of mutual gains outcomes through joint problem-solving, most notably a radical redesigning and modernising of the apprenticeship system.

Statutory rights to training. More could be done to promote statutory training rights and enhance upskilling. This could be based on the mutual gains principle of encouraging employees and their representatives to become more effective participants in the joint 'management' of workplace change. Coat's (2005) refers to a need to encourage 'intelligent interlocutors' on the worker side to promote cooperation with change, and refers to the benefits of state funding for this.

Workplace Policies

In addition, the following employment relations issues 'inside' the workplace are likely to be important for practitioners engaging in partnership initiatives:

- Senior management endorsement is vital for partnership to take root and survive. Also, the provision of leadership skills and training for management at all levels is important for promoting more competent managers – perhaps the key factor in successful partnerships. Similarly, training for worker representatives in partnership skills is also vital.

- In so far as possible, it is important that a relatively equal share of mutual gains is generated for all workplace stakeholders if partnership is to 'work' and maintain credibility. The balance of gains should not be perceived as being too heavily skewed towards the employer.

- The strategic 'bundling' of complementary partnership and HR practices that 'fit' with technology/production systems and wider business strategy is crucial for conveying a coherent set of messages to the workforce. The bundle should contain core elements like partnership forums, direct employee participation, training, financial stakeholding, and efforts to secure employment.

- Despite the increasing formalisation of employment regulation, informality and informal interaction are vital for partnership to flourish. Without the existence of informal dialogue, trust and goodwill, it is impossible to progress with formal partnership structures and processes.

- Careful thought needs to be given to the role of middle managers and front line managers for they are both the agents and objects of change.

- Capital-intensive (especially continuous process) technology would seem to be particularly suitable to the introduction of partnership.

- When partnership is being developed, the structural tensions created by the co-existence of employee autonomy and management control needs to be carefully managed and balanced.

- Some kind of explicit management commitment to employment security is a crucial factor in generating a positive employee response to partnership. Employees are unlikely to offer their consent when their jobs might come under threat as a result of partnership. Creative measures are required to manage the contradictions between employment security and flexibility, hence interest in the new buzzword of 'flexicurity'.

- Attention needs to be given to opportunities for employee development in partnership organisations with flatter organisational hierarchies. Adequate resourcing of skills training and employee competencies is important.

- As pay levels, structures and systems are frequently a focal point for employee discontent it is important that, as far as possible, they should be fair, equitable and transparent. Partnership may operate best in conjunction with employee financial involvement schemes such as gainsharing and profit sharing.

- Independent worker voice is a vital component of partnership. Where trade unions are present, the strategy of securing union cooperation is vital for promoting wider employee consent. Even where unions are not present, shared decisions (pluralism) are likely to command greater legitimacy than those imposed by management unilaterally, though, obviously, there will be times when management has to lead and act unilaterally.

- In relation to the last point, to gain legitimacy from workers, successful partnerships need to involve and encompass as large a proportion of the workforce as possible (from the point of production right up to strategic decision-making level), as opposed to just a 'chosen elite'.

- Provision of strong communications and employee 'voice' mechanisms at all organisational levels is vital for providing the flow of information necessary for partnership to flourish.

Pointers to Future Research

In terms of future research, there is an undoubted requirement for further in-depth case studies to uncover the realities of workplace partnership, as experienced by management, employees and their representatives. There is a need to recapture some of the contextual richness contained in the classic workplace industrial relations studies of the 1950s-1980s (Gouldner, 1954; Flanders, 1964; McCarthy, 1973; Burawoy, 1979). There is a danger that recourse to an overly unitarist and managerialist research agenda, often using large-scale quantitative surveys, will mean that the complex nuances of workplace relations will be lost. In view of this, the task is to 'get back into' workplaces, and examine the nitty-gritty of relations between managers and employees on the ground, so to speak. By definition, this necessitates a 'return' to a pluralist line of workplace enquiry placing the views of employees and their representatives, as well as managers, centre stage: to flip the coin by examining what employees expect from management, rather than just what managers expect from employees in performance terms, as is now becoming more and more the norm. Also, much industrial relations research, including this study, still takes place in unionised firms, but there is clearly a need to discover more about industrial relations patterns in newer non-traditional non-union workplaces, particularly as private sector union density has been receding in Ireland in recent decades. Accordingly, detailed case studies examining new forms of employee voice in non-union companies, particularly from an employee perspective, would be an invaluable addition to the literature. A key research issue would be whether genuine pluralist mutual gains partnership is possible in non-union enterprises.

Appendix

RESEARCH METHODOLOGY AND TABLE OF INTERVIEWS

Given that the employment relationship is shaped by its context, it was considered critical to utilise a research method sensitive to context. This is the key reason why a case study methodology was deployed to examine workplace partnership and its potential for mutual gains at Waterford Crystal and Aughinish Alumina. Too much research on partnership is dominated by quantitative surveys, many relying on single (mostly management) respondents – a somewhat paradoxical phenomenon when workplace partnership involves multiple stakeholders. It is also critical that such case investigations incorporate a breadth of perspectives and long-term engagement with participants. The case studies at WC and AAL met these criteria. Exceptional (and perhaps) unique access was granted at all levels in the two organisations, from top management down. It was crucial that very good access to trade union representatives and employees was given, because this is a constituency often under-represented in studies of this nature. Furthermore, the study incorporated an important longitudinal element, which meant the two organisations could be studied over a fairly lengthy period, involving repeat visits and 'follow-up' discussions. In sum, the comprehensive nature of the case study investigations greatly strengthens the validity of the findings.

Waterford Crystal (WC) and Aughinish Alumina (AAL) were chosen because they constitute 'ideal/critical' case sites for in-depth empirical analysis of partnership. Both are long established, highly unionised manufacturing firms, now owned by multinationals (Waterford Wedgwood and United Company RUSAL [UCR]), and have experienced serious industrial conflict over the years. Responding to intensified international competition, both attempted to move away from adversarial IR towards a cooperative industrial relations style by engaging in partnership with unions and employees.

Various primary and secondary research methods were deployed. The findings are based largely on semi-structured interviews (lasting between one and three hours) with all levels of management, trade union officials and shop stewards, as well as shorter interviews of up to one hour with a sample of employees drawn from different occupational groups. In total, this amounted to 91 interviews over a two-year period (29 with managers, 12 with union officials and shop stewards and 50 with employees), summarized in Table A1.

Table A1: Summary of Interviews

Waterford Crystal	Aughinish Alumina Limited
Training/communications manager	HR director
Manufacturing director	Plant manager
Employee relations manager	Technical/materials manager
Health and safety manager	HR manager
Finance director	Turnaround team facilitator
Communications officer	Shift plant facilitator
Auto cutting manager	Engineering co-ordinator
Quality assurance manager	Accounting co-ordinator
Tank furnace manager	Former HR director
Two plant managers	TEEU official
Training and safety manager	SIPTU official
Manufacturing manager	Chairman of Group of Unions (AEEU)
HR manager	TEEU shop steward
Four front line managers	Two SIPTU shop stewards
Industrial engineering manager	
Former HR director	
ATGWU official	
ATGWU chief shop steward (convenor)	
Four ATGWU shop stewards	
Retired ATGWU official	
Sample of 28 workers from main production areas: blowing, cutting and engraving, polishing and packing.	Sample of 22 workers from various areas of plant: local areas 1, 2 and 5 plus central stores.

At WC, in-depth semi-structured interviews took place with 20 senior, middle-level and front line managers. The senior and middle managers were drawn from the HR function, as well as manufacturing, quality, finance, health and safety, industrial engineering, communications – in other words, right across the management spectrum. Front line managers were interviewed in different sections, including cutting, blowing and packing. Interviews were also conducted with an Amalgamated Transport and General Workers Union (ATGWU) official, and senior shop stewards. Next, shorter but relatively detailed interviews were conducted with shop stewards and a random sample of 28 workers, drawn from the three main sections/production stages of the plant: 10 from glass blowing; 10 from glass cutting and engraving; and 8 from polishing/packing. The employee interviewees were drawn from different skill levels: craft/maintenance, semi-skilled and operatives.

A similar methodology was deployed at AAL, which is a much 'flatter' organisation. Semi-structured interviews were conducted with three out of four members of the top management team, as well as with 'lower-level' HR management, management facilitators (9 managers in total). Interviews took place with union officials, along with shop stewards. Shorter interviews were then conducted with a random sample of 22 electrical/instrumentation workers, maintenance fitters and operators. These interviewees were also drawn from different skill groupings. Interviews with workers were spread across the main production areas (digestion, filtration and mud washing, hydrate filtration & calcinations, and central workshops).

It was also considered important to deploy an element of ethnography in the form of non-participant observation. This was operationalised through widespread informal contact with people in their work areas, and during meal/tea breaks and proved critical in getting a 'feel' for the realities of shop-floor life. The findings were also informed by discussions with previous senior managers and external industrial relations 'experts'. Finally, secondary research methods consisted of extensive internal (company/union) and external archival and documentary material, derived over almost four years and too numerous to detail here.

BIBLIOGRAPHY

Ackers, P. (2002). 'Reframing employment relations: The case for neo-pluralism'. *Industrial Relations Journal,* Vol. 33, No. 1, 2-19.

Allen, K. (2000). *The Celtic Tiger: The Myth of Social Partnership in Ireland.* Manchester: Manchester University Press.

Aughinish Alumina (1987). 'Comprehensive Agreement'.

Aughinish Alumina (1993). Grading and Flexibility Agreement.

Aughinish Alumina (1993). 'The 'Future' Document'.

Bacon, N. and Blyton, P. (1999). 'Co-operation and conflict in industrial relations: What are the implications for employees and trade unions?' *International Journal of Human Resource Management,* Vol. 10, No. 4, 638-654.

Bacon, N. and Blyton, P. (2002). 'Militant and moderate trade union orientations: What are the effects on workplace trade unionism, union-management relations and employee gains?' *International Journal of Human Resource Management,* Vol. 13, No. 2, 302-319.

Batstone, E. (1986). 'Labour and productivity'. *Oxford Review of Economic Policy*, Vol. 2, 32-42.

Batstone, E. (1988). 'The Frontier of Control'. In D. Gallie (ed.) *Employment in Britain.* Oxford: Blackwell.

Batstone, E. (1988). *The Reform of Workplace Industrial Relations: Theory, Myth, and Evidence.* Oxford: Clarendon Press.

Belanger, J. and Edwards, P. (2007). 'The Conditions Promoting Compromise in the Workplace'. *British Journal of Industrial Relations,* Vol. 45, No. 4, 713-734.

Boxall, P. (1996). 'The strategic HRM debate and the resource-based view of the firm'. *Human Resource Management Journal,* Vol. 6, No. 3, 59-75.

Burawoy, M. (1979). *Manufacturing Consent: Changes in the Labor Process Under Monopoly Capitalism.* Chicago: University of Chicago Press.

Burawoy, M. (1985). *The Politics of Production.* London: Verso.

Cappelli, P., Bassi, L., Katz, H., Knoke, D., Osterman, P. and Useem, M. (eds.). (1997). *Change at Work.* New York: Oxford University Press.

Central Statistics Office (CSO) (2007). 'Average weekly earnings – industrial workers 1964-2006'. Cork/Dublin: CSO.

Clegg, H. (1979). *The Changing System of Industrial Relations in Great Britain.* Oxford: Blackwell.

Coats, D. (2005). *An agenda for work: The Work Foundation's challenge to policy makers.* Work Foundation Provocation Series, Vol. 1, No. 2.

Collinson, M., Edwards, P. and Rees, C. (1997). *Involving Employees in Total Quality Management.* London: Department of Trade and Industry.

Crouch, C. and Streeck, W. (1997). *Political Economy of Modern Capitalism.* London: Sage Publications.

D'Art, D. and Turner, T. (2005). 'Union recognition and partnership at work: A new legitimacy for Irish trade unions?' *Industrial Relations Journal,* Vol. 36, No. 2, 121-139.

Danford, A., Richardson, M., Stewart, P., Tailby, S. and Upchurch, M. (2005). *Partnership and the High-Performance Workplace – Work and Employment Relations in the Aerospace Industry,* London: Palgrave Macmillan.

Department of Enterprise, Trade and Employment (2003). 'Consultation Paper on Transposition of National Information and Consultation Directive into Irish Law'. Dublin: Department of Enterprise, Trade and Employment.

Dobbins, T. (2006). 'Can consultation law create new workplace bargaining agenda?' *Industrial Relations News,* No. 19. Dublin: IRN Publishing.

Donovan Commission (1968). *Report on the Royal Commission on Trade Unions and Employers' Associations.* London: HMSO.

Dundon, T. Curran, D, Ryan, P. and Maloney, M. (2006). 'Conceptualising the dynamics of employee voice: evidence from the Republic of Ireland', *Industrial Relations Journal,* Vol. 34, No. 5, 492-512.

Edwards, P. (1986). *Conflict at Work.* Oxford: Blackwell.

Edwards, P. (1990). 'Understanding Conflict in the Labour Process: The Logic and Autonomy of Struggle'. In D. Knights and H. Wilmott (eds.), *Labour Process Theory.* London: Macmillan.

Edwards, P. (2003). *Industrial Relations* (2nd edition). Oxford: Blackwell.

Edwards, P. (2007). *Justice in the workplace: Why it is important and why a new public policy initiative is needed.* Work Foundation Provocation Series, Vol. 2, No. 3.

Edwards, P. and Wright, M. (1998). 'HRM and commitment: A case study of teamworking'. In P. Sparrow and M. Marchington (eds.), *Human Resource Management: The New Agenda.* London: Financial Times Management.

Edwards, P. and Wright, M. (2001). 'High-involvement work systems and performance outcomes: the strength of variable, contingent and context-bound relationships'. *International Journal of Human Resource Management,* Vol. 12, No. 4), 568-585.

Fisher, R. and Ury, W. (1999). *Getting to Yes: The Secret to Successful Negotiations.* Boston: Houghton-Mifflin.

Flanders, A. (1964). *The Fawley Productivity Agreements.* London: Faber & Faber.

Flanders, A. (1970). *Management and Unions.* London: Faber & Faber.

Fox, A. (1966). *Industrial Sociology and Industrial Relations.* London: HMSO.

Fox, A. (1974). *Beyond Contract: Work, Power and Trust Relations.* London: Faber & Faber.

Fox, A. (1985). *Man Mismanagement.* London: Hutchison.

Gallie, D, White, M, Cheng, Y. and Tomlinson, M. (1998). *Restructuring the Employment Relationship.* Oxford: Oxford University Press.

Geary, J. (2003). 'New Forms of Work Organization: Still Limited, Still Controlled, but Still Welcome?' In P. Edwards (eds.), *Industrial Relations* (2nd edition). Oxford: Blackwell Publishing.

Geary, J. and Dobbins, T. (2001). 'Teamworking: A new dynamic in the pursuit of management control'. *Human Resource Management Journal,* Vol. 11, No. 1, 3-23.

Geary, J. and Roche, W. (2005). 'The Future of Employee Information and Consultation in Ireland'. In J. Storey (ed.), *Adding Value Through Information and Consultation.* Palgrave Macmillan.

Godard, J. (2001). 'High performance and the transformation of work? The implications of alternative work practices for the experience and outcomes of work'. *Industrial and Labor Relations Review.* Vol. 54, No. 4, 776-805.

Godard, J. (2004). 'A Critical Assessment of the High-Performance Paradigm'. *British Journal of Industrial Relations,* Vol. 42, No. 2, 349-378.

Goodrich, C. (1920). *The Frontier of Control: A Study in British Workshop Politics.* Harcourt, Brace, New York.

Gouldner, A. (1954). *Patterns of Industrial Bureaucracy.* New York: Free Press.

Guest, D. and Peccei, R. (2001). 'Partnership at Work: Mutuality and the Balance of Advantage'. *British Journal of Industrial Relations,* Vol. 39, No. 2: 207-236.

Gunnigle, P. (1998). 'More Rhetoric than Reality: Enterprise Level Industrial Relations Partnerships in Ireland'. *Economic and Social Review,* Vol. 28, No. 4, 179-200.

Hamel, G. and Prahalad, P.K. (1994). *Competing for the Future.* Boston, Mass.: Harvard Business School Press.

Hastings, T. (2003). *Politics, Management and Industrial Relations.* Dublin: Blackhall Publishing.

Hastings, T., Sheehan, B. and Yeates, P. (2007). *Saving the Future.* Dublin: Blackhall Publishing.

Hodson, R. (1999). 'Organizational Anomie and Worker Consent'. *Work and Occupations,* Vol. 26, No. 3, 292-323.

Hodson, R. (2005). 'Management Behaviour as Social Capital: A Systematic Analysis of Organizational Ethnographies'. *British Journal of Industrial Relations,* Vol. 43, No. 1, 41-65.

Huselid, M. (1995). 'The impact of human resource management practices on turnover, productivity and corporate financial performance'. *Academy of Management Journal,* Vol. 38, No. 3, 635-70.

Hutton, W. (2002). *The World We're In.* London: Little, Brown.

Hyman, R. (1987). 'Strategy or structure: Capital, labour and control'. *Work, Employment and Society,* Vol. 1, No.1, 25-26.

Ichniowski, C, Kochan, T, Levine, D, Olson, C. and Strauss, G. (1996). 'What works at work: Overview and assessment'. *Industrial Relations,* Vol. 35, No.3, 299-333.

Industrial Relations News (IRN) various editions. Dublin: IRN Publishing Limited.

Irish Business and Employers Confederation (2002). 'IBEC's Initial Submission on the Implementation of the Directive for Informing and Consulting Employees'. Dublin: Irish Business and Employers Confederation.

Irish Congress of Trade Unions (1995). *Managing Change.* Dublin: Irish Congress of Trade Unions.

Irish Congress of Trade Unions (2003). 'Submission to the Department of Enterprise Trade and Employment on the Transposition of Directive 2002/14/EC on the Establishment of a General Framework for Informing and Consulting Employees in the European Community'. Dublin: Irish Congress of Trade Unions.

Kelly, J. (1996). 'Union Militancy and Social Partnership'. In P. Ackers, C. Smith and P. Smith (eds.), *The New Workplace and Trade Unionism*. London: Routledge.

Kelly, J. (1998). *Rethinking Industrial Relations*. London: Routledge.

Kelly, J. (2004). 'Social partnership agreements in Britain: Labor cooperation and compliance', *Industrial Relations*, Vol. 43, No. 1, 267-292.

Kochan, T. and Osterman, P. (1994). *The Mutual Gains Enterprise*. Cambridge, MA: Harvard Business School Press.

Kochan, T. and Rubinstein, S. (2000). 'Toward a Stakeholder Theory of the Firm: The Saturn Partnership'. *Organization Science*, Vol. 11, No. 4, 367-386.

Korczynski, M., Shire, K., Frenkel, S. and Tam, M. (2000). 'Service work in consumer capitalism: Customers, control and contradictions'. *Work, Employment and Society,* Vol. 14, No. 4, 669-88.

Lazonick, W. (1990). *Competitive Advantage on the Shop Floor*. Cambridge, Mass: Harvard University Press.

Locke, R, Kochan, T. and Piore, M. (eds.) (1995). *Employment Relations in a Changing World Economy*. Cambridge: MIT Press.

Lukes, S. (2005). *Power: A Radical View* (2nd edition). Basingstoke: Palgrave.

Marchington, M. (2000). 'Teamworking and employee involvement: Terminology, evaluation and context'. In S. Procter and F. Mueller (eds.), *Teamworking*. Basingstoke: Macmillan.

Marchington, M, and Wilkinson, A. (2000). 'Direct Participation'. In S. Bach and K. Sisson (eds.), *Personnel Management*. Oxford: Blackwell.

Marks, A., Findlay, P., Hine, J., McKinlay, A. and Thompson, P. (1998). 'The Politics of Partnership? Innovation in Employment Relations in the Scottish Spirits Industry'. *British Journal of Industrial Relations,* Vol. 36, No. 2, 209-26.

MacDuffie, J.P. (1995). 'Human Resource Bundles and Manufacturing Performance: Organizational Logical and Flexible Production Systems in the World Auto Industry'. *Industrial and Labor Relations Review,* Vol. 48, 197-221.

McCarthy, C. (1973). *The decade of upheaval: Irish trade unions in the nineteen sixties*. Dublin: Institute of Public Administration.

National Centre for Partnership and Performance (2004). *Achieving High Performance: Partnership Works – The International Evidence*. Dublin: NCPP.

Nichols, T. (1986). *The British Worker Question*. London: Routledge & Kegan Paul.

Nolan, P. and O'Donnell, K. (2003). 'Industrial Relations, HRM and Performance'. In P. Edwards (ed.), *Industrial Relations* (2nd edition). Oxford: Blackwell.

O'Connell, P.J., Russell, H, Williams, J, and Blackwell, S. (2004). *The Changing Workplace: A Survey of Employees' Views and Experiences.* Economic and Social Research Institute/National Centre for Partnership and Performance.

O'Dowd, J. (2006). *Voluntary Management-Union Partnerships in Ireland: A Theoretical and Empirical Study.* PhD thesis, University College Dublin.

Oxenbridge, S. and Brown, W. (2004). 'Achieving a new equilibrium? The stability of cooperative employer-union relationships'. *British Journal of Industrial Relations,* Vol. 35, No. 5, 388-401.

Partnership 2000 (1997). Department of the Taoiseach. Dublin.

Pfeffer, J. (1994). *Competitive Advantage through People: Unleashing the Power of the Workforce.* Boston, Mass: Harvard Business School Press.

Pfeffer, J. (1998). *The Human Equation: Building Profits by Putting People First.* Boston, Mass: Harvard Business School Press.

Piore, M.J. and Sabel, C.F. (1984). *The Second Industrial Divide.* New York: Basic Books.

Pontusson, J. (1992). 'Unions, new technology and job redesign at Volvo and British Leyland'. In J. Pontusson and M. Golden (eds.), *Bargaining for Change: Union Politics in Europe and North America.* Ithaca: Cornell University Press.

Procter, S. and Mueller, F. (2000). *Teamworking.* Basingstoke: Macmillan.

Ramsey, H. (1977). 'Cycles of Control'. *Sociology,* Vol. 11, No. 3, 481–506.

Regini, M. (1995). *Uncertain Boundaries: The Social and Political Construction of European Economies.* Cambridge: Cambridge University Press.

Roche, W.K. (2005). 'The Changing Industrial Relations Landscape in the Republic of Ireland'. Paper presented to seminar on changing approaches in industrial relations – the Republic of Ireland/Northern Ireland and the UK, November 21, 2005.

Roche, W.K. (2006). 'Social Partnership and Workplace Regimes in Ireland'. British Universities Industrial Relations Association Annual Conference, Galway, 28-30 June.

Roche, W.K. (2008). 'Who Gains From Workplace Partnership?' *International Journal of Human Resource Management,* (forthcoming).

Roche, W.K. and Geary, J. (2000). 'Collaborative Production and the Irish Boom: Work Organization, Partnership and Direct Involvement in Irish Workplaces'. *Economic and Social Review,* Vol. 31, No. 1, 1-36.

Roche, W.K. and Geary, J. (2006). *Partnership at Work: The quest for radical organizational change*. London: Routledge.

Roche, W.K and Turner, T. (1998). 'Human Resource Management and Industrial Relations: Substitution, Dualism and Partnership'. In W. Roche, K. Monks and J. Walsh (eds.), *Human Resource Management in Ireland*. Dublin: Oak Tree Press.

Rogers, J. and Streeck, W. (1995) (eds.). *Works Councils: Consultation, Representation, and Cooperation in Industrial Relations*. London and New York: University of Chicago Press.

Rubinstein, S. (2000). 'The impact of co-management on quality performance: The case of the Saturn Corporation'. *Industrial and Labor Relations Review,* Vol. 53, No. 2, 197-218.

Rubinstein, S. and Heckscher, C. (2002). 'Partnerships and Flexible Networks: Alternatives or Complementary Models of Labor-Management Relations?' In T. Kochan and D. Lipsky (eds.), *Negotiations and Change: From the workplace to society*. Ithaca: Cornell University Press.

Rubinstein, S. and Heckscher, C. (2003). 'Partnerships and Flexible Networks: Alternatives or Complementary Models of Labor-Management Relations?' In T. Kochan and D. Lipsky (eds), *Negotiations and Change: rom the workplace to society*. Ithaca, NY: Cornell University Press.

Rubinstein, S. and Kochan, T. (2001). *Learning from Saturn*. Ithaca, NY: ILR Press.

Sennett, R. (1998). *The Corrosion of Character: The Personal Consequences of Work in the New Capitalism*. New York: W.W. Norton.

Sheehan, B. (1993). 'Industrial relations change at Waterford Crystal', *Industrial Relations News*, No. 31 and 32. Dublin: IRN Publishing Limited.

Strauss, A, Schatzman, L, Ehrlich, D, Bucher, R, and Sabshim, M. (1971). 'The hospital and its negotiated order'. In F.G. Castles, D.J. Murray and D.C. Porter (eds.), *Decisions, Organizations and Society*. Harmondsworth: Penguin.

Streeck, W. (1987). 'The uncertainties of management in the management of uncertainty'. *Work, Employment and Society,* Vol. 1, No. 3, 281-308.

Streeck, W., 1995. 'Works Councils in Western Europe: From Consultation to Participation'. In J. Rogers and W. Streeck (eds.), *Works Councils: Consultation, Representation, and Cooperation in Industrial Relations*. London and New York: University of Chicago Press.

Streeck, W. (1997). 'German Capitalism: Does it Exist? Can it Survive?' In C. Crouch and W. Streeck (eds.), *Political Economy of Modern Capitalism*. London: Sage Publications.

Streeck, W. (1997). 'The End of the New Industrial Relations'. Seminar at International Industrial Relations Association conference. Graduate School of Business, University College Dublin, Dublin.

Tailby, S., Richardson, M., Upchurch, M., Danford, A. and Stewart, P. (2007) 'Partnership with and without trade unions in the UK financial services: Filling or fuelling the representation gap?' *Industrial Relations Journal*, Vol. 38, No. 3, 210-28.

Terry, M. (2003). 'Employee Representation'. In P. Edwards (ed.), *Industrial Relations* (2nd edition). Oxford: Blackwell.

Thompson, P. (2003). 'Disconnected capitalism: Or why employers can't keep their side of the bargain'. *Work, Employment and Society,* Vol. 17, No. 2, 359-378.

Visser, J. (1998). 'Two Cheers for Corporatism. One for the Market. Industrial Relations, Wage Moderation and Job Growth in the Netherlands'. *British Journal of Industrial Relations*, Vol. 36, No. 2, 269-292.

Wallace, J., Gunnigle, P. and McMahon, G. (2004). *Industrial Relations in Ireland* (3rd edition). Dublin: Gill & Macmillan.

Walton, R., Cutcher-Gershenfeld, J. and McKersie, R. (1994). *Strategic Negotiations: A Theory of Change in Labor-Management Relations*. Boston: Harvard Business School Press.

Walton, R. (1985). 'From control to commitment in the workplace'. *Harvard Business Review,* Vol. 53, 77-84.

Waterford Crystal (1990). 'Comprehensive Agreement for Profit Improvement'.

Waterford Crystal (1992). 'Terms and Conditions of Employment and Union Representation/Union Time/Procedures Agreement'.

Waterford Crystal (1993). 'Cost Improvement Agreement'.

Waterford Crystal (1994). 'Investment in Competitiveness Agreement'.

Waterford Crystal (2002). 'Plan for Renewal and Growth Agreement'.

Watson, T. (1995). *Sociology, Work and Industry.* London/New York: Routledge.

Williams, J., Blackwell, S., Gorby, S., O'Connell, P.J. and Russell, H. (2004). *The Changing Workplace: A Survey of Employers' Views and Experiences*. Economic and Social Research Institute/National Centre for Partnership and Performance. Dublin.

Womack, J., Jones, D. and Roos, D. (1990). *The Machine that Changed the World.* New York: Rawson Associates.

GLOSSARY

This short glossary provides definitions of some key concepts contained within this book.

Annual hours: a pay system which brings flexibility into working time. Instead of a set number of hours per day or per week, the employee is contracted to work a certain number of hours per year.

Collective bargaining: negotiations between organised workers and employers concerning wages, working conditions, etc.

Compliance: describes situations where employment relations are characterised by the use of power by employers to control and coerce employees.

Consensus: the degree to which there is a commonly agreed position or set of values.

Consultation: the exchange of views and establishment of dialogue between employers and employee representatives with a view to reaching an agreement on decisions likely to lead to substantial changes in employment, work organisation or contractual relations.

Contradiction: forces pushing in opposite directions, such as the paradox of management's dual search for cooperation and control in the employment relationship.

Direct employee participation: refers to direct methods of employee involvement in managerial decision-making at the point of production, notably teamwork. Can be contrasted with indirect worker participation through representatives.

Flexibility: the attempt to secure managerial manoeuvrability in work organisation and employment practices in two broad ways: flexibility for tight control and flexibility for adaptability and innovation.

Frontier of control: concept referring to whether management or unions/ workers control details of work organisation at the point of production/service delivery.

Front line managers: managers responsible for controlling, coordinating, directing, facilitating work activities at the point of production/ service delivery.

Globalisation: a trend in which economic, political and cultural activities in different countries influence each other and become interdependent.

Indulgency pattern: the ignoring by management of infringements of formal rules by workers, and acceptance of informal 'custom and practice' in return for cooperation with overall company goals.

Industrial relations (IR): the activities and institutions associated with employment relationships between employers, employees and their representatives.

Labour process: process driving employment relations whereby management design, control and monitor work tasks and activities to ensure that surplus value is extracted from the labour of employees so that commodities can be exchanged in the market place for profit.

Management control: the sets of roles, rules, structures and procedures managerially designed to co-ordinate and control employee activities.

Mutuality/mutual gains bargaining: management engage employees, both directly as individuals and indirectly through representatives, in a cooperative and integrated relationship to pursue mutual gains such as participation, employment security and productivity.

Negotiated order: patterns of employment relations and accompanying rules and expectations are (re)created by the outcomes of interactions and power relations between employers, employees and their representatives.

Performance management: a systematic attempt to evaluate employees' performance in terms of stated or agreed indicators.

Pluralism: perspective that recognises different interest groups at the workplace, and consequently, accepts the inevitability of conflict between the interests of employers and workers, but considers ways in which conflict can be contained and institutionalised to maintain workplace order.

Power: the capacity of any interest group or individual to achieve their aims regardless of resistance.

Pragmatic cooperation: employers, employees and unions decide that their respective interests are best fulfilled by pragmatically cooperating in response to difficult and uncertain economic conditions.

Psychological contract: explicit or implicit expectations and norms governing management-employee relations.

Radical pluralism: recognises the plurality of groups and interests in society (and welcomes social pluralism in principle) whilst observing the more basic patterns of power and inequality which tend to shape, and be shaped by it

Responsible autonomy: approach to the design of work tasks that gives discretion to employees on the understanding that they accept the managerial trust put in them and perform tasks in accordance with overall management goals.

Semi-autonomous teamwork: the grouping of individual jobs into a general whole work 'process' with team members being granted considerable discretion over how work is organized and completed.

Social partnership: national level pluralist consensus, whereby senior representatives of Government, employers and trade unions engage in centralized bargaining over key economic and social priorities.

Structured antagonism: rather than just being a surface problem with industrial relations institutions and procedures, conflict is 'structured into' the very core of the employment relationship due to the dynamics of the labour process (see above). Employment relations will always be governed by conflicting <u>and</u> common interests, because of this.

Unilateral management prerogative: a management style whereby most or all the important decisions affecting companies are best decided and enacted solely by management, rather than through negotiation or consultation with employee representatives.

Unitarism: perspective on employment relations which assume that the interests of employers and employees are the same, with mutual commitment to common goals. Management is seen as the sole source of authority. Conflict is seen as pathological rather than normal.

Voluntarism: the traditional system of industrial relations in Ireland, whereby employers and trade unions engage in 'voluntary' negotiations over workplace issues. Based on traditional view that IR system should be characterised by lack of legal intervention and binding regulation.

Workplace partnership: employment relations based on recognition of a common interest to achieve competitive, productive and participatory enterprises. Involves ongoing commitment from employees to improve productivity, and employer acceptance of employees and their representatives as independent stakeholders with rights and interests to be considered in the context of major decisions.

WORKPLACE PARTNERSHIP
IN PRACTICE